Little
America

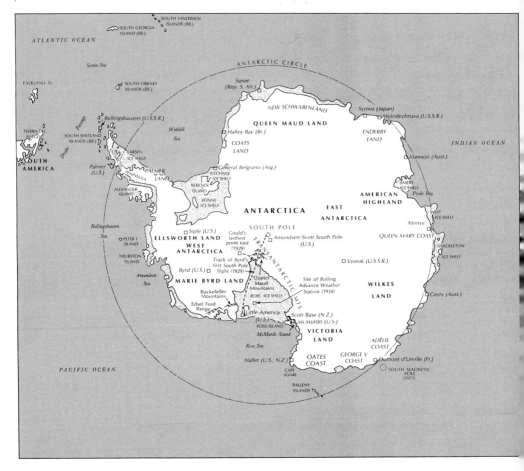

Antarctica. From The New Columbia Encyclopedia (*New York: 1975*), p. 114. Used by permission.

Little America

America

Town at the End of the World

Paul A. Carter

NEW YORK   COLUMBIA UNIVERSITY PRESS   1979

Paul A. Carter is Professor of History, University of Arizona, Tucson

Library of Congress Cataloging in Publication Data

Carter, Paul Allen, 1926–
  Little America.

  Includes index.
  SUMMARY: Details American explorations of Antarctica.
  1. Antarctic regions—American exploration.
[1. Antarctic regions—American exploration] I. Title.
G860.C324   919.8′9   79–13727
ISBN 0–231–04682–

Columbia University Press
New York   Guildford, Surrey
Copyright © 1979 by Paul A. Carter

THIS BOOK IS FOR
BRUCE CARTER

Who Wonders Wondrously
at the World's Wonders

Contents

List of Maps

Preface

This book is my personal tribute to the fiftieth anniversary of the first flight to the South Pole (November 29, 1929) and to the twentieth anniversary of the signing of the Antarctic Treaty (December 1, 1959). The first of those events was a point of transition between the old style of exploration conducted by Lewis and Clark and the new mode pioneered by Neil Armstrong; the second was a civilized exception to the kinds of international relations that have generally prevailed in the twentieth century. But the book is also a tribute to a town which was built on the edge of the Ross Ice Shelf to support the polar flight and which continued at intervals to have a major share in Antarctic history until the year of the Treaty, when Little America was finally closed. People seem to remember Richard E. Byrd's historic flight rather better than they recall the community which made it possible, and my primary purpose here is to tell the story of that last American frontier town.

Admiral Byrd's own papers have not generally been available to scholars. He quoted liberally, however, from his own journals in his many books and articles. Fortunately, others who lived at Little America also kept diaries, wrote books, and saved papers. Several members of the First Byrd Antarctic Expedition contributed such materials to the Center for Polar and Scientific Archives in the U.S. National Archives, and this book could not have been written without the use of the Arnold Clarke Papers, the Victor Czegka

Papers, the Dana Coman Papers, the Epaminondas Demas Papers, the Laurence Gould Papers, the William C. Haines Papers, and (for the Second Expedition) the John Dyer Papers. In addition another member of the First Expedition, Henry Harrison, kindly photocopied many pages of his own diary and sent them to me; he also answered many questions.

These personal papers, and other sources, are fully cited in the notes which appear at the end of the book. I shall not say anything more of a bibliographical nature here, except to offer one invitation and utter one warning. The warning is that when going through these expedition diaries a reader must question and mistrust one of the historian's most cherished axioms. Ordinarily, the rule in dealing with historical sources is "the closer to the event, the more authentic." However, when people are shut up together in an Antarctic camp for a months-long winter, as one wise survivor of such a winter has cautioned me, they are likely to write things down about each other which they would never say after the healing return of the sun. A far more gossipy account of Little America than I have written could have been compiled from these same sources. I have tried to balance people's long-term judgments against the short, and be fair to both.

The invitation, for anyone interested in learning more about Antarctica, is to go and look at maps. The coasts and hinterlands of the once-unknown seventh continent now leap into vivid life in the American Geographic Society's *Antarctic Map Folio Series* (New York, 1964–), which include, as well as the maps themselves, informative essays on Antarctic plants and animals (both terrestrial and marine), glaciers, atmosphere, ocean currents, terrestrial magnetism, geology, and history. Authoritative and literate, they invite the reader with access to a good library map collection to browse indefinitely. For more detail, the U.S. Geological Survey's standard 1:250,000 *Reconnaissance Geologic Maps* (1962–) are executed with rare cartographic beauty.

From there one goes to the general works on Antarctica, which vary greatly in quality. Many are handsomely illustrated, but some have insipid texts. The eye should linger over the pictures, however. They explain something about which newcomers to the subject seem, usually, skeptical: how any place as bleak and empty as Antarctica could be accounted beautiful. (But that is exactly the point, many of Antarctica's devotees would reply.)

Apart from present-day description, the history of Antarctic exploration has been told by the explorers themselves, and retold by scholars imaginatively following in their track. It is an uncommonly rich literature, and the notes to this book's Prologue will indicate some of it to the reader. A little of it—not as much as I should like—remains in print; less here than in Britain, which has kept alive the tragic Scott tradition. More may be forthcoming in the current modest revival of interest in polar affairs, which the media have picked up in the past year or so. I hope this book may contain a clue as to why that revival is taking place.

Many persons have contributed to purging the manuscript of the kind of errors inevitable for a writer who has not known Antarctica at first hand. Foremost is Laurence McKinley Gould, whose office in the University of Arizona's Geology Building—adorned with fossils, a relief map of Antarctica, photos of dogs and penguins, and other Antarctic memorabilia—has been a frequent stopping-place for me during the writing of this book. Professor Gould, who has carefully read the entire manuscript, has been kind far beyond the requirements of scholarship; loaning to me, for example, the irreplaceable fifty-year-old negatives from which were made the Little America photographs which appear in this book. He has also given his permission to quote here some comments he made to me on several occasions. Henry Harrison, who was with Gould on the First Byrd Antarctic Expedition, has similarly read and criticized the five chapters dealing with the first settlement at Little America and with the South Pole flight. Gerald Pagano, of the Center for Polar and Scientific Archives, Washington, has taken similar care with drafts of chapters 6 and 8, which quote material from the Paul

Siple Papers. A conversation with Herman R. Friis during one of my visits to the Polar Archive was helpful, as was a letter from Commander Richard E. Byrd, Jr.

The University of Arizona made it possible for me to extend two visits to Washington, undertaken for a different purpose, in order to spend time at the Polar Archive. There, Mr. Pagano, Ms. Alison Wilson, and Director Franklin Burch gave the kind of unstinting aid which is a researcher's delight. The good people of National Public Radio in Washington, for whom I was functioning as a consultant, during recreational breaks provided a sympathetic audience when I felt the urge to tell tales of Antarctica. One of their number—sharply, but to an ultimately kindly purpose—corrected a number of my landlubberly nautical terms.

Students at the University of Arizona have listened with apparent willingness to early drafts of the Prologue and the first four chapters, and my colleagues in the Department of History have been uniformly supportive. Sitting among Larry Gould's own undergraduate students in glacial geology, during the 1978 spring term, was also beneficial. Typists Marilyn Bradian, Dorothy Donnelly, and Dawn Polter have borne patiently with my hand-emended manuscript—which, as they received it, was often far less legible than the fifty-year-old, snow-stained, pencil-written diaries upon which it was based. Without their cheerful, accurate, and rapid work this book would never have made its deadline with Columbia University Press. (They also confess that they have all become Antarctica fans.) This is the third of my books for Columbia to have had the good fortune to be edited, with taste and intelligence, by Mr. Leslie Bialler. My wife, Julie Raffety Carter, has gone through the manuscript with her usual care and good sense, rescued it from many a dreadful *faux pas,* and seen to it that I hit the nail on the head rather than taking the long way around. Special thanks to Florence Raffety, who prepared the index.

Little
America

Prologue: Finding a Way to the Bay of Whales

Although many of the scenes about these islands are highly exciting, the effect produced on the mind of their general aspect is cold and cheerless to an unusual degree, for on their lonely shores the voice of man is seldom heard: the only indication of his ever having trod the soil, is the solitary grave of some poor seaman near the beach, and the only wood that any where meets the eye, are the staves that mark its dimensions; no sound for years disturbs the silence of the scene, save the wild screech of the sea-birds as they wing their way in search of their accustomed food—the incessant chattering of the congregated Penguins—the rude blasts, tearing among the icy hills—the sullen roar of the waves, tumbling and dashing along the shores, or the heavy explosions of the large masses of snow falling into the waves beneath, to form the vast ice-bergs which every where drift through the southern ocean.

—James Eights (1833)[1]

Of the nine planets in our solar system only Mars and Earth are adorned with ice caps at their poles. The pole at the northern tip of Earth's axis is surrounded by the frozen portion of a polar ocean, and therefore it knows the (comparatively) moderating influence of the sea. At the south, however, Earth's pole lies in the midst of an upland, the crown of a great continent whose average height rises eight thousand feet above the ocean's surface. Therefore, in the thin dryness of its frigid atmosphere (dry despite all the water locked up underfoot in ice and snow) and in its all but unimaginably low temperatures, Earth's south polar cap is the closest we can come on this planet to experiencing the climate of Mars.

When the Viking lander settled down on its splayed feet at the surface of our red planetary neighbor in 1976 and hoisted all its sensors, one of the first messages it beamed back through space to Earth was a weather report. "Light winds at 15 m.p.h.," announced Viking meteorologist Seymour Hess: "Temperatures Tuesday ranging from a low of $-122°$ F to an early afternoon high of $-22°$ F [$-85.5°$ C to $-30°$ C]." Since both planets have 24-hour days and approximately the same axial tilt, such highs and lows can be fairly compared, and by Antarctican standards these figures were not too unreasonable. The Americans at their south pole base in 1957 had recorded a hundred degrees below zero on the Fahrenheit scale ($-73°$ C); the Russians at their Vostok station in 1960 had posted an even more spirit-numbing $-126.9°$ F ($-88.2°$ C). Vostok's night temperatures regularly drop below the mark at which carbon dioxide would naturally freeze out of the atmosphere ($-109°$ F, or $-78.5°$ C, at normal Earth surface pressures), a phenomenon which may also happen on Mars.[2]

Earth's polar caps, however, are far more extensive than their Martian equivalents. In our north polar regions Greenland, which has its own, smaller, ice cap, has been likened to "a great apple pie with a thick mound of ice-cream piled high all over the top crust and oozing out between the scallops on the edge." That description still more accurately fits the Antarctic ice cap, whose millions of oppressive tons—piled up thickly enough to extend *below* sea level in some parts of Marie Byrd Land—are hemmed in by mountains that range in height up to fifteen thousand feet above the sea. But there is an important difference between the far north and the frozen south. Greenland's icy mountains bar much of that island's interior ice from contact with the Arctic Ocean, so that most of the icebergs that break off to float on down to the North Atlantic are the front faces of relatively small glaciers molded by the mountains down which they flow. In contrast many of Antarctica's mighty glaciers, as they emerge from the gaps between the mountains, flow together into great sheets of ice hundreds of feet thick, anchored on the shore but extending far out to sea. One such mass, the Ross Ice Shelf—the setting for the narrative that follows—is as large as France or Texas. The ice masses that break ("calve") cleanly away from the leading edges of such shelves,

Tilted iceberg in the Bay of Whales
The Antarctic seawater, never far above freezing, quickly refroze around this tipped berg, solidly enough to give firm support to a dog team.

unlike Greenland's irregularly shaped icebergs, commonly sail away across the southern ocean in square-sided tabular bergs that may be dozens of miles across. In addition, during winter the inlets and bays along Antarctica's coasts freeze over. Much of this bay ice breaks up in summer, but rather than melting away it moves out to sea, where it becomes part of that bane of navigation, the Antarctic ice pack.

Sunshine plays on the frigid southern land during Earth's long polar summer day, as it does also, more feebly, on Mars, but the white face of the ice cap reflects most of that radiance back out into space. Earth's albedo—its reflectivity—is nearly three times that of Mars, and a large part of that difference is made by Antarctica and its surrounding ice pack. As a result the polar plateau is a great heat sink, into which falls a never-ending column of cooling air. This heavy, dry, refrigerated air flows outward from the pole and down off the highland to the coasts, where—sometimes at two hundred miles an hour!—it strikes moister air from the ocean and begets storms. (Mars, in contrast, lacking available surface water, cannot afford such luxuries as blizzards; its foul weather is made by great clouds of blowing dust, to the exasperation of watching astronomers on Earth.)

Life on Mars, from the fragmentary and disputed evidence snatched so far by the Viking probes, remains at best a matter for debate. At the fringes of Antarctica, on the contrary, life is abundant. The polar ocean teems with it, far more so than any tropic waters. In the south polar seas one finds both the blue whale, the largest creature that has ever lived, and the tiny shrimplike krill which may, on some not-far-off day, be harvested for Earth's starving humans by the tens of millions of tons. Yet only a short distance from the water's edge, beyond waddling distance from the last penguin rookery, the Antarctic population dramatically drops off. Inland, away from the nurturing sea, life reduces to mosses, lichens, one or two stunted grasses, microorganisms, and a few insects—forms similar to what might be viable on present-day Mars. "While not 'Martian'," writes George A. Llano, a specialist on Antarctic biology, "the dry valleys of Victoria Land, Antarctica, approach expected conditions in terms of low magnetic field, comparatively high ultraviolet irradiation, desiccating winds and low humidities, similar temperature conditions ($-50°$ to $+20°$ C [$-58°$ F to 68° F] versus $\sim -70°$ to $+20°$ C [$-94°$ F to 68° F] for Mars), diurnal freeze-thaw cycles, permafrost, moisture-holding salts and surface or subsurface microbial life as the only possible life form." In this austere corner of our own planet, "some soil samples were collected from which no visible microorganisms could be obtained."[3]

Earth's south polar continent also resembles Mars in that first-hand knowledge about it has come to us rather late in history.

"When King Alfred reigned in England the Vikings were navigating the ice-fields of the North," notes Antarctic explorer Apsley Cherry-Garrard; "yet when Wellington fought the battle of Waterloo there was still an undiscovered continent in the South." Until the end of the nineteenth century's second decade Antarctica was the only continent which had never known the inquisitive trespass of man. For centuries it existed, like Mars, not as a field of direct human experience but rather as an object for fanciful storytelling or for abstract intellectual speculation. The Greeks, as usual, were the first to think systematically about the subject. The very word *Antarctica* derives from *antarktikos*—"opposite to the Bear," referring to the star group which from great antiquity has been associated with the polar north. There had to be a southern continent in the midst of all that water, savants assumed, in order to balance the great landmasses of the northern hemisphere, and—so they reasoned, out of pre-Newtonian notions of gravitation—to weight down the Earth at its bottom end. Christianity added a complication: could such an antipodean continent be inhabited? Not by the descendants of Adam by way of Noah, Saint Augustine argued; "It is utterly absurd to say that any men from this side of the world could sail across the immense tract of the ocean, reach the far side, and then people it with men sprung from the single father of all mankind." In the eighth century A.D. the Venerable Bede, a highly enlightened man for his times (or any times) wrote of the inhabited northern hemisphere, but carefully termed the southern merely "habitable." To believe in the existence of human beings not involved in Adam's fall and not within reach of Christian missionaries, a medieval consensus insisted, would be heresy; there could be, therefore, no native Antarcticans.[4]

In the end Bede, if not Augustine, turned out to have been right. The Antarctic continent was habitable—just barely—but until the nineteenth century it was empty of human beings, and it remains nearly so even today. However, when Western civilization exploded out of Europe's narrow confines, a more exuberant view of the great south came for a time to prevail: Antarctica might be a second (and equally profitable) America. Newly discovered Tierra del Fuego and Tasmania were assumed, until further exploration proved otherwise, to be the outer edges of the Greek geographer-astronomer Ptolemy's southern *Terra Incognita,* optimistically rechristened *Terra Australis Nondam Cognita*—the southern land not *yet* known. Antarctica was imaginatively filled up with milk and honey, given a mild climate, and peopled with inhabitants eager to trade with Spain or England or France, depending on the imaginer's own nationality. To be sure, reports from the cheerless, storm-swept islands which European (notably French) voyagers from time to time chanced upon at high southern latitudes were not encouraging. Nevertheless, as late as the time of Paul Revere and George III, British publicist Alexander Dalrymple maintained that at least fifty million probably civilized Antarcticans awaited the beneficent advent of the Union Jack.

By that time a new way of thinking about Earth's place in the cosmos had come generally to prevail, which changed the way poeple thought about the hypothetical southern continent. Attempts to measure the transits of the planet Venus across the sun in 1761 and 1769, which were given a certain urgency by the astronomers' knowledge that it would be 105 years before the movements of Venus and Earth would allow them another such chance, required simultaneous accurate observations from widely separated spots on the globe. The intercolonial and overseas collaboration required in the venture, cutting across the national and imperial rivalries of the time, foreshadowed the effective international cooperation of the modern, nationally established Antarctican stations for scientific research during and since the International Geophysical Year (1957). This requirement, newly sensed in the eighteenth century, that further progress of human knowledge would demand a world-wide exchange of accurate scientific information, gave exploration an entirely different rationale from that of the *conquistadores.*[5]

Three days after the bells rang in Philadelphia for American independence, a British naval officer who was not connected with the invasion fleet then gathering to strike at New York sat down near Plymouth Sound in England to write a general introduction to a book. Its subject seemed remote indeed from revolution and war. "Whether the unexplored part of the *Southern Hemisphere* be only an immense mass of water, or contain another continent, as speculative geography seemed to suggest," wrote Captain James Cook, R.N., "was a question which had long engaged the attention, not only of learned men, but of most of the maritime powers of Europe." Accordingly, His Britannic Majesty in 1772 had directed that a voyage be undertaken toward the southern pole. As he told the story of that expedition, Cook cautioned the public not to expect "the elegance of a fine writer, or the plausibility of a professed book-maker," from a plain man "who has not had the advantage of much school education, but who has been constantly at sea from his youth." The captain need not have apologized. Cook, whose careful planning of physical detail and whose concern for the welfare of his men (unheard-of, in a contemporary of Captain Bligh!) set high standards for all subsequent leaders of Antarctic expeditions, established a literary precedent also. Antarctic explorers as a class, unlike the tongue-tied astronauts who are their spiritual descendants, write uncommonly well.

Setting forth in two specially constructed exploring vessels, *Resolution* (462 tons) and *Adventure* (336 tons), James Cook's South Pole expedition struck twice across the Antarctic Circle, probing at the encircling ice pack. It was becoming apparent that Dalrymple's affluent southern continental citizens were phantoms; Captain Cook was, in effect, de-Eldoradoizing Antarctica. During a pause to take up ice for fresh drinking water on December 23, 1773, as he observed many sea-birds, the expedition leader logically inferred "that there is land to the South. If not, I must ask where these birds breed?" Unlike his more credulous predecessors Cook observed with scientific caution that his question might never be

"The Ice Islands"
An engraving from Capt. James Cook, R.N. A Voyage Towards the South Pole and Round the World. Performed in His Majesty's ships the *Resolution* and *Adventure, in the Years 1771, 1773,*

1774, and 1775. (London: Printed for W. Strahan and T. Cadell
in the Strand, 1777), 1:36–37. (Courtesy Kenneth A. Lohf Li-
brarian For Rare Books, Columbia University.)

answered, "for hitherto we have found these lands, if any, quite inaccessible." A month later, on January 30, 1774, at Lat. 71° 10′ S., 106° 54′ W., the expedition reached its farthest South, off what is now called the Walgreen Coast between Ellsworth Land and Marie Byrd Land. Counting 97 hills of ice in the glaring, crumpled mass that blocked their way, the captain—along with "most on board"—decided "that this ice extended quite to the pole, or perhaps joined to some land, to which it had been fixed from the earliest time."

In that case there was little point in attempting to go on. "I will not say it was impossible any where to get farther to the South," Cook conceded; "but the attempting it would have been a rash and dangerous enterprise, and what, I believe, no man in my situation would have thought of." The history of exploration, polar and otherwise, teems with suicidal Faustian madmen, but this rational, matter-of-fact, self-made eighteenth-century Englishman was not one of them. Indeed, Captain Cook greeted this check to the expedition's further progress almost as a deliverance; the terrible, unsentient encumbrance of the Antarctic ice pack had gotten him honorably off the hook:

> I, who had ambition not only to go farther than any one had been before, but as far as it was possible for man to go, was not sorry at meeting with this interruption; as it, in some measure, relieved us; at least, shortened the dangers and hardships inseparable from the navigation of the southern polar regions. Since therefore we could not proceed one inch farther to the South, no other reason need be assigned for my tacking, and standing back to the North.[6]

So matters rested for another 45 years. What daunts personal ambition or scientific curiosity, however, may yield to ordinary commercial greed. Before the end of the century a sealing ship out of Boston, it was said, had sold a cargo of 13,000 fur seal pelts for fifty cents a skin to a buyer in New York who in turn had had them reloaded for Canton, where they fetched five dollars apiece, a bonanza profit of 900 percent. When word of this coup got out, abetted by continuing good prices in China, it ignited a seal-killing boom. Unlike whaling, in which hunter and prey were almost equal hazards for each other, there was no sport in this business; the seals, by the thousands, placidly let themselves be clubbed on the head or stabbed in the breast. With club and lance and gun the sealers speedily depopulated the islands off the coast of Chile, moved on to the known islands beyond the tip of Cape Horn, and pressed on southward into the unknown.

We shall probably never know who actually "discovered" the mainland of Antarctica. Protecting their newfound sealing grounds from poaching by competitors, the sealers felt little urge to publish the exact whereabouts of their findings. The British traditionally have given the laurels to Captain Edward Bransfield, for a reported sighting on January 30, 1820; while Americans have usually credited the young captain of the *Hero,* Nathaniel Palmer, for a logbook entry on November 17, 1820 that described "2 small Islands and the shore every where Perpendicular." American maps of the great cape that thrusts up past the Antarctic Circle toward South America used to name it the Palmer Peninsula; British maps from about 1830 just as regularly referred to it as Graham Land. The Soviets in similar fashion credit the discovery of the Antarctic continent, also in 1820, to Faddei Faddeevich Bellingshausen of the Imperial Russian Navy, whose ships *Vostok* and *Mirny* (after which two present-day Soviet bases on Antarctica are named) discovered what Bellingshausen called by a Russian word usually rendered as "ice mountains," which may or may not mean that he had found solid land and understood what he had found. All three claims still have their partisans; but, warns Antarctic scientist and explorer Laurence M. Gould, "the assumed achievement of the discovery of Antarctica on the part of all three rests on the interpretation of imperfect records by modern investigators. It is unlikely that the matter will ever be settled to the satisfaction of all concerned."[7]

Historically, the most puzzling of these three missions is that of
Bellingshausen. With minutely detailed instructions from the Russian Admiralty—including an enlightened order to treat kindly any
native peoples he might meet, and in dealing with them to avoid
any use of firearms—he had sailed roughly parallel to the track of
Captain Cook a generation before. Seeing to it that his crews observed their Lenten duties and celebrated the Tsar's name day, the
Russian skipper brooded over the fact that men under modern
scurvyless conditions might be still physically fit after a long sea
voyage, only to be at once ruined by drink and disease at the first
inhabited landfall. Of the high southern latitudes Bellingshausen
told much the same kind of story as had Cook: close calls with
icebergs, penguin on the menu (not bad eating once you got used
to it, he claimed, especially if seasoned with vinegar), and the terror of fog so thick that *Vostok* could not see *Mirny* even when the
crew could hear the other ship's bells striking the hours. But what
was a *Russian* naval task force doing at the opposite end of the
world—far indeed from those "warm-water ports" which for
many generations were supposedly the ultimate goal of Russia's
foreign policy? Did the government of Tsar Alexander I envision
another, antipodal, Alaska? Or was this a subtler form of nationalism than the straightforward scramble for commercial advantage
that had characterized the eighteenth century; a mode of national
noteworthiness, such that sending out major exploratory missions
had come to be something countries accounting themselves "Great
Powers" did as a matter of course?[8]

Secretary of State John Quincy Adams, as ghostwriter in 1823
of the Monroe Doctrine, dealt a polite rebuke to that same Tsar
Alexander for attempting to extend his Alaskan dominion further
into North America. Elected President the following year, Adams
told Congress in his first annual message that voyages of discovery, such as the major European nations had endorsed and set into
motion during the half-century since the U.S. Declaration of Independence, were activities of a kind in which a self-respecting

American government ought to engage also. With "generous emulation" the governments of France, England, and Russia had "devoted the genius, the intelligence, the treasures of their respective nations to the common improvement of the species" in astronomical and geographic knowledge. Americans had benefited from these British, French, and Russian discoveries, and they owed therefore a debt "of equal or proportionate exertion in the same cause." Besides, exploration was cheaper than militarism; a hundred circumnavigatory expeditions like Cook's would not cost a nation's treasury as much as a single season's campaign in war. Finally, Adams told the Congressmen, "liberty is power," and when other countries "less blessed with that freedom which is power" advanced with great strides along the frontiers of knowledge, "were we to slumber in indolence, . . . would it not be to . . . doom ourselves to perpetual inferiority?"[9]

That last nagging question reminds one of John F. Kennedy (who, not coincidentally, much admired J. Q. Adams), as he urged his fellow Americans to take the great leap into space and put a man on the moon. The quest for unknown Antarctica was the space race of its day, and it generated some of the same questions—including, inevitably, "Is this trip really necessary?" Adams, both as president and afterward as a respected if maverick elder statesman in the House of Representatives, nagged again and again at Congress to launch a great exploring expedition, one of whose missions would be to solve the age-old mystery of *Terra australis nondam cognita*. His Democratic opponents shot down his proposals while they came from an opposition president, but after Adams's defeat at the polls in 1828 the Jacksonians embraced the same cause as their own. After exasperating, crippling delays (which remind one of the troubles of America's post-Apollo space program) and with unseemly squabbles as to who were to be chiefs and who Indians, an unknown young lieutenant, Charles Wilkes, brashly lobbied for and got the job—the great United States Exploring Expedition of 1838–42 was born.[10]

Motives more quirky, but no less typically American, than John Quincy Adams's were also involved. Jeremiah N. Reynolds emerged in the 1830s as one of the most effective lobbyists with Congress for an Antarctic expedition; he told an enthralled House of Representatives in 1836 that he envisioned American explorers "pushing their adventurous barks into the high southern latitudes" all the way to the pole, and there planting and leaving "our eagle and star-spangled banner . . . to wave on the axis of the earth itself." Reynolds, however, had gotten into the Antarctic lecture circuit in the first place as an advocate for the strange theory of J. N. Symmes that our Earth is hollow, with openings at the poles, and that ships traveling to either of them should be able to sail inside. The idea had a considerable vogue in America; hollow-earth believers were to the nineteenth century what UFO people have become in the twentieth. (Indeed, as will be seen in chapter 8 eventually the two theories became connected.) Edgar Allan Poe was familiar with the concept of holes in the poles, and the climax of his short science fiction story "MS. Found in a Bottle" (1831) describes a ship being drawn to the ultimate southern abyss by an irresistible current: "The ice opens suddenly to the right, and to the left, and we are whirling dizzily, in immense concentric circles, round and round the borders of a gigantic amphitheater, the summit of whose walls is lost in the darkness and the distance." Idly daubing at a folded sail with a tar-brush, the tale's narrator just before the catastrophe sees that sail unfolded and set, "and the thoughtless touches of the brush are spread out into the word DISCOVERY." The message seems to be that discovery has its limits; that man and the Antarctic really were not meant for each other; that those who came after Cook ought to have left well enough alone.[11]

Poe's shudder of Gothic aversion—it is even stronger in his longest story, the *Narrative of Arthur Gordon Pym* (1837–1838), whose narrative of shipwreck, murder, and cannibalism is topped off by an Antarctic voyage so awful that even the southern realm's

Huge tabular berg in the Ross Sea
*It has recently been suggested that such great ice masses, towed
from the Antarctic to some such port as Long Beach, California,
could become a novel means for relieving water shortages in the
American Southwest.*

winsomely funny birds become objects of horror—was not the
only imaginative response available. Antarctica was beginning to
find a niche in polite literature "as a place which, by its remote-
ness from everyday experience, sets man's existence in a new and
truer perspective." That perspective might be as haunted as Poe's;
it might be didactic, as in *The Sea Lions,* by James Fenimore Cooper (1849), who used the sealing grounds beyond the South Shet-
lands as a place where impious reason gets its comeuppance: "The
icy barriers of Antarctica become the analogues of the mysteries
which ultimately confront all rational inquiry and mark its farthest
limits." Or, it might be a last flareup of literary Romanticism,
contemplating a sea- and icescape so vast and austere as to justify

fully that overworked nineteenth-century adjective *sublime*. James Eights, the first American naturalist known to have traveled south of the Antarctic Convergence (the place where the cold currents from the southern continent meet and slide under the milder waters from the north), and the first to have used the term "tabular" to describe the typical Antarctic-born iceberg, reported that one's first actual sight through the mist in those admittedly "dreary and uninhabitable regions" prompted at once an "all-absorbing sentiment of delight."[12]

Eights, one of the few American scientists in that era who could claim any previous Antarctic experience, was chosen to go south in 1838 as geologist with the Congressionally approved United States Exploring Expedition; at the last moment, just before the ships sailed, for no accountable reason, he was dismissed. It was an episode all too typical of the dissension-wracked history of the Wilkes Expedition. To some extent its troubles were typical of *all* polar exploration; "My experience," says Finn Ronne, who in 1947–48 led a notably quarrelsome Antarctic venture, "is that in general the members of expeditions do not get along very well with each other." A great many of the Wilkes Expedition's specific problems, however, rose out of the moment in American history when it was launched. Charles Darwin's personal and intellectual adventure aboard H.M.S. *Beagle* in 1836 had only just been completed. A pre-Darwinian era in science, of gentleman-amateur "natural philosophers," was ending, and a new era of academic/scientific professionals, self-consciously and at times jealously concerned for the integrity of their burgeoning sub-sub-sub-specialties, was just beginning. The relationship between science and government, however—in a time when only one microscope could be found in the whole city of Washington!—was rudimentary. More subtly, a perennial American tension between the empirical and the theoretical, between "practical" and "useless" learning, became particularly acute in the Age of Jackson, when one person's opinion was considered democratically to be just as good as anyone else's. Furthermore, the expedition was an experiment in cooperation between civilians and military personnel; scientists, seeking to spend as many precious minutes as possible ashore collecting specimens on some unknown island, clashed with Navy men insistent upon a sundown curfew lest the specimen collectors be themselves taken as specimens by hostile, conceivably hungry, native islanders.

In addition, the personality of the expedition's commanding officer was—and, among Antarctic historians, remains!—highly controversial. Charles Wilkes, who would gain renown or notoriety two decades later as the Union officer who provoked a first-class crisis with Great Britain by intercepting a civilian British vessel and taking off it Confederate diplomats James Murray Mason and John Slidell, was a man who—to say the least—knew his own mind; and it was, very often, not the mind of his fellow officers, the scientists, the ships' crews, or the politicians back home. Nevertheless, the achievement of the expedition he commanded was very substantial. Antarctic exploration was only a fraction of its mission. In the Oregon Country, still in dispute with Britain, it contributed toward the establishment of the American claim; in the South Pacific it produced hydrographic charts of such excellence that the Navy was still using them a century later in the Second World War; and everywhere the Wilkes Expedition went it collected and sent back treasure troves of scientific specimens. By the end of 1841, with the ships themselves not yet returned, Washington's facilities—the Navy Department, the Patent Office, and eventually the Smithsonian—were swamped with 1500 bird skins, 160 quadrupeds, 3000 insects, 50,000 botanical items, 7000 mineral specimens (collected by the great founder of American mineralogy, James Dwight Dana), some 30 or 40 bushels of seashells, and 200 glass jars, two barrels, and ten kegs filled with molluscs, fishes, and reptiles.[13]

Logically, explorers in Antarctica might have been expected to take up where Palmer and Bellingshausen had left off, crossing

over from South America and then along the Antarctic Peninsula
closer to the Pole. The sub-Antarctic climate of the offshore islands and of the tip of the Peninsula was believed to be relatively
less rugged than that which prevails farther to the south, and Captain James Weddell's discovery in 1823 of the sea that is named
after him, upon which not a particle of ice of any description was
to be seen, seemed to bring the South Pole a long jump nearer.
Captain Weddell, however, had been extraordinarily lucky; the
Weddell Sea was not to be so clear again in February for another
hundred and thirty-four years!

Wilkes, arriving at Tierra del Fuego on February 17, 1839, was
not so fortunate as he launched his first Antarctic probes. By the
time he arrived it was rather late in the southern summer season,
and neither ships nor men were fitted out for polar conditions. Icy
spray smashed unhindered through the warships' open gun ports,
and the crews faced the cold in ordinary Navy foul-weather clothing. One last-minute purchase for the expedition, the *Flying Fish*,
was a small (96-ton) former pilot boat in New York Harbor—a
superb sailer, but dwarfed by a whale that hairraisingly came up
one day and "rubbed his vast sides" against its hull! Yet it was
Flying Fish which on March 22, 1839, after dodging past great
bergs and forcibly breaking through what its captain termed "su-
tures" in the sea ice, attained a mark of 70° South, 101° 11' West.
Although short of Cook's record, this was a very creditable showing indeed; sailing southwest of the Antarctic Peninsula its fifteen-
man crew had unknowingly come within a hundred-mile hands-
breadth of the mainland itself. (A sister ex-pilot ship, the *Sea Gull*,
was shortly afterward lost with all hands in a gale off Cape
Horn.) [14]

The following season the Wilkes Expedition tried again, this
time forsaking the tip of South America as a launch area and instead operating out of Sydney, Australia. Between January 16 and
February 21, 1840, the sloops-of-war *Peacock* and *Vincennes* and
the gun-brig *Porpoise* made or claimed sightings along the coast of
what is now called Wilkes Land. By the end of that cruise Lieu-

tenant Wilkes had coasted far enough (more than 1500 miles) to be
convinced that what they had seen was in fact an Antarctic continent, not merely another collection of circumpolar islands such as
exist in the Arctic Ocean. It was well into the twentieth century
before Wilkes's sweeping claim was allowed to stand. Sir James
Ross, to whom Wilkes helpfully sent a tracing of what he had
found for use in Ross's own voyage of Antarctic discovery, paid
no attention to the claimed American landfalls. Wilkes Land was
not nailed down on the map for certain as an American discovery
until 1956, when aerial photomapping definitely settled the question. (Meanwhile the whole vast territory, except for a small sliver
claimed by the French, had been annexed to Australia.)

Sir James had been sent out to search for the South Magnetic
Pole, surely a useful objective for a maritime commercial nation
quite aside from its intrinsic interest for science. He entered the ice
pack on January 5, 1841, with two unsinkable but constantly rolling Royal Navy bomb-ships, *Erebus* and *Terror*. (Now, *there* are
dark names worthy of the forbidding Antarctic, in contrast to the
Americans' more frisky christenings *Porpoise* and *Flying Fish!*)
Four days later Ross broke through into clear water in the great sea
that now bears his name. Passing (and naming) Cape Adare, the
Ross Sea's western portal, the ships proceeded southward alongside a mighty mountain range, pausing at one rocky offshore island to claim that region for Britain as Victoria Land. Still farther
to the south Ross entered McMurdo Sound, which is now the humming center of American and New Zealand scientific activity in the
Antarctic. On the eastern shore of the sound he found two volcanoes towering above Ross Island, one of them active, which he
named respectively Mount Erebus and Mount Terror. It was
Ross's eyewitness description of this awesome mass of fire and
ice, with "streams of lava pouring down its sides until lost beneath
the snow," that prompted Edgar Allan Poe in 1847 to write of

> *The lavas that restlessly roll . . .*
> *In the realm of the boreal pole.*

("Boreal" unfortunately refers to the *north* pole, but perhaps that can be charged off to poetic license.)[15]

Thwarted from sailing to the South Magnetic Pole, which at that time lay far inland behind the mountains, Ross turned eastward, coasting along the front of his greatest discovery: the Ross Ice Shelf, or, as it was more graphically named until fairly recently, the Ross *Barrier*. A barrier to further navigation it assuredly was, "a perpendicular cliff of ice, between 150 and 200 feet above the level of the sea, perfectly flat and level at the top and without any fissure or promontories in its seaward face," and extending off to the south as far as the eye could see. From that point onward, obviously, one got out and walked! At the Barrier's western end, in the shadow of smoking Mount Erebus, the great British south polar expeditions of the early twentieth century were to be based; nearer its eastern end, where the ice shelf crumples up against buried Roosevelt Island, would be the sites of Roald Amundsen's Framheim and of Richard Byrd's Little America—the setting for the chapters that follow.[16]

"The expeditions came and went through the rest of the nineteenth century," as Lennard Bickel aptly puts it, "like mice nibbling at the edge of a vast, chilled cheese." Few U.S. citizens, however, took part in them. After the Wilkes Expedition returned in 1842, Antarctica was definitely on America's back burner. Charles Wilkes came home from four strenuous years on the farthest seas, not to a victory parade but to a chilly reception: a court martial (he was charged with arbitrary and unfair discipline) and a formal reprimand from the Secretary of the Navy, in a Whig administration which had little enthusiasm for an expedition not of its own making. The wider visions and designs of Jefferson and John Quincy Adams were fading. America's interest turned inward, toward its own continental hinterland; the sea story gave place, as a genre of popular fiction, to the Western dime novel. Penguins and icebergs were all very well, no doubt, but there were cattle to be run in Texas and there was gold to be dredged in California.

As a result, Americans by and large did not take part in Antarctica's Heroic Age of Amundsen and Shackleton and Scott. They
had their own West to digest, and to the extent that they thought at
all in polar terms it was the Arctic, or sub-Arctic, of Alaska and
the Yukon that attracted them, not the frozen far south. Yet in its
psychic effect upon the men who trudged through it on snowshoes,
America's silent Last Northwest—in the words of its greatest
chronicler Jack London a land that was "lifeless, without movement, so lone and cold that the spirit of it was not even that of sad-
ness," but rather had "a hint in it of . . . laughter cold as the
frost"—was much akin to Antarctica. There, on the final North
American frontier, evolved that special symbiosis between civilized man and half-wild sledge dog in which both dog and man,
while becoming deeply bonded to each other, were at the same
time permitted to be more forthrightly barbarian than respectable
society allowed either of them to be back at home; a relationship
without which the conquest of Antarctica would not have been
possible. And there, where the aurora's silent music lifted one's
eyes to the wispy fringes of Earth's atmosphere and the bitter wind
howled with a deadly touch of outer space over huddled human en-
campments, the ever-wandering, fire-building *Homo sapiens* found
himself at last approaching the outer limits of the biosphere. The
Arctic, and even more the Antarctic, constituted a transitional zone
comparable to the shallow tidal waters where Paleozoic ocean life
had made ready for its great leap to the land four hundred million
years before. A leap as comparably stupendous awaits Earth life
today, if we but have the will to take it, and the polar experience
has been our spiritual preparation.[17]

The ostensible motive for getting us up out of our comfortable
ocean into those transitional tidewaters, regrettably, must sometimes be rather crass: finding gold in the Yukon or outwitting the
Russians on the moon. Yet the Yukon gold rush was also an opportunity "to see and take part in a most picturesque and impressive movement across the wilderness," reminisced participant

Hamlin Garland. "I believed it to be the last march of the kind
which could ever come to America, so rapidly were the wild
places being settled up." In 1897, the year of the Yukon rush, at
least one wandering American sought his picturesqueness not in
the Arctic but in the cold south; Dr. Frederick A. Cook—better
known, a decade afterward, for a controversial and generally re-
jected claim to have been first at the North Pole—shipped aboard
the ship *Belgica* with Adrian de Gerlache for an Antarctic cruise.
(Another shipmate was young Roald Amundsen, who later on may
have saved that expedition by nagging a despondent captain into
eating seal meat for his health; Antarctic history, ever since Nat
Palmer quite by chance encountered the Tsar's two ships in 1820,
has abounded in coincident meetings and associations of this
kind.)[18]

On January 23, 1898, Cook and others piled eagerly into a boat
and landed on unknown terrain well along the Antarctic Peninsula's western shore. The American doctor captured in his diary
the interplanetary character of the site:

> It was a curious evening. Everything about us had an otherworld ap-
> pearance. The scenery, the light, the clouds, the atmosphere, the
> curious luminous grey of the water—everything wore an air of mys-
> tery. There was nothing in our surroundings which resembled any part
> of the antipodes or any part of the Arctic.

Two geologists were first to step out of the boat, one of whom was
shortly "turning up the stones along the shore," wrote Cook,
"where he found mysterious crawling things which he hailed with
as much delight as if he had found nuggets of gold."[19]

A few days later the Gerlache expedition became the first in history to engage in overnight tent-camping on Antarctica, and at the
end of February it recorded another first: the *Belgica* was beset by
pack in the Bellingshausen Sea and was iced in for 347 days,
thereby making its crew—quite unintentionally!—the first of the
great Antarctic wintering-over parties. The *Belgica's* experience,

in the course of which it had taken a shore party seven hard, man-hauling days to penetrate only a mile into the interior, raised the logical question: might there not be an easier way of doing Antarctic exploration? For example, by air? En route to his first winter quarters at Hut Point on McMurdo Sound, Captain Robert Falcon Scott essayed a tentative answer to that question.

Anchoring his ship *Discovery* at a small indentation in the Barrier, on February 4, 1902, Scott had his crew unpack and inflate with hydrogen an army balloon named Eva. (One sailor, nonchalantly standing nearby with a lighted pipe, was suddenly seized by the scruff of the neck and pulled away!) "The Captain, knowing nothing whatever about the business, insisted on going up first and through no fault of his own came down safely," Dr. Edward Wilson wrote in his diary that day. At an altitude of 800 feet one could see further over the Ross Shelf than ever before, and so Ernest Shackleton went aloft to take photographs. Dr. Wilson considered "the whole ballooning business . . . an exceedingly dangerous amusement," and reported that "happily, after lunch, the balloon was found to have leaked to such an extent that an ascent was impossible, so no one went up and the balloon was emptied." So ended the first aeronautic experiment in Antarctic history, the precursor of Richard Byrd's stout trimotored Ford in 1929 and of the chattering U.S. Navy helicopters of today. Edward Wilson, meanwhile, before another decade was over, was to discover in anguish that other, earthbound Antarctic activities can be far more dangerous than ballooning.[20]

In 1908 Scott's former colleague Sir Ernest Shackleton, leading his own South Pole expedition, steered for the little inlet in the Ross Shelf at 78° 28′ South, 163° 45′ West that Scott had named Balloon Bight. It was gone, swept out of existence by a cataclysmic calving of the Barrier ice; in its place was a broad shallow natural harbor, whose blithely frolicking inhabitants prompted Shackleton to name it the Bay of Whales. "It was bad enough to try and make for a port that had been wiped off the face of the earth," the

How the Bay of Whales got its name

Briton declared, "but it would have been infinitely worse if we had landed there whilst the place was still in existence. . . . The thought of what might have been made me decide that under no circumstances would I winter on the Barrier, and that wherever we did land we would secure a solid rock foundation for our winter home."

Shackleton did secure such a foundation, at Cape Royds on Ross Island, from which members of his party climbed Mount Erebus for the first time. The following Antarctic summer (1908–9) he struck for the South Pole, but fell short of his goal by a tantalizing ninety-seven miles. (Had the ice not calved at the other end of the Shelf, Admiral Lord Mountevans, his fellow voyager with Scott, believed, "and had Shackleton made a landing there, it is possible that he and not Amundsen would have been the first to reach the Pole.") Captain Scott, returning to Antarctica for his second (and last) expedition in 1910, adhered to Shackleton's solid-rock theory and wintered again on Ross Island, at Cape Evans. Roald Amundsen, however, Scott's great rival, when he came to look over the ground—or ice—upon which he would build his Framheim, decided that the Barrier in the Bay of Whales area was stably grounded on a submerged island. So he took the calculated risk of wintering there—at least fifty miles nearer to the South Pole, he reasoned, than Scott's base would be. Both locations, at Ross Island and at the Bay of Whales, were logical, intellectually defensible choices—and life and death would turn upon them.[21]

"Modern civilization," Thorstein Veblen wrote in 1906, "is peculiarly matter-of-fact." Yet sometimes, even in the statistical, nit-picking twentieth century, the facts transcend themselves into legend. To understand the task confronting those explorers, a *New York Times* science editor later suggested, one must imagine the United States and Mexico entirely covered with snow, and a man walking from New York—the only harbor yet discovered on that mythical continent—all the way to Chicago, hauling a sledge. The story of the race for the South Pole between Roald Amundsen and Robert Falcon Scott in 1911–12 was prosaically pieced together from cablegrams, set up on linotype machines, and run off on high-speed rotary presses; in an archaic time it would more fittingly have taken the form of anonymously composed poetry.[22]

A skald, in a drafty hall illuminated by smoking pine torches, might have sung the Amundsen-Scott Saga, telling the tale of how a high-spirited Captain Scott fared forth aboard the *Terra Nova*, torn between sheer curiosity ("Won't it be fun when we've got all this Pole business out of the way and can do some real scientific work") and national pride ("It *must* be an Englishman who first gets to the Pole"); how a grimly pragmatic Roald Amundsen, bound for the *North* Pole with Fridtjof Nansen's old ship the *Fram,* learned that Robert Peary had beaten him to that prize and so told his crew on the high seas that they were going south instead; how Scott and his men, unwilling to use dogs and unable to employ effectively the ponies they had brought to lay down their supply depots, exhaustingly man-hauled their sledges all the way to the Pole; how Amundsen, after reducing "the weight of provisions to be carried by calculating the flesh of the dogs which carried it as part of the food supply of us men," on the day appointed for the slaughter turned up the hissing primus stove in his tent in order not to hear the shots—but feasted on dog cutlets next day nonetheless; how Scott's party came at last to its goal, only to find there a black flag, ski and sledge tracks, and paw prints, mute evidence that "the Norwegians have forestalled us and are first at the Pole"; how Amundsen's party raced home in triumph to Framheim, the surviving dogs sleek and eager from a diet of fresh meat, while Scott's men, worn out and discouraged, one by one died along the homeward trail; and, finally, how a rescue party eight months later found Scott frozen in his tent, only eleven miles from the supply cache that might have saved him, one arm flung across the body of Dr. Wilson, and under his shoulders the journal with his last entry: "It seems a pity, but I do not think I can write more. For God's sake look after our people."[23]

After Amundsen's conquest of the South Pole there remained yet one great objective for an Antarctic land journey: the crossing of the continent from sea to sea. In 1914 Sir Ernest Shackleton undertook it, and plunged into an adventure even more incredible than the struggles of Amundsen and Scott. Beset by pack ice in the Weddell Sea on January 19, 1915, his coal-powered barkentine *Endurance* drifted with the pack all through the following Antarctic winter, and on November 21 sank beneath the floes. Meanwhile Shackleton had evacuated all hands to a camp on the ice, where they floated for another four months until they were able to launch the ship's boats and land just north of the Antarctic Peninsula on miserably barren Elephant Island. On April 24, 1916, with another winter coming on, six men in a decked-over lifeboat with a small storm sail set out to get help from the nearest outpost of civilization, on South Georgia—eight hundred miles away! They made landfall on May 9, but on the wrong side of the island, so that three of them had then to climb its icy, three-thousand-foot spine and guess which of its treacherous valleys led down to its only settlement. They chose the right place to descend—cued by the early-morning whistle of a whaling factory, an incongruous note of industrialism—and were welcomed, when the word got around, by captains and mates and sailors who had sailed the stormy southern ocean for many years without having heard a tale the like of this, and who felt it an honor to meet with Sir Ernest and his comrades and shake their hands.

The news of Shackleton's exploit reached England at the end of May, 1916, just in time to be unceremoniously shoved off the front page of the British press by news of the naval battle of Jutland. Ironically, although Sir Ernest had brought his entire crew through the ordeal alive and well, a number of them soon afterward perished in the First World War. "When dying gladly for your country was the norm," bitterly writes Duncan Carse, who has himself climbed those glaciated South Georgia hills, "explorers who went to the ends of the earth were in bad taste—though you couldn't quite proffer them the white feather." And in the postwar climate of skepticism and disillusion, the motives of both the warmakers and the explorers could be called into question: "There had been in four and a half years of unbridled blood-letting such a prodigal expenditure of patriotism and loyalty, courage and discipline, to such little apparent purpose that their validity as founder-virtues of the good life was no longer an article of faith. . . . Antarctica," Carse concludes, was out of fashion."

Fashions come and fashions go. Since America's Bicentennial (and that date may not be entirely coincidental), there has been a modest revival of interest in polar affairs. When the New Haven Repertory Theater in 1977 presented Ted Tally's play *Terra Nova,* a dramatization of Scott's last march, it was well received. "For a generation, the educated young of the U.S. have been taught to

deride or satirize the heroic,'' reviewer T. E. Kalem wrote in
Time. "It is moving to watch their rapt attention at *Terra Nova*,
for they are famished for models of honor.''[24]

Models of honor may have been sparse in the 1970s, a time
whose bitter folklore told us that young, high-spirited knights *sans
peur et sans reproche* are invariably either cut down by skulking
assassins or corrupted by their own quest for success. Fifty years
ago, however, such models were more readily available. The decade of the 1920s was not so hopelessly sunk in cynicism as
Shackleton's admirer Duncan Carse assumes. Everyone knows of
Charles Lindbergh's role in momentarily recalling the public of the
Roaring Twenties to its better self, but a later generation is less familiar with the Arctic and Antarctic aerial odysseys of the same
decade. One of the greatest such adventures came to its climax
with Richard Byrd's flight to the South Pole on November 29,
1929—a month and year which Americans usually remember in
quite another way. It is time in the longer run of history that we
made room, beside our painful memory of what Americans were
doing on Wall Street in 1929, for a more constructive recollection
of what Americans were doing that same year at the Bay of
Whales.

One newspaper cartoon prompted by the Lindbergh flight, reprinted in the *Literary Digest* for June 25, 1927, was captioned:
"It is a big relief to be looking up instead of down.'' A figure
labeled "Public" is standing on a junkheap inscribed "Hollywood,'' "Elmer Gantry,'' and the like. Over "Public's" head
pass airplanes, buzzing him with clouds labeled "Human stead-
fastness''—"Human courage''—"Faith''—"Romance''—"Constructive science''—"Inspiring youth''—and "Indomitable will.''
That same issue of the *Digest* carried an article on "The Rocket-
Ship of the Future,'' by Max Valier, who predicted a trans-Atlantic rocket crossing in two hours: "Colonel Lindbergh's feat, with
which the world is now ringing, will look like the expedition of a
snail across the street.'' That theme also is present, by implication

at least, in any twentieth-century account of Antarctic discovery. The great white south, as its own explorers well know, is not the conclusion of man's search for the geographic unknown; it is a prelude, pointing toward the stars.[25]

Pitching anticline in ice, Bay of Whales
Ice, as glaciologists like to point out, is geologically a rock, and it behaves the same way as rock when subjected to pressure.

1

The Ross
Ice Shelf
or Bust

*There you stand, lost in the infinite series of the sea, with
nothing ruffled but the waves. . . . A sublime uneventfulness
invests you; you hear no news; read no gazettes; extras with
startling accounts of commonplaces never delude you into un-
necessary excitements; you hear of no domestic afflictions;
bankrupt securities; fall of stocks; are never troubled with the
thought of what you shall have for dinner—for all your meals
for three years and more are snugly stowed in casks, and your
bill of fare is immutable.*
        —*Herman Melville,* Moby-Dick, *chap. XXXV*

"If you stuck a hatpin in the globe at Spitsbergen," a distinguished polar explorer has written, "and drove it down through
the center, the point would come out at the Bay of Whales." It is
at Spitsbergen, on the opposite side of the earth from Little
America, that Little America's story really begins, on May 10,
1926. At Kings Bay, at that time the northernmost year-round
community in the world—a drab huddle of buildings backed by a
breathtaking snow slope—the man who reportedly had just come
back from the first flight over the North Pole was enjoying a victory dinner with his associates, rivals, and friends. One of them,
fifteen years before, had been the first human being to walk to the
planet's other pole. They made an incongruous pair: the pleasant-
faced, wavy-haired American naval officer, scion of an ancient
colonial family that had been in Virginia since the seventeenth
century, and the craggy, jut-beaked old Viking.[1]

"Well, Byrd, what shall it be now?" Roald Amundsen asked.

"The South Pole," Richard E. Byrd lightly replied.

The Norwegian at once became serious. Byrd had the right idea,
Amundsen said. "The old order is changing. Aircraft is the new
vehicle for exploration. . . . Look here!" And he began to plan;

to suggest other Norwegians he knew for the expedition; to recommend a ship. Antarctica's age of legend, of wooden ships that vanished for two or three years into the great white unknown, was ending; Antarctica's mechanical age, of gasoline and radio waves, had begun.[2]

Amundsen had to get up early the next morning. He was scheduled to float in a dirigible from Spitsbergen across to Alaska, thereby becoming the first man in history to have visited *both* poles. That put him one up on Richard Byrd, who, moreover, was unable to act at once upon Amundsen's south polar suggestions. Byrd had a prior commitment to fly across the ocean from New York to Paris, carrying the first transatlantic airmail. One month before his departure on that flight, however, Charles Lindbergh dramatically upstaged him by crossing the Atlantic alone. Byrd nevertheless took off as planned on June 29, 1927, with three companions—Bert Acosta, George Noville, and one of Amundsen's North Pole group, a rugged young Royal Norwegian Air Force flier named Bernt Balchen. Le Bourget airfield, where Lindbergh scant weeks earlier had come down into a Hollywood scene of blazing car headlights under a clear sky, this time was pounded into invisibility by a driving rain. The people on the ground could hear the drone of the engines, but the airplane could not land. After circling the field for nearly three hours, with the gas tanks almost empty, Balchen flew the Byrd party back over the French coast and set the plane down safely in the surf at Ver-sur-Mer—a place better known to Americans of a subsequent, war-torn generation as Omaha Beach.[3]

For Byrd, a lucky American in the boom year 1927, this was a typical adventure: the fatal accident that did *not* happen. It was a good omen for the Virginian as he went on afterward to seize his chance, as he put it, "to take off the maps for the schoolchildren of the ages to come, a part of that great blank white space at the bottom of the world." By (northern) midwinter 1928, the Byrd Antarctic Expedition had set up shop in a small fifteenth-floor room on West 45th Street, New York, with space enough for a desk, a typewriter, a filing cabinet, and a couple of chairs. Within weeks it had expanded into a suite of rooms at the Biltmore, donated by the hotel. There Commander Byrd planned, made lists, lined up equipment, listened to prospective recruits, and of necessity engaged in the "beastly job" of raising money. That task in turn required publicity, and Byrd's calmly conceived scientific and geographic venture had to compete for attention with the big-time sports of the golden twenties, not to mention the scandals and gang wars. Therefore, on March 11, 1928, the *New York Times* in exchange for exclusive coverage of the adventure blazoned "Byrd's Plans for his South Polar Expedition" across page one of its fat Sunday edition.[4]

No gain without loss, in this kind of bargain; if the *Times* got exclusive coverage, some of its rivals—most particularly the Hearst newspapers[5]—were bound to criticize the polar venture for extravagance or uselessness. Moreover, in the mass-media packaging of history a kind of Gresham's Law operates: no matter how much genuine intrinsic drama a historic moment may contain, the event has to be oversold. It soon developed that Richard Byrd was not the only explorer with his heart set on the Antarctic that year. At the same time that the Byrd expedition would be crunching its way through the pack ice in the Ross Sea south of New Zealand toward Amundsen's old polar invasion route, the Australian explorer Sir Hubert Wilkins planned to be flying out of Deception Island, in the other area whence men traditionally had made approaches to Antarctica: the great archipelago, then thought to be a peninsula, that lies below South America like a mirror-image of the Andes. Inevitably, therefore, in the American and British press the cry of "Antarctic Derby" went up: would Wilkins beat Byrd to the Pole?

Sizing up the two expeditions in an article for the *Nation,* with subtle, acrimonious echoes from the old controversies over Scott and Amundsen, arctic explorder Earl Hanson gave the preference to the Australian: "Commander Byrd's million-dollar expedition is too ponderous, too cluttered up with materials and safety plans and specialized experts who are still absolute greenhorns under polar conditions." Wilkins, with two planes and two other men, operating without a base-ship, and dependent on "a chance whaler" to get him out afterward, had a better—if riskier—chance of getting there first. It was an unkind cut, and somewhat unfair since the Byrd expedition would be, for scientific purposes, definitely *under*-supplied with specialists. But Richard Byrd declined to play this media-encouraged game. "I am not engaging in a race to the South Pole," he flatly told the *New York World*. "The Antarctic expedition which I am leading will go forward exactly as planned, and without change due to the plans of any one else, in the interests of science and aviation."[6]

A few old Antarctic hands pointed out that science and aviation had never before faced such a challenge as Antarctica. Herbert Ponting, who had gone south with the ill-fated Robert Falcon Scott—and who, using the clumsy box camera and glass plate equipment available in 1910, had made some of the greatest photographs ever taken in that frozen wilderness—praised Byrd's successful flight from Spitsbergen to the North Pole. However, Ponting warned, "Spitzbergen in Summer is a pleasant place with almost a temperate climate," quite unlike the frigid, windswept shores where Byrd would have to begin his south polar flight. Likewise, Captain Charles S. Wright, who had the proud, sad distinction of having found Scott's frozen body on the polar trail, feared tragedy: "If Byrd is forced to make a landing on the ice, I do not see how he can ever take off again." The polar interior provided no way of "living off the land," and Antarctica had no natives, friendly or unfriendly. "In the immediate region of the pole," as one writer summed it up for *Popular Mechanics,* "the airmen will look down on . . a scene of sheer lifeless desolation such as one might imagine upon the face of the moon." Man, as noted in the Prologue, was now approaching his ultimate biological limit; beyond Antarctica lay only outer space.[7]

Before an aircraft could get itself into such a predicament as Captain Wright described, however, it had to be loaded on board a ship and carried to Antarctica, along with a mountainous cargo of food, fuel, dogs, and men. The expedition needed an ice-ship, like Fridtjof Nansen's sturdy old *Fram,* in which Amundsen had gone south. It would have to be second-hand; "new ships," Byrd ruefully noted, "are very expensive." He took Amundsen's advice, therefore, and cabled to Tromsoe, Norway, for an old sealer built in 1882, the *Samson,* a windjammer with an overall length of 162 feet, 31 feet abeam, and a capacity of 502 gross tons. It had an auxiliary steam engine that could barely get up 200 horsepower—no more, as one of the crew observed long afterward, than a modern automobile. It had a hull 34 inches thick, however, and that, in the grinding Antarctic pack ice, would be what mattered.

En route from Norway to North America the *Samson* came near ending its days when the boiler buckled in a storm, but the Norwegian skipper brought the old vessel (slowly!) the rest of the way across the Atlantic under sail. Stripped of its rotted old sails and rigging, converted into a bark (square-rigged on the fore and main masts; fore-and-aft rigged at the mizzen), and rechristened *City of New York,* the expedition's flagship lay at dockside on the Hudson looking to one bystander like "an ideal craft . . . for Peter Pan and the Pirate Captain, not to mention the revengeful crocodile." The contrast between the romantic antiquity of the ship and the aeronautical and scientific modernity of its mission was stark: *"The City of New York,"* second mate Harry Adams believed, "is probably the last vessel of her kind in the world." Captain Frederick C. Melville, who claimed the author of *Moby-Dick* as his father's first cousin, was chosen to sail the *City* to the Bay of Whales; ship and master were a historically appropriate match. A veteran of thirty-one years at sea, mostly—and by preference—on sailing vessels, Melville was a man who prudently respected sailors' superstitions, such as the belief that it is an ill omen to kill an albatross.[8]

Commander Byrd, taking two of his backers on an inspection

tour of the ship after reconditioning, tried to see the brighter side:
"Things look great," he declared. "She almost looks like a regular yacht." Privately the expedition leader was more skeptical.
Durable the *City of New York* undoubtedly was, but it was also
slow and small; in fact the *Resolution,* one of the ships that had
carried Captain Cook to his farthest south back in 1774, had had a
greater carrying capacity. Also, the *City*'s deadweight had greatly
increased with advancing age as water soaked into the ancient hull.
Worst of all, the crate built for the Ford Trimotor airplane that was
going to the Pole would not fit into the hold. So the expedition had
to buy a second vessel, a rusty iron cargo ship named the *Chelsea,*
high in the bow and with a low, overhung stern—"a worn iron
pot, bent into the general shape of a ship and riveted haphazard,"
as Harry Adams later described it. With dimensions of only 174 by
34 feet, this second ship had no more overall carrying capacity
than the *City of New York,* but it possessed two good-sized cargo
holds; it would do.

Byrd renamed the new acquisition after his mother, Eleanor
Bolling. Its crew, as they watched the green water tumble over the
decks, sometimes reaching as high as the bridge, would soon learn
to call it the *Evermore Rolling;* and they would have the additional
aggravation that the newsreel cameramen ignored their vessel in
favor of the *City of New York*'s picturesquely photogenic yards and
sails. The *Bolling,* declared Harry Adams, who was to serve on
both ships before the expedition was over, "stood in the public
eye as a sort of step-child who is hardly noticed, while the romantic *City of New York* occupied the headlines of every newspaper in
the world." Perhaps because of that public neglect, the *Eleanor
Bolling* nevertheless had ardent partisans among its own crew. Arnold Clarke, who shipped as a fireman aboard the *Bolling,* regularly and studiously referred to the *City of New York* in his diary
merely as "the other vessel," and concluded that "it was a mistake to expect a vessel of its type to play a useful part in a modern
expedition."[9]

(*above*) The City of New York
*Built in Norway in 1882 as a sealer and re-rigged in New York
for the first Byrd Antarctic expedition, the* City *struck one on-
looker as "an ideal craft . . . for Peter Pan and the Pirate Captain, not to mention the revengeful crocodile." But its 34-inch
planking could be expected to survive the pounding ice floes.*

(*below*) The Eleanor Bolling
*Purchased primarily because it had a hold large enough for the
Ford trimotored airplane that was going to the South Pole, the
Bolling otherwise, said Commander Byrd, "had little to recommend her." Nonetheless, this ugly duckling inspired partisan loyalty in its crew, despite news photographers' attention to the
more glamorous* City.

"We purchased her," Byrd later said of the *Bolling,* "because she was cheap, available and suitable for the job we had in store; otherwise, I candidly confess, she had little to recommend her." Even so, in one expedition leader's judgment, the Commander had been robbed: the *Eleanor Bolling* had been bought for $34,000 when it could have been obtained for one-fourth or one-third of that figure, and the *City* likewise had been "purchased without being seen at a terrifically and unnecessarily high price." Commander Byrd, expedition second-in-command Laurence Gould concluded, "is not a business man." However, to assess those purchases in terms of Byrd's "cost overruns," as we would nowadays call them, many have been to put the question the wrong way. When Galahad rode out to look for the Grail, did he stop to ponder how much his horse was worth?[10]

Like the astronauts of a later day, Antarctic explorers in 1928 could not go chasing back to the supermarket for items they had forgotten. Down into those little ships' holds, and into those of the commercial whalers that would carry much of their gear part of the way, went the mass of supplies Byrd's people would need for a stay of a year and a half at the bottom of the world. Except for what could be picked up in Dunedin, New Zealand, on the way,— eggs, it was said, were cheaper there—and for the seal and penguin flesh that would help to sustain them and their dogs in Antarctica, it all had to be put together in New York: 4000 pounds of pork loins, one ton of fresh hams; two tons of smoked ham, three of bacon; half a ton each of lamb and mutton, one ton of veal; five tons of beef, two of corned beef, 1000 pounds of hot dogs; 3500 chickens, 2500 turkeys; ten tons of sugar, five of flour, one of dried milk; 1500 pounds of calves' liver, for vitamins during the long winter darkness; 1000 pounds of cigarettes, 1000 pounds of pipe tobacco, 500 pounds of chewing gum; 450 pounds of ether, 200 packages of tetanus antitoxin; 6 guitars, 15 harmonicas, 12 ukuleles, and an electric player piano; sledges, special footwear, skis, and snowshoes; eight thousand dollars' worth of dog food, much of which turned out to be unsatisfactory and had to be replaced in New Zealand; radio equipment, scientific instruments, mechanical tools, a large drum of alcohol, for photo purposes, and other liquor which in prohibitionist America had to be described as "medicinal only." The expedition's doctor, Byrd assured the press, would keep it under lock and key.

All this was beginning to count up as costing a good deal of money, even for affluent 1928. The support of government, with Calvin Coolidge in the White House, was primarily only moral; even Byrd's own Navy Department, from which Byrd had technically retired, was bound up in the outlook of Washington Conference retrenchment. So the proud Virginian, quite gallingly, had to borrow and beg. Lindbergh gave a thousand dollars; so did heavyweight champion Gene Tunney. Fourteen-year-old Theodore Roosevelt, III, painted his porch roof, weeded the garden, and did other work around the house to raise ten dollars. ("I asked mother if ten dollars would be enough to come in handy if sent to you," he wrote to Byrd, "and she said 'yes.' ") Larger gifts came from John D. Rockefeller, Jr., the National Geographic Society, and Edsel Ford.

Ingenious ways were found of inducing corporate America to part with a little of its treasure trove. Amelia Earhart, for example, endorsed a cigarette and turned the $1500 she earned from that commercial over to the Byrd expedition. Fur merchants in New York furnished some of their wares, in return for a tribute to their product's warmth and comfort near the South Pole. An equipment exhibit was held in Gimbels.[11] Dr. Coman, Little America's physician, persuaded the Army Medical Corps to part with equipment for the chemical sterilization of water, and coaxed medical supply and drug companies to donate surgical sutures, dressings, and seasickness remedies; Coman even got the Rogers Brothers Seed Company, of Idaho Falls, Idaho, to promise 3000 pounds of potato flour, delivered to Dunedin.[12]

Inevitably some gifts came in which were not especially welcome, but which under the circumstances could not be refused. Much of this unwanted cargo would have to be unpacked when the expedition got to New Zealand, and left behind; as airplane pilot Bernt Balchen recalled three decades later, "two hundred kegs of chutney sauce, which some bright genius had purchased for the expedition, may be in the warehouse in Dunedin to this day." Many of these donations in kind, however, were highly welcome. The Beechnut Company put up a large quantity of peanut butter and jelly; Swift & Company provided 3500 pounds of butter in six-pound sealed tins; Maxwell House donated all the coffee. The Ford Trimotor, the photographic supplies, and $2500 worth of office supplies were all donated. On the very day the *City of New York* left for Antarctica, an advertisement placed close to one news story proclaimed that "Commander Byrd takes along OAKITE Cleanser." Yet expenditures and cash outlays were running neck-and-neck when the *City* sailed, and business firms did not yet have the urge for tax-deductible grants that the New Deal would inadvertently trigger with its drastic revisions of the internal revenue.[13]

To the question, what was the use of raising so much money to explore millions of acres so many thousands of miles away? (analogous to the critics' complaint of a later day, "Why go to the moon?") Richard Byrd had no ready answer. "We lack, most of us, the universal, philosophical point of view," he admitted. "As is natural in our own crowded affairs, we see things narrowly . . . in trite, personal and commercial terms of worth." Antarctica could not be appraised on such limited terms. "Vainly did I try to impress this fact upon a well-known American business man. 'But where's the money in it? Where's the profit?' he demanded." The *conquistadores* had gone out to far lands for loot; the California and Klondike pioneers had gone for gold; and Helen's face, 'tis said, launched a thousand ships to Troy. But most of Byrd's volunteers, working their passage on those lumbering ships only to face long weeks of hard work, monotony, darkness, and biting cold, could expect no more than the satisfaction of having gone to

Antarctica the way men went to Everest, "because it is there." A few might take heart at the thought of having a nunatak or a glacier named after them; the rest, unsung, would stolidly take their turns shoveling snow or chopping blubber. There would be no gold, and no Helens; they were on their way, Byrd wrote in his journal, to "a new place, where wealth and fame and power count for nothing, and where men will not strut because there are no women about."

A century earlier such volunteering would have been no cause for surprise. American literature and legend abound with young people who run off to sea or light out for the territory. However, even allowing for the fact that few of the expedition's newcomers had any clear idea what they were letting themselves in for, theirs was an astonishing vocational choice to be making in the (supposedly) self-indulgent, money-mad twenties. Three thousand had already applied for posts on the Byrd Antarctic Expedition when the *New York Times* ran its first big story on March 11, 1928, and many hundreds more would come clamoring to go before the ships sailed in August and September. If Byrd had trouble drawing dollars from American capitalists, he had equal trouble turning American volunteers away. Perhaps they sensed that this might be their last chance for this kind of adventure. Such opportunity was "lessening all the time," Byrd noted; consequently, when such a chance did present itself, there was a "rush for admission to the party. With only one major expedition in sight this year . . . and a United States population of 110,000,000 people, this rush threatens at times to become a riot."

They came in droves—the cranks, some with mysterious inventions they wanted to test out at the South Pole; the parents, some of them rich and well-connected, insistent that their boys go with Byrd; and, most painfully of all, Byrd's own friends, lobbying like " a little Battalion of Death" to make him take along some young protégé. One adviser suggested that he have a board of Army and Navy surgeons give all his applicants the standard recruiting test, to winnow down the field, and then select his party by lot from the survivors of that screening. Byrd, in spite of his own Annapolis training, saw no merit whatever in that idea: ''The trouble with such a plan is that a year of isolation and hardship on the polar sea . . . does things to men that are never even dreamed of in ordinary military service.'' Well he knew that two members of the first crew to winter over in Antarctica, in 1898 on board the *Belgica,* had gone mad, and he grimly took the appropriate precautions. Press reports revealed to the public that the expedition's medical supplies included handcuffs and a strait-jacket. It is a measure of leadership or luck that these ''social safety appliances,'' as the *Boston Globe* tactfully called them, never had to be used.[14]

The only announced choice for membership in the expedition as of March 11, 1928, half a year before departure,[15] was Floyd Bennett, who had flown with Byrd on the North Pole venture and who, on another Arctic flight, had unhesitatingly climbed out of the cockpit onto the wing and loosened the oil tank cap to lower the pressure; evidently a man one could count on. That same spring, however, Bennett, en route for a rescue mission to a downed German airship in Newfoundland, took sick with pneumonia and died—a shocking blow to Richard Byrd, who sadly renamed the Ford Trimotor after his departed friend and turned instead to Bernt Balchen, the powerful young Norwegian who had successfully ditched their plane off the French coast the year before. Other veterans of previous Byrd expeditions were recruited; fourteen of them, all told, ended up spending the winter in Little America. Martin Ronne, the expedition's 68-year-old sailmaker, held the ultimate Antarctic credential: he had wintered over with Amundsen at the Bay of Whales. It was a silk tent made by Ronne, left behind by Amundsen, that Scott had found at the South Pole. Arthur Walden, the sturdy old New Englander who would be in charge of all the sledge dogs, likewise had a long polar pedigree; he had driven huskies in Jack London's Yukon. For the most part,

Martin Ronne
*The oldest member of the wintering-over party at
Little America, he had been at Framheim with the
legendary Amundsen. His son, Finn Ronne, also
became an Antarctic explorer and eventually led
an expedition of his own.*

however, in mustering his forces, Commander Byrd had to fall
back upon his own intuitive sense of a man's temperament and his
potential for handling stress. "A lot of it was sheer accident,"
recalls Laurence M. Gould, the expedition's geologist and second-
in-command. Scientists for the expedition volunteered themselves,
or were proposed by leading lights in America's scientific es-

James Feury
*The former ice cream manufacturer's specialties
in Antarctica were nursing the Ford Snowmobile
until its untimely demise, and making Eskimo
Pies for all.*

tablishment. But "a great many of the nonscientific staff were people who burgeoned into the office at the Biltmore," Gould continues, "and if Byrd liked them, they got in." [16]

Despite Richard Byrd's conscientious preparation of all the material details, according to Amundsen's dictum that "an adventure
is merely a bit of bad planning," there was thus a refreshing amateur spirit about the whole enterprise. This was a chance not only

to go off on man's last great geographic frontier short of the moon, but also to do so without taking a battery of tests and filling out a host of forms—and without being particularly trained or qualified for the job, on the traditional bumptious assumption that any American can do anything. Although there are no trees in Antarctica, a forester went to Little America; so did a prizefighter; so did an ice cream manufacturer! When asked how this hastily, even haphazardly, assembled team actually performed out on the ice, Professor Gould is quick to say, "For the most part, magnificently," in implicit rebuke to the meticulously specialized ways of a later generation. In return, Little America's aerologist Henry Harrison pays tribute to the expedition's leaders. "If I had to try a thumbnail sketch of the expedition, I would put it this way," Harrison writes:

> Byrd had the imagination and organizing brains to put it together.
> Balchen had the mechanical brain and technical skills to make flying safer and surer than it had a right to be at that time.
> With Gould at the helm, the scientific program was assured of success from the start.[17]

The closest any expedition member came to the elaborate psychological screening, security clearances, and other bureaucratic tests of suitability that are taken for granted nowadays (compare the red tape involved in volunteering for the Peace Corps!) was the selection of a senior Boy Scout to go to Little America; he was chosen in a nationwide competition. The formal application that was circulated among 28,400 scout troops had blanks for certification by one's scoutmaster or troop committee (including spaces to show observance of the Scout Oath and Law, Motto, and Good Turn); for specifying the merit badges earned; for evidence of winter and other camping experience; for school records, physical examination results, proof of age, and a photograph. Paul A. Siple, of Troop 24, Erie, Pennsylvania, with 59 out of 88 possible merit badges and other impressive credentials, was the winner,

chosen from six national finalists. Typically of the pace of that expedition, as it scrambled to get everybody and everything together
in time to get down to the Ross Sea under optimum ice conditions
(comparable to the "launch window" of time within which a
spacecraft must lift off for an interplanetary rendezvous), the vic-
torious Scout learned of his appointment only five days before
sailing. He showed up at expedition headquarters on August 22 in
regulation Scout uniform with a blue kerchief, and was promptly
given a dental examination; there was not much, except simple ex-
traction, that could be done if an aching cavity developed in the
polar snow.[18]

Three days later, on the morning when the *City of New York*
weighed anchor, a headline proclaimed:

13 DEAD, 100 HURT IN SUBWAY CRASH IN TIMES SQUARE;
TWO CARS OF RUSH-HOUR I.R.T. EXPRESS JUMP FAULTY
    SWITCH;
SUBWAY MAINTENANCE MAN IS ARRESTED, CHARGE IS HOMI-
    CIDE

As they read newspaper accounts of the panic in the dark under
Manhattan's hot and noisy streets, the expedition members could
have reflected that Antarctica might not be so much worse after
all. Perhaps it was high time they got out of there; ten thousand of
the *City*'s paper drinking cups had already been filched for souvenirs. And so the "little bark, her yards akimbo, her stout sides
wallowing through the lumpy waters of the Hudson, put out from
Hoboken" on the afternoon of August 25, 1928.

It had been a long time since a square-rigged ship had dropped
down the Hudson into New York Harbor, and the spectacle drew
forth hails and whistles from every boat that passed. Down the bay
came the *Leviathan*, America's mightiest ocean liner, giving a
deep-voiced greeting to this "little bark that could have been
placed on her boat deck." Some of the *City*'s crew waved their

hats and grinned; the first mate "climbed into the rigging and balanced, semaphoring his arms, then ran out and stood on the end of
the jib boom." Another man went out on the main yard and
worked his arms like a trombone. Amidst the festivities, however,
there was also pain: "Far aft a radio operator stood, alone and
quite white in his loneliness, with his eyes fastened on his wife
and child, a little girl gay in a red hat who waved her doll at
him."[19]

The expedition's own members had now to separate temporarily. If they were all to make rendezvous together in the South Pacific, the lumbering old square-rigger had to be given a long head
start. As Coney Island and Far Rockaway dwindled into "long,
low lines of distant golden fire," Byrd had all hands summoned aft
so that he might make his farewells. Standing a little above them
near the wheel, speaking slowly in his soft Virginia accent, he told
them that Mrs. Byrd had their wives' and mothers' addresses and
would keep in touch with their families. If there was sickness or
trouble, she would know about it, and "a good friend" had arranged for any necessary hospital care. The men listened in a
silence broken only by the lapping water under the hull and the
low throb of the engine. At the end arose a burst of applause, from
"strong and heavy hands." The commander said a personal word
to each man and climbed down the ladder to the pilot boat's
dinghy. The pilot boat threw a searchlight on the old ship's bowsprit; somebody sang out "Three cheers for Commander Byrd,"
and "they cheered him in the night where the binnacle light
glowed on the face and figure of the man at the wheel."[20]

The Byrd party went ashore. So did two of the three stowa-
ways—one of them an unemployed Wall Street runner—who had
been discovered on the *City of New York* just before the tug cast
off. They had betrayed their presence by quarreling over possession of a hiding place. (A third youth, a black who aspired to emu-
late Matthew Henson, the black American who had sledged with
Peary to the North Pole, was given the chance to stay in the crew

and work his passage; he shipped with the Byrd Expedition as far as Panama.) Life back home went on as if not much of any consequence had happened. The Hoover-Smith presidential campaign that the explorers were leaving far behind them continued, and two days after the sailing the morning papers headlined the signing in Paris by fifteen nations of the Briand-Kellogg treaty for the renunciation of war.

Two weeks after the square-rigger's departure it was the airplanes' turn. The Fairchild monoplane *Stars and Stripes* flew from Long Island to Washington on September 8, and the next day to the naval air station at Hampton Roads, Virginia, where the aviation personnel started disassembling and crating it. On September 16, despite the warning of "a bewhiskered old fellow with a Bible in his hand" who came on board to prophesy the expedition's doom, the rusty *Eleanor Bolling* sailed from Brooklyn. "Full speed ahead, the Eleanor Bolling is on her way," fireman Arnold Clarke hopefully wrote in his diary. Next day he had to add: "Yes and damn slow too but you can't burn dirt"—a reference to the poor quality of their coal. So dowdy-looking was the *Bolling* that off Cape May it was boarded by the Coast Guard as a suspected rum-runner; and off Hampton Roads it nearly foundered in a hurricane. Not long afterward, on September 20, the airplane pilots and mechanics went on board the whaler *C. A. Larsen*. "Motion picture and still photographers took pictures of the gang," airplane mechanic Pete Demas noted at the time, but "there were no ceremonies. A very quiet departure." The celebration would come later, when they called at San Pedro, California, to pick up Commander Byrd.[21]

Now that the *Larsen* was under way, having the expedition's aircraft, gasoline, and oil securely stowed in its hold, and with another whaler, the *James Clark Ross*—named after the discoverer of the great sea and ice shelf to which they were bound—en route carrying 40 tons of dog biscuit and 94 yapping sledge dogs, Commander Byrd thought he would be able to relax for a few days with his family before traveling across the country by train to join the expedition. Instead he was presented with a final statement from the expedition's fund raiser. They had a deficit of $300,000, most of it incurred in overhauling and outfitting the *City* and the *Bolling*. Just to rub it in, his New York manager added, "I have also learned this: an article is being written for a powerful syndicate of newspapers attacking the expedition for lavish equipment."

"Great," Byrd replied. "Now let's have some more good news."

It was a sad truism, in those days before the coming of government sponsorship, that the organizers of polar exploration typically teetered on the edge of financial ruin; "I have never known an explorer," Byrd wrote, "who was not either bankrupt or close to it." (Government sponsorship had its own drawbacks, however, as will be shown in chapter 8.) The American explorer was perfectly aware of how his Norwegian colleague Amundsen had jumped off for the Northwest Passage aboard the *Gjoa* at midnight on June 16, 1903, in a pouring rainstorm, one jump ahead of a creditor who threatened to garnishee his ship.[22]

Byrd's contemporaries and successors, unless they were privately wealthy, continued the same melancholy tale. "Compared to the brutal toil of raising funds for an expedition in these days," Finn Ronne (Martin's son) was to write in 1949, "the work of the expedition itself is almost a vacation." Particularly for a descendant of the Virginia plantation gentry, fund-raising—"begging, it really is"—was "the most disagreeable job in the world." Byrd had intended originally not to leave the United States if a large deficit piled up, but "the expedition gathered so much momentum that it could not be stopped." Owing to that launch window situation, another month's delay in New York would have meant another year's delay in Antarctica. And now, committed as they were, if they failed to get their winter base established on the ice the outcome would be "bankruptcy and disgrace." In spite of the very different economic circumstances of the twentieth century, their experience was echoing that of the nineteenth-century American frontier: the expedition's choice could well have been expressed as the Ross Shelf or bust.

The money was raised and the deficit reduced, somehow; the Fisher Brothers and others came through. But Byrd, as he sat on board the Twentieth Century Limited en route to San Pedro, after an all-too-short visit with his children, confessed that this interlude was "a time of heart-sinking doubt." Why was he doing this anyway? Could any joy in exploration compensate for the pain of leaving the eight-year-old who at their parting had shoved "shyly into my hand his most treasured toy"? "Half of human instinct drives away from the center, and makes for enlarging the outline of what we know," Byrd mused as the train clattered along. "Half of it drives toward the center, seeking to confirm and make secure the goods that are there." At that moment he was seized by "the instinct toward digging-in," even though his intellect insisted that "home-building is never finished, until we know all that is outside that charmed circle." Meanwhile it would be Marie Byrd, after she left him at dockside in San Pedro, who would hold that circle together, and her task as she fended their children from America's pitiless publicity machines would be the harder one. As Anne Morrow Lindbergh could have told her a few years later, no Antarctic blizzard could compete with the howling of the media for psychological horror, and Mrs. Byrd in their home at 9 Brimmer Street, Boston, would have to stand alone.[23]

On the seat opposite Commander Byrd lay an open suitcase, and in it was an old newspaper which headlined his "Million Dollar Expedition" as the "Costliest on Record." That kind of treatment, after Byrd's grueling fund-raising stint, scant days earlier, rankled deeply. "To the man who wrote the article, an attack on Antarctica with a shoestring would have been the desirable thing," Byrd fumed. "There would then be more high adventure to it, more sport, more drama and so, more news value. I fear we shall pay for that impression." As if in reply to that reporter, Byrd noted how the purchasing power of the dollar had diminished since the great expeditions of Shackleton and Scott. Furthermore, the use of the airplane must dramatically increase not only the speed of exploration but also its expense. Salaries for the four pilots alone would come to $35,000; airmen, the elite of the 1920s labor force, could not be asked to work only for room and board. "No," Byrd concluded, "we are not half so well fixed as this fellow believed." [24]

The Commander could have taken comfort from friendlier accounts in other newspapers. "The million dollars is a small item, indeed, compared to the human lives and reputations that are likewise at stake," was the *Washington Star*'s rejoinder. "The World's progress is largely due to man's desire to see what is just around the corner," the *Tacoma Ledger* added. "The youngster who escapes his mother's vigilant eye for the first time and toddles up to the corner is doing what his ancestors have always done. . . . So long as there is one spot of this old world of ours which holds a secret, just so long will there be explorers." "It will be a sad day," said the *Salt Lake Telegram*, "when there are no more Arctic or Antarctic regions to explore." The work of Hubert Wilkins and Richard Byrd was

only a new chapter in the old, old story that was begun countless centuries ago by the first Phoenician captain who dared to poke his rickety craft out beyond Gibraltar. . . . To be dauntless, to be everlasting inquisitive—these are two traits in us that will not die out. So long as they last—so long as the Byrds and the Wilkinses persist, daring death for knowledge about a land that the race can never use—we can have hope. [25]

"I do hope they let us get away quietly and without too noisy a show," Byrd wrote on October 7, 1928, from their hotel room in Los Angeles. It was, of course, not to be; when he, Mrs. Byrd, and their fox terrier Igloo (who was going on to Antarctica) showed up on the docks at San Pedro on the 10th "the crowd just

went wild, hats confetti and yells.'' And now, as the *C. A. Larsen*
got under way, Byrd had worries other than financial. One was
discipline. There could be neither promotion nor pay increases for
work well done, nor any lawful punishment for misdeed or failure:
''There is no brig, with bread and water diet. There can be no
court-martial for disrespect, or overstaying liberty, or desertion.''
(Where in Antarctica, indeed, could anyone *go* to desert?)[26]

Scott and other of Byrd's predecessors had solved this problem
by invoking the class-distinct tradition of the British Navy, with
the officers dining separately and toasting the King. A sketch sur-
vives, comic to the modern reader, of the interior of an ice-roofed
cave on a desolate Antarctic island where six members of Scott's
last expedition had to spend the polar winter of 1912. There was
barely room for their sleeping bags and a tiny galley area—but the
proprieties were observed; on opposite sides of that very small
space, three of those bags are marked ''officers'' and the other
three ''men.'' But that sort of thing, in the essentially civilian venture whose ships were now converging on the great South Sea,
was out of the question. On the *Larsen* itself, Byrd wrote on October 30th, ''it has already been necessary to rebuke one man, an
officer in the military, for high-hatting one of the men who happens to be in the enlisted ranks.'' It was not really that officer's
fault; ''He hasn't had time to learn that special privileges will not
obtain on this expedition.''[27]

Laurence Gould, sailing down aboard the *Eleanor Bolling* as
second officer—or, as he preferred to say, bosun—had similar
worries. When the *Bolling* and the *City of New York* made rendezvous in Tahiti, it became apparent that their masters had sharply
differing philosophies of how to manage their men. Any effectively governed vessel, civilian or military, may be described from
a disciplinary standpoint as either a ''tight ship'' or a ''happy
ship,'' and these were no exceptions. ''Instead of the good fellowship that prevails aboard the Eleanor Bolling one finds the City of
New York sharply divided into fore and aft gangs,'' Gould ob-

served. The scientists, in particular, objected to being treated "as though they were ordinary seamen on a bark of the old days." It was an echo from an old, old quarrel in the annals of Antarctic exploration, for just such friction between scientists and naval officers had dogged the great Wilkes exploring expedition of 1838–42.[28]

Crew members, also, compared notes and came to a similar conclusion. "It seems on this ship as if it was composed of one large family of brothers," *Bolling* crewman Pete Demas observed. "From what I hear the 'City of N.Y.' is far from being as well managed." Nevertheless some natures thrive on just such tautness, and it is not on every day in the twentieth century that one gets the chance to ship before the mast. At least one crewman on the *City of New York,* Boy Scout Paul Siple, despite the long exhausting watches afloat and the coalheaving and barnacle-scraping ashore, was evidently having the time of his life.[29]

There is a famous chapter in *Moby-Dick* titled "The Masthead," in which Herman Melville describes standing lookout in the tropics: "The tranced ship indolently rolls; the drowsy trade winds blow; everything resolves you into languor. . . . There is no life in thee, now, except that rocking life imparted by a gently rolling ship; by her, borrowed from the sea; by the sea, from the inscrutable tides of God." On the ship skippered by Melville's younger relative, Scout Siple on night watch experienced a similar illumination—and, like Ishmael, had to confess at one point that he had "kept but sorry guard":

The light breeze wafting down the jib cools my face, and plays through my shirt so refreshingly that I throw back my head and fill my lungs. The occasional snap of a fluttering sail overhead, a creaking block or a rasping stay forces me to the consciousness of the ship's presence. I had almost forgotten I was on watch. . . .

In the half light of the moon, as I look back over my shoulder, the ship is a magnificent sight. Every sail is set, partly filled, and quivering in the light breeze. The tall phantom-like masts towering above me roll gently from side to side. I feel wide-awake, yet dreaming; strangely contented and free, but with the desire to soar—high, higher yet, up to the velvet sky.

"Why didn't you strike two bells? It was struck aft," break in the words of the mate, as he comes up silently behind me.

"What! So soon? I never saw a watch go so quickly. Isn't this a wonderful night?" I answer all in one breath.

"Yes, it's a nice night, but keep your eyes open."[30]

2

They
Named It
Little America

*The wilderness masters the colonist. It finds him a Euro-
pean in dress, industries, tools, modes of travel, and thought.
It takes him from the railroad car and puts him in the birch
canoe. It strips off the garments of civilization and arrays him
in the hunting shirt and the moccasin. It puts him in the log
cabin of the Cherokee and Iroquois and runs an Indian pali-
sade around him. Before long he has gone to planting Indian
corn and plowing with a sharp stick; he shouts the war cry
and takes the scalp in orthodox Indian fashion. In short, at
the frontier the environment is at first too strong for the man.*
—Frederick Jackson Turner, "The Significance
of the Frontier in American History"

Dunedin, New Zealand, was a considerably more comfortable
place from which to make a polar jumpoff than barren, coalmine-
pocked Spitsbergen. Low, red-roofed homes perched along a
graceful arc of green hills that ringed its sunken crater harbor. The
city possessed a first-rate university, an Anglican cathedral, and a
chocolate factory; its hinterland was a source of butter and excellent wool. Scottish Free Kirk settlers, one of them a nephew of
the poet Robert Burns, had founded the town eighty years before,
as "New Edinburgh." Their descendants—85,000 of them by
1928 (and not so many more today)—lived in apparent harmony
alongside the descendants of New Zealand's native Maoris. A
more recent map of the metropolitan area still intersperses British
with Polynesian place-names. The place lies almost exactly halfway between the Equator and the South Pole, at latitude 45°50′
South, comparable in northern hemispheric terms to the location of
Portland, Oregon—or if one prefers a more bracing climate, that
of Greenville, Maine; in short, near enough to the Pole to see an
occasional aurora. If you dropped down its meridian of longitude,

170°30' East, you would strike Cape Adare, the northwest entrance to the Ross Sea.[1]

Shortly after the Byrd Antarctic Expedition arrived there, near the end of 1928, Boy Scout Paul Siple went with the other men to a wharf shed beside Dunedin's harbor to receive his winter clothes. He was shocked when he was handed ordinary ship's crew clothing instead of the heavier garments suitable for life in Antarctica. Siple was down on the expedition's roster as Commander Byrd's "orderly," and all along he had assumed he was going to winter over at the Bay of Whales. Had he won his way this far, in competition with 650,000 other Scouts, only to holystone decks and heave sacks of coal? Mustering up his courage, he approached Byrd on the dock and asked, "rather disappointedly," whether the leader's decision was final. "Nobody knows who is going to stay on the ice," the Commander sternly replied. Everyone who stayed would have to have a definite reason for doing so, and some of the men would be needed to bring the ships back for the winter party the following year. With an anxious heart, but with the mature stoicism that also characterized this young man, Paul Siple returned to his chores.[2]

The last-minute preparations went feverishly on. It was November 25—late spring in the southern hemisphere—when the *City of New York* finally came lumbering in to Dunedin, and the season for getting established in Antarctica was growing perilously short. They had to go in after the pack had broken enough to let them through, and still have enough solid bay ice to tie up alongside in order to unload. Also, before they sailed, the cargo from the whalers had to be unpacked and re-stowed. "The decks of the *City* were jammed with houses, airplanes, gasoline drums and crates," Siple later recalled. "On top of this mess, which was piled so high the mainsail couldn't be set, rode eighty-five sledge dogs who barked continually." (This was a hazardous arrangement, as the formal written report on the Fairchild monoplane was to point out, should the ship encounter a storm; "if any bad weather had been encountered on the voyage, dogs and plane would have been washed overboard.'')[3]

Watching the crews as they loaded the *City of New York* alarmingly above the Plimsoll line, toiling half the night and then turning out again at four in the morning, one dockside spectator in Dunedin seemed disappointed:

> "Why, they look just like ordinary men," she said, with a sad astonishment.
> A scornful snort came from one who was groggy with weariness. "What does she expect, wings?"

It was *New York Times* correspondent Russell Owen's job to persuade such landsiders of the reality of those wings. As a newsman Owen had seen other men off on desperate adventures. He had covered Byrd en route to the North Pole, Amundsen with his dirigible, and Lindbergh. But all the ''brass-band emotion'' that was so easy to conjure out of a typewriter in a newspaper office seemed far away, Owen morosely reflected, as he sacked out a few days later on a pile of fur bags piled high in the ship's saloon just under the beams. When the *City* and the *Eleanor Bolling* at last got under way on December 2, 1928, lifting and dropping on the great Antarctic ocean swell, the *Times* man missed seeing the New Zealand coast drop behind them out of sight; he was hopelessly seasick. Days later he greenly emerged, threading his way cautiously between the tiers of dog crates to the galley, only to be raucously greeted by the crew: "My God, here's little Eva. When did you come to? Been telling the world about us heroes today?"[4]

They sighted their first iceberg on December 9, and even Owen felt better. ("I've never seen an unbeautiful iceberg," says Larry Gould.) The next day they met the *C.A. Larsen,* from which they took on ninety more tons of coal, itself not a simple operation in those heaving seas. The *Larsen*'s skipper had generously offered them a tow, so that the *Eleanor Bolling* need not risk its thin metal

William C. Haines
*Meteorologist on both the First and Second Byrd
Antarctic Expeditions, "Cyclone" Haines takes
a turn at the* City of New York's *helm. Seaman-
ship was a trait discovered en route; some of the
ablest at steering through the pack turned out to
be the airplane pilots.*

sides until later in the season when the ice hazard would be less.
Accordingly, as planned, the *Bolling* turned back to Dunedin for
more cargo, and together the *Larsen* and the *City of New York* hit
the pack. It was at once apparent that another stroke of proverbial
Byrd luck had befallen the expedition. "What a boon this tow by
the Larsen is to us," wrote Gould, who by that time had been told

Russell Owen
*His daily dispatches from Little America sent by
Morse code to New York and published in the
following day's* Times *earned him a Pulitzer
Prize.*

he was to be Byrd's lieutenant when they got to shore. "Without it
we should be at a standstill, for with our puny power plant we
should never be able to push our way through this ice."[5]

Even so it was no easy affair. Towing a boat at the end of a line
is tricky enough work in open water, and here they had to batter
their way into or shoulder between the ice masses. Down in the
engine room, as Russell Owen reported in one of his radio dispatches to the *Times*, they were getting as many as forty signals

from the bridge in an hour; the engineer on watch, "his hands working the throttle and reversing gears back and forth, moves as fast as if he were shadow boxing." Constantly they were stopping and starting their ancient 200-horsepower steam engine, and if that engine stayed shut down long enough to cool appreciably they were in trouble. It was cold work; there was "the constant sound of stamping feet." Topside and forward, "the second mate occasionally shoots a stream of tobacco juice to the leeward, waves his arms and yells back to the man at the wheel: 'Hard left! That's right; steady her now . . . Half astern there! Right! Full steam ahead!' And wham! we go into an ice cake." Yet amidst all this uproar, the calm planning for the expedition went on; Byrd, Gould, and seaman engineer George H. Black—the erstwhile prizefighter—at this same hectic time were quietly working on lists and weights and food values of the rations for the sledges, on a trip that was yet ten months away.

"It is nervous and tiresome work finding a way through these leads in ice fields," Russell Owen continued his story. "The airplane pilots have been especially good at it. They seem to get the feel of the ship instinctively, and as she swings meet her in time with the wheel." The helm kicked viciously, and one had to be alert not to be caught. Scout Siple, now weighing in at almost 200 pounds, had turned into one of the best helmsmen aboard; "he stands in front of the wheel and swirls it with one hand as if he were cranking a car."[6]

Radio chatter filled the frigid Antarctic air as never before. Owen's news stories from the *City of New York* winged their way in Morse to the *Times;* on the *Bolling,* the ship's receiver picked up a Chicago station with an orchestra playing "See You In My Dreams." For those who might still be worried about the "Antarctic Derby" aspect of their quest, there was more ominous traffic in the air. While the *Larsen* and the *City of New York* struggled on toward the open Ross Sea, Sir Hubert Wilkins began his own Antarctic aeronautics as planned. On December 20 he flew southward, mostly along the Weddell Sea side of the Antarctic Peninsula (or Archipelago); at 71°20' S., with half his gasoline gone—Cook's farthest southing had been 71°10'—Wilkins turned back, returning to his base on foggy, sulfurous Deception Island after a triumphant round trip of twelve hundred miles.

Sir Hubert's expedition was, in a sense, a retort by William Randolph Hearst to Byrd's. If the *New York Times* got exclusive coverage of the Byrd Antarctic Expedition, the Hearst newspapers received the same favor from the Australian. On his December 20 flight Wilkins discovered and named Hearst Land, and he immortalized another of his sponsors in the name Mobiloil Bay; within a month's time the Virginian in Antarctica would by paying similar compliments to his own patrons. Such commercial christenings were not without precedent; there are stretches of the Antarctic shore to this day that bear the names of nineteenth-century sealing firms, alongside those of explorers, explorers' wives, and kings and queens. (The mystique of commerce, however, yields at last to the mystique of nationalism: in 1947 the Argentine Navy would anchor at Deception Island and indignantly rename Mobiloil Bay *Bahia Eva Perón*.)[7]

On December 23, 1928, three days after Wilkins's pioneering flight, the Byrd Antarctic Expedition broke out of the ice pack into the open waters of the Ross Sea. The *Larsen* cast off the tow line and resumed its profitable pursuit of whales, those dwindling buffalo on that last frontier.[8] The *City* was at last on its own. Christmas Day found the crew around an evergreen tree in the forecastle, opening presents handed out by the chubby little physicist Frank Davies, resplendent in an absorbent cotton Santa Claus beard and "a red parka the color of his round apple cheeks." The party was never finished. One of the men glanced over his shoulder, left the group quietly and climbed to the bow. Another joined him, then another. "Barrier on starboard bow!" sang out First Mate Sverre Strom from the crow's nest. All hands rushed out to see the high, clean line of cliffs, towering above their ship's tall masts (as Bernt Balchen put it) "like a Great Wall of China carved in ice." Of course, they cheered—but, Paul Siple noticed, "there was an eerie quality about the barrier that made the men fall silent."[9]

Silence, however, is not one of the modern mechanical world's virtues. Speakers on deck and in quarters carried the strains of Pittsburgh's radio station KDKA, broadcasting a Christmas program especially for the expedition as the venerable square-rigger moved on up to the bay ice that fringed the great Ross Shelf. "It is weird and almost ghostly," Owen mused, "to hear words from home coming to us as we move through these ice-filled waters to our base." Yet they were 2400 statute miles from the nearest human dwelling, in the only part of the world where a ship could get so far from civilization. "This day we have carried the American flag further south than it has ever been before," Owen reported to the *Times*, "and have taken with us to that point an American airplane." Byrd radioed Navy Secretary Curtis Wilbur to the same effect: "It seems fitting that an airplane, that instrument of good-will, should reach its furthest south on Christmas Day."

In any other twentieth-century year except 1928, the year of the Kellogg-Briand peace pact, such words would have rung with horrible irony. Ask any non-German European over the age of forty if the scream of a Stuka, ask any Southeast Asian if the thunder of a B-52, carries to their ears the Christmas angels' message of good will! Yet at that moment in history Commander Byrd's innocent remark had considerable point. Up near the other pole, through all the pioneering Arctic flights of the 1920s, the aloof Soviets had always stood ready with their ice ships to help capitalist British, Americans, Norwegians, even fascist Italians, when they got into trouble. Symbolically, Fridtjof Nansen, the greatest of all the north polar voyagers, had moved on from Arctic exploration to international philanthropy, becoming Norway's delegate to the League of Nations where he earned a Nobel Peace Prize for his labor on behalf of persons left stateless by World War I. Possibly at the materially useless bottom of the world, where the "strenuous honor and disinterestedness" that went with martial valor could prevail without actual resort to the clash of arms, a basis existed for the philosopher William James's "moral equivalent of war."[10]

The *City of New York* made for Discovery Inlet, where Captain Scott had anchored in 1902. Perhaps that area would make a better anchorage and airfield for the Byrd Expedition than Amundsen's base farther east. Where the inlet narrowed to a width of two or three miles the crew threw out two iron ice anchors and made the ship fast. "The marines are always the first ashore," Marine Corps flier Alton Parker exclaimed as he vaulted over the side to the ice. A moment later most of the ship's company were ashore, pelting each other with snowballs; the dogs, released from their cramped crates for a romp in the snow, went "wild with joy."[11]

Then came the natives. From some distance off the expedition members saw a long file of slowly moving objects approaching. To Scout Siple they seemed like a procession of "monks filing in reverence from a monastery." Closer up they proved to be representatives of those First Citizens of Antarctica, the emperor penguins. Collectively ponderous and grave, while individually ridiculous ("A penguin walks much like Charlie Chaplin in his more abandoned moments," Russell Owen observed), they stopped, clustered into a group, and put their heads together to discuss the situation. Then they turned as one to face the intruders, and one of the largest—three and a half feet tall, and weighing 75 or 80 pounds—stepped forward, clucking his approval:

> Very slowly he lowered his head upon his breast in a gracious bow, so low that his beak almost touched the snow, and delivered a long welcoming speech which lasted for several seconds and sounded like the clear blare of trumpets playing a range of several notes. Then very, very slowly he raised his head and looked at us. . . . Seeing that we did not comprehend, he began to shake his head in disgust. A critical member of his delegation, who evidently thought this speech had not

been properly presented, approached the chairman and nudging him to one side proceeded to deliver the welcoming speech himself, but to no avail. We humans were too ignorant of the penguin dialect to understand what was expected of us.

After another conference among themselves, the Antarcticans gave up on these dumb outland specimens, and started to march off in single file as they had come. Encountering several curiously sniffing sledge dogs, the penguins easily fended them off with stinging flipper-slaps to the nose, then dove forward and slid swiftly along the ice on their white breadbaskets, easily outdistancing the heavy-booted humans.[12]

To provide fresh food for the dogs after the crowded sea journey, parties of men went off to hunt the big Weddell seals, so winsomely tame—they enjoy rolling over like house pets, to have their tummies scratched—and so pathetically easy to kill. Other men went skiing, several of them for the comical first time. Master of the dogs Arthur Walden took Captain Melville for a sledge ride, and one hopes Herman's ghost approved. After persistent efforts airplane pilot Harold June finally succeeded, football-style, in tackling a penguin. Byrd with four others went inland to look for a landing field, meanwhile granting permission for people to go exploring in groups of three or more provided they carried safety lines and took all proper precautions.

One such party, which included Dr. Coman, meteorologist "Cyclone" Haines, machinist Victor Czegka, and several others, made for a dark hole in the Barrier about four miles away. Roping themselves together they passed under a 25-foot archway fringed with enormous icicles. "Along the walls from the arched roof hung ice crystal tapestries that reached to the floor, so delicate that a slight touch would bring down a great shower with a sound like the rustle of dry leaves." All was lit with a living blue. Carefully they worked their way back into the cavern until halted by inner darkness. "In one place we found what was evidently an old seal hole leading into the water below, and on all sides pieces of ice and snow made fine ghosts and goblins that spattered into shapeless wreckage as we touched them.'' Single hexagonal crystals several inches in length had grown there undisturbed for many years. The Americans were at last in physical touch with Antarctica's unhuman mystery—and nobody had remembered to bring a camera![13]

Byrd's report from the hinterland was negative: too hilly for aircraft. The sky had clouded over, the sea was rising, and the bay ice was starting to break up. Leaving behind many of the seals which had been killed, in the necessitous haste and waste that have characterized every American frontier, the dog teams rushed aboard and the *City of New York* cast off. On December 28th they came at last into the Bay of Whales, whose shape, as the ice walls pushed forward and calved into the sea, had changed dramatically since Amundsen's time. Nonetheless, along its eastern shore Martin Ronne's bright old eyes could pick out familiar landmarks. The expedition leaders hoped to use ''Framheim''—the base from which Amundsen had set out for the Pole, named after his (and Nansen's) ship the *Fram*—as its headquarters; not only because of the historical sentiment associated with it but also because, buried under snow, the house and much of the equipment were probably still in good condition. Accordingly six men with two dog teams, led by Byrd, fared forth to look for Framheim. The weather remained ominous: ''Still the low hanging steely blue clouds,'' Gould wrote in his journal, ''and away from the ship's noise a silence which fairly presses one down from all sides, it is so deadly.''[14]

Commander Byrd, camped out on the bay ice, felt the awesome quiet also, a silence ''so deep one could almost reach out and take hold of it.'' But Antarctica's ages-old interplanetary stillness was ending. By New Year's Eve a bamboo pole was up at Byrd's tent camp to serve as a radio antenna, and messages were flying between the camp and the ship. Byrd, instead of communing with the great white unknown, was replying as an executive must to messages relayed from New Zealand about the loading of the *Bolling*. "The radio beyond doubt has ended the isolation of this ice cap," the expedition leader wrote at 1 A.M. on January 1, while operator Carl Petersen busily worked the key. "As a practical thing, its help is priceless," the Commander admitted. "But I can see where it is going to destroy all peace of mind, which is half the attraction of the polar regions."[15]

The *New York Times*, needless to say, did not view this matter from the same perspective. Its correspondents dwelt rather upon the triumphant scientific annihilation of time and space: "Over the sub-zero fields of crackling ice, over the gray and restless desolation of berg-infested seas . . . through blinding blizzards that drive across the Pole and through the terrific gales that sweep the floor of the world, radio, fleet messenger . . . , will carry the story." With the means of communication available only a decade earlier Russell Owen would have had to wait at least a year to file a story; today it might be in the copyreaders' hands sooner than that of a local police reporter, telling a rewrite man over the phone the details of the most recent murder. The first part of Owen's dispatch could be set in type before he had finished sending the last paragraph; as he concluded the story, the sentence with which it had begun would very likely be on linotypes in every quarter of the United States, perhaps also in Buenos Aires, London, Paris, and Tokyo. Short waves carried so many thousands of words to the *Times,* Owen afterward recalled, that "many radio engineers could not believe that all the stuff pouring into the office was actually sent from Little America; they thought it was being padded out in New York."[16]

Moreover, it was even easier to send to Antarctica than to receive from there. "The loneliness of exploration is gone," the *Times* moralized. Unlike previous expeditions, totally cut off for two or three years at a time from civilization, the Byrd Antarctic

Expedition could be subjected to the same raucous music, the same self-serving political chatter, and the same unfulfillable advertising seductions that likewise came booming into the living-room sets of the folks back home. The old, old frontier cycle was being played out again: fleeing from the hassles and hustle of civilization to an unspoiled wilderness, one had to spoil it by bringing in all the clutter of civilization. "Our external difficulties," Byrd regretfully concluded in the small hours of the New Year 1929, "must always be with us"—and where, after Antarctica, could one go?

Back at the ship, meanwhile, Paul Siple was busy solving his own problem, of how to justify staying on shore in Antarctica when the ships left. The expedition, whose primary mission was simply to get Byrd and an airplane to the Pole, was rather short-handed in its scientific staff; it lacked, for example, a fulltime biologist. The Commander had indicated in one of his magazine articles that the expedition's doctor would double as biologist. But Dr. Coman's specialty, which he taught at Johns Hopkins when not off on exploring expeditions, was dietetics, not taxidermy! Professor Gould in an incautiously generous moment had promised the American Museum of Natural History that he would bring them back a barrel each of seal and penguin skins. But now Gould was second in command, and "with his advance in status, hard rock geologist Larry was quite anxious to turn over this messy job to anyone else who would take it." Paul Siple, possessing the right Boy Scout merit badges, was more than eager to volunteer. Pete Demas, who as one of the mechanics nursing the all-important aircraft would of necessity be wintering over, offered to help Siple make his Antarctic animal and bird collection; Gould, pleased with this decision, told Demas he would recommend the arrangement to Byrd, and "try and get Paul to stay on the ice." Happily the two younger men made a shopping list of tools and chemicals they would need, sending for them in New Zealand by

At anchor in the Bay of Whales
*Dog sledges are ready to haul ashore the supplies to build Little
America.*

radio, the supplies to be brought down on the *Bolling* when she returned. The next day, January 1, 1929, they started to work,
skinning a petrel.[17]

Commander Byrd that same New Year's Day was trudging with
Bernt Balchen up an easy slope which ascended gradually from a
little inlet they had found the day before—they named it Ver-sur-
Mer Bay, after the small French coastal indentation where they
had made their stormy trans-Atlantic landing—to the top of the
great Ice Shelf. They had never found Framheim; but just past the
top of the Barrier they came into a shallow basin, protected by a
high snow rim from the winds in every direction but west. This,
they decided, was the place; their Jamestown, their Plymouth
Rock. They named it Little America, much as explorers from

Spain had named a New World island Hispaniola (Little Spain), or as settlers from old England had named a region New England.

Racing back to the ship with their dogs, Byrd and Balchen broke the news, and at once preparations were begun to unload. Boxes and barrels scraped and rolled down the planks the men had rigged from the deck to the bay ice, and other hands pulled these cargoes away to a safe distance lest they break through into the sea. Before lunch five dog teams were on their way; "the dogs' tails waved like plumes, and the drivers hurried behind, cracking their long whips and chattering incessantly in the mad monologue that passes as language between driver and dogs." These dog teams, however, unlike Amundsen's, were radio-dispatched, and it was not long until Gould was able to radio the ship that his advance party had found the site; that they had put up several tents; and that "Little America, the most southern American community, was formally colonized."

They had started that colony not a moment too soon. The next day, January 2, a crack opened across the dog trail, forcing the teams to detour. Shortly afterward a jagged ice field bore down upon the ship from the east; the *City of New York* hastily got up steam and put out to sea, then hoisted its sails and stood off and on all night to conserve coal. Then it was back to work, impressing every hand that could be spared from the ship and "every dog that could move its bones" to haul the supplies across the bay ice and up the trail. Sledge load by sledge load, with almost railroad regularity, the coal and man-food and gasoline moved up over the Barrier to Little America—but with frustrating slowness. If they did not get all the supplies landed by mid-February, Byrd estimated on January 6, the old *City of New York* might have to freeze in.[18]

While the building of Little America went on, Commander Byrd had to stay with the ship, moving it from berth to berth as the bay ice broke. But the hours and days were not all drudgery. In the intervals while waiting to load sledges the airplane pilots played bridge in the cabin and told old war stories. Outside, adding a pas-

Building Little America II
Far in the distance is the great Ross Ice Shelf's edge.

toral note, the whales from which the Bay had received its name
"played constantly, their spouts echoing from the snow cliffs that
lined the bay like the exhausts of switching engines in a freight
yard." Down in the forecastle on the afternoon of January 11 "the
boys were shooting craps," Pete Demas wrote, "and the Commander happened to come down so he joined in the game and lost
a dollar. He isn't a gambler but he got in the game to work a point
of his psychology and gain confidence with the boys." (It was certainly a different leadership style from that of Amundsen, who,
Martin Ronne remembered, had demanded that his men snap to attention when he entered the room!) On the 20th, a Sunday, they
got out the wind-up phonograph and afterward the boxing gloves.
First, aerial photographer Ashley McKinley sparred with Arthur
Creagh, the ship's cook; then the big Norwegian pilot Bernt Bal-

chen and the former pugilist George Black ("Blackie") treated the men to "three very good rounds of light and very interesting boxing."[19]

Meantime at Little America Larry Gould, as executive officer, was trying to sort out the incoming sledge loads and organize the rough trail camp into a permanent home. The crews started digging foundations in the ice for the first of the buildings on January 8, cutting four feet down into the firn or nevé. Two days into the work they were interrupted by a blizzard. Finally "we succeeded in getting the floor down," Gould wrote in his little red leather pocket notebook on January 11, "though none of the pieces fitted"; it was "a nasty job, this business of assembling such a complicated house—designed by a New York architect who had no notions as to the difficulties of temperature and wind that one encounters in the Antarctic." But the work went on, and the houses went up. To Americans bossing a job, as Byrd and Gould were doing, it all seemed an endless series of exasperating delays; to the Norwegian Sverre Strom, however, the *City's* first mate, who had been driving one of the dog teams, the process seemed to go with breathtaking speed: "Only the 'Yanks' could do such a job as we have done in getting all our supplies and equipment out here and getting houses up and all that sort of thing. 'Why,' he exclaimed, 'if Amundsen had been confronted with such a problem he would not even have tried to do it.' " However unfamiliar they may seem in the retrospect of fifty years, they are specimens of those fabulously productive American workers of whom one heard so often during World War II.[20]

By that time other hard-working men had hoisted the *City's* most expensive cargo, the Fairchild monoplane *Stars and Stripes,* over the side and down onto the ice. Uncrated, greased, and oiled, with the help of a blowtorch to warm the oil and the engine, the aircraft was ready by January 15 for a little test flying, even though icicles froze onto the ailerons and eight men had to hang onto the wing when the plane taxied crosswind. Marine Corps pilot Alton Parker was the first to take the plane aloft; the three airplane mechanics cut cards from a deck donated by aerologist Henry Harrison to see who would accompany him as the first passenger on the test flights. (The winner was Benny Roth, one of the luckier members of the expedition; he had survived a fall into the icy Ross Sea, thanks to a heroic diving rescue by Commander Byrd himself.)

After the mechanics it was *Times* reporter Russell Owen's turn. The weather was so fine that day, as it was not again to be for a fortnight, that pilot Dean Smith, a veteran of the early airmail service—one of only four survivors of the first 32 pilots who during the barnstorming twenties had opened the New York–Cleveland mail run—took Commander Byrd and Harold June up for an hour's flight of exploration. They soared above the old square-rigger, "a toy ship with a black toothpick for a mast stuck against a curving crescent of flat ice," and within five minutes were looking down on a region never before seen by man; the great rolling surface of the Ross Ice Shelf had hidden it from the sight of Amundsen's adventurers. They scared a few seals (most paid no attention), appropriately named a newly found formation Lindbergh Inlet, and returned, having surveyed within a few hours territory that foot travelers would have taken weeks to cover. When they got back newsreel cameramen Rucker and Van der Veer went up for pictures, and then Harold June and Bernt Balchen with Larry Gould flew the *Stars and Stripes* out to Little America for the night. On January 20, 1929, Gould trudged down the orange-flagged trail to collect his gear at the ship and Balchen flew him back—the first of the party to be permanently located ashore.[21]

When Russell Owen came back from his first plane ride, ship's mate Strom who had been out dog sledging sadly said to him: "I stopped the dogs and watched you go by and said to myself: 'Here I am a thousand years behind the times.' Ja, a thousand years, sweating and pulling and doing in three hours what you do in ten minutes. It makes me feel old, like an Eskimo." Yet it was dogs

Oolie
*Although he was part wolf, like any other sledge
dog he was amenable to being scratched behind
the ears.*

such as those Sverre Strom drove that were making Little America
possible, not the airplane. (Motorized ground vehicles were landed
from the ships, but they humiliatingly broke down; besides, as an
observer in the 1950s would add, "Divertingly maddening as dogs
can be, they offer certain compensations not possessed by internal
combustion engines.")[22]

Hour after hour, day after day, the huskies tugged selflessly at
their punishing loads. Like the men of Little America the dogs

were a poignant mixture of young and old. Pups yet unborn would be hauling sledges the following spring; but Arthur Walden also brought with him his grand old lead dog Chinook, who had logged nearly a dozen years on the trail. Semi-retired now, Chinook started out from Little America on the morning of his twelfth birthday, in harness at the head of Walden's team just "to limber him up a bit." After they got past the worst of the pressure ridges the driver turned him loose with just his collar on, and the old dog began to lag behind. When the team returned to Little America that afternoon, Chinook had not showed up; Byrd, who by that time had started the flight program, instructed the planes to keep a lookout for him, but the old dog had vanished. Arthur Walden believed his veteran lead dog was brokenhearted after a fight with three other huskies from which Chinook had had to be rescued, no longer able to hold his own. The night before the disappearance, Walden later recalled, "he woke me up twice by placing one of his forepaws on my face just as his father 'Kim' did the night before he died. Perhaps that was his way of trying to tell me good-by." [23]

Commander Byrd did not come out for his first visit to Little America until January 25. He brought written instructions for Gould, should the geologist have to take command if anything happened to the aeronauts on the longer flight for which they now awaited a break in the weather. On the 27th the break came. At 2:53 P.M. the *Stars and Stripes* lifted its skis clear of the snow. Balchen was forward at the controls, June crouched aft on a sleeping bag working the radio, and Byrd with his charts found himself sitting on a primus stove. The 700 pounds of emergency equipment they would need should the plane be forced down filled the cabin to overflowing: a tent, two sledges, three sleeping bags, skis, snowshoes, crampons, alpine rope, an ice axe, a portable radio transmitter, first aid kits, tools for engine repair, a blowtorch for heating the engine, a funnel for draining oil from the engine, mukluks, windproofs, fur mittens, and enough food to keep them alive for three months. If they had to abandon the aircraft it would be a long walk home.

From an altitude of 3000 feet the high, sharply cut edge of the great Ross Shelf "seemed relatively a few inches of beautifully carved alabaster." Flying, Byrd had to admit, "does deprive an observer of much of the awe that seizes the surface traveller." Shortly they picked up Scott's Nunatak, to which three of Amundsen's men had fought their way on foot in 1911. It gave Byrd an odd sensation to be rushing at a rate of two miles a minute (boosted by a good tail wind) toward this lonely spur, which his predecessors "had struggled weeks to gain; to be over it and gone in a few minutes, whereas they had lain, shivering and wet, in a tent, beset by snow storms, while Prestrud, to pass away the time, conjugated Russian verbs."

Even in the air age, however, the Antarctic is ruthless toward the explorer it catches napping. While the men on the *Stars and Stripes* were carefully examining the scenery, they flew into a snow squall. The horizon vanished; the impression they had was that of "flying in a bowl of milk." It was a "white-out," the condition polar fliers most dread, in which all sense of direction is lost. Bernt Balchen flew them out between two squalls, and again they could see a murky red sun. Then, together, came two pleasant surprises. Radioman Harold June handed the commander a message from the operator at Little America: *"Bolling* sighted." A nagging weight of worry lifted, for the old freighter carried the indispensable trimotored plane that was going to the Pole. Immediately afterward, Balchen beckoned Byrd to come forward:

> I looked out over the nose of the ship, through the shimmering play of the propeller. Far ahead, but perfectly distinct, was a splendid mountain peak, with the slate gray of bare rock showing. Then as we advanced a second peak, then a third, and more lifted their summit above the southern horizon until we had counted fourteen. . . . Here was no jammed-up continuous range, but rather a group of highly individualistic mountains, solitary and stern.[24]

What should Byrd call them? "The names of several of the men who had befriended the expedition came to mind" as they headed back toward Little America, their gas running low:

> Foremost among these was that of John D. Rockefeller, Jr. And it occurred to me that his true inner life is as little known as these peaks which we had just seen. His character is in keeping with that of these austere mountain masses. He stands, steady as a rock, in the chaos of life, and the great power he controls is directed wisely and unselfishly for the betterment of the world.

Byrd's second-in-command puts it less poetically. "These are the Rockefeller Mountains," Professor Gould told his class of undergraduate geology majors in 1978 as he flashed a slide upon a screen—"named after the signature on the hundred-thousand-dollar check." [25]

While they were still in flight the *Bolling* had come in alongside the *City of New York* and tied up. The work began of unloading two more airplanes, 7500 gallons of gasoline, and additional dogs. The breaking pack ice endangered both ships; the *Eleanor Bolling* rolled sidewise and broached, saved only by the lines securing the iron ship to the *City,* and they nearly lost the Ford through the ice. At length the task was done, and the *Bolling* got its vulnerable hull away from those ice cakes and sailed for New Zealand, flying a United States Mail flag and "carrying the first mail from an American colony in the Antarctic." Byrd now had an additional smaller aircraft, considerably reducing the risks; one plane would be able to back up the other. Accordingly on February 18, 1929, in the Fokker monoplane *Virginia,* Byrd flew eastward again; this time discovering and naming after his wife the vast terrain that became known on Antarctic maps as Marie Byrd Land.

The short Antarctic summer was hurrying on. "Ice, like lily pads, was beginning to form on the surface of the bay, and the Mate used to look over the side and shake his head," Russell Owen observed. "Long experience in the North had taught him

Antarctica enters the Air Age
Fokker monoplane Virginia *in its first flight over Little America.*
This aircraft not long afterward crashed in the Rockefeller moun-
tains.

that those tiny, thin cakes meant danger for a ship, and he wanted
to see her leave.'' The *City of New York* was to sail on Washington's Birthday, and apparently the cruel suspense as to who would
go with the ship and who stay on the ice was maintained until the
very end. ''Sorry for the stoker with tears streaming down his face
because he was going back, sorry for the little engineer who had
so cheerfully taken his dismissal after working for our comfort,''
the wintering party stood at the edge of the ice in the biting wind
and watched the *City* go:

> The ship moved farther into the mist, her sides faintly showing, her
> dark masts and yards becoming indistinct, the maintop sticking high
> above the shroud. There was a faint cheer from the wraithlike figures

on her deck and in the rigging, and then she merged with the shifting fog and slipped away. . . . The fuddlements of nations, the breaking of stock markets, bills, telephones, money, love, and all the bedazzlements of civilization were beyond the mist through which the ship was leaving. We did not regret them.[26]

February turned into March, and in Washington Herbert Hoover was inaugurated as President. Byrd, via the Navy Department, radioed his congratulations. But March in the great white south is the equivalent of September in the frozen north; the season of flyable weather was rapidly ending. Commander Byrd, when he first saw the Rockefeller Mountains, had felt sure that "when he learned about this discovery our geologist, Dr. Gould, would insist upon flying to these mountains to make a special investigation of their structure," but time was growing short. On March 7, 1929, Bernt Balchen, Harold June, and Gould flew out in the Fokker against a strong head wind and camped on a frozen lake at the foot of the Rockefeller Mountains.[27]

"For the next three days and nights," as Gould described it, "we were occupied in a strenuous struggle with the wind." At 6:30 A.M. on the 9th they woke up and "found it snowing and blowing pretty hard—too hard to do any work," so they stayed in their sleeping bags until 11. Then Bernt Balchen looked outside the tent. "The plane has moved!" he shouted. They flung a line over the wing and hung on for three hours in the driving, snow-stinging wind while Balchen tried to pile up snow blocks high enough to get a line through a ring at the tip of the wing and secure it to a ski. The wind snatched most of the blocks away as fast as they were cut. Meantime in the tent "sleeping bags and everything were fairly saturated with snow. We cleaned things out as best we could and turned in.

"With early morning," Gould's narrative continued on the 10th, "the wind was on the increase—our tent was cracking and snapping—sounded like a broadside of muskets. One cannot imag-

(*above*), Bernt Balchen (*below*) Harold June
These pictures were taken by Professor Gould immediately after the losing struggle to save their airplane, which literally blew away from their tent camp below the Rockefeller Mountains. Later, Balchen and June both participated in the South Pole flight (chapter 4).

ine the din inside even a small tent in such a gale. He must experience it.'' They endured that gale for two more days; then it calmed down enough for them to resume their surveying and rock collecting. On March 14, with the sun shining, it looked like a day to fly home. They started to shovel the snow away from the plane and began the tedious process of heating the motor and oil. But then the wind came up again, and there were no words, Gould wrote in his journal the following morning, to describe what happened next.[28]

''When I got in the plane to try and make radio contact'' with Little America, as Harold June later told the story,

> the needle on the airspeed indicator was registering 88 mph, and although she was only banging up and down on the snow, the aircraft was going through all the motions of flying. I looked out and saw Gould hanging onto a rope attached to one of the wing tips; he was blown straight out, horizontal, like a flag. . . . It was blowing so hard, we could scarcely breathe. . . . When it stopped it was so quiet that it hurt.

Then it started again, violently. ''A sudden gust tore the plane loose from its moorings, lifted it bodily into the air and literally flew it tail foremost for more than half a mile and dropped it onto the ice a total wreck.'' The specimens of ''a greenish mosslike growth'' that they had found among those inhospitable mountains were blown away with the plane.

Byrd and Dean Smith, with Malcolm Hanson as radio operator, alarmed at the complete radio silence from the 15th onward, flew the *Stars and Stripes* out in dirty weather on the evening of the 18th and, in the gathering twilight, located the three men by their ground signals—a smoke column, a flashing light, and a landing ''T'' marked out with flags. Harold June and Bernt Balchen went back to Little America with Smith, who returned on March 22 with June to pick up the rest of the party at the mountain camp. The next day, March 23, the rescuing airplane was drained of gas and buried in the snow for the long polar night. The first summer's aviation season quite obviously was over.[29]

The lost, wrecked aircraft stayed at its resting place 150 miles away among the Rockefellers—and twenty-seven years later it was still there! Looking for a downed airplane of their own, Navy fliers in 1956 during "Operation Deepfreeze" found "an old plane, much weathered" which turned out to be the one last used by Balchen, Gould, and June. Antarctica destroys; but it also preserves, seeming to stop time itself in the utter, abysmal cold.[30]

3

Wintering Over

Hath the rain a father? Or who hath begotten the drops of dew?
Out of whose womb came the ice? and the hoary frost of heaven, who hath gendered it?
The waters are hid as with a stone, and the face of the deep is frozen.

—Job 38:28–30 (KJV)

Little America, as the supply ships sailed away early in 1929, had the unfinished clutter of any hastily built new town. Behind the half-buried orange-sided houses "scores of crates and boxes lay in a shapeless pile, with the yellow heads of gasoline drums showing here and there above the snow." Sixty-five feet above the busy village the three radio masts spread their spidery filaments of wire, and near the three houses bulked the spectral, snow-covered shapes of the anchored planes. Mere yards away, beyond the shouts of men, lay the heavy silence of the great ice shelf. In the days that followed, perceptibly shortening as the sun circled closer to the cold horizon, "a rain of radiant iridescence seemed to drop softly upon the chill gray of the Barrier, warming and nourishing it into flame. . . . The cliffs surrendered none of their color as twilight approached, the somber sweep of Ross Sea none of its darkness; and the effect of night marching over the scene was inexpressibly strange."[1]

The pack ice closed in early that year, and it drastically changed the colonists' lifestyle. While the *City of New York* was struggling away from the Bay of Whales the *Eleanor Bolling* was trying once more to work its way in, but at the end of February Byrd had to radio Captain Brown to abandon the effort as hopelessly hazardous. Three more houses that were supposed to have been erected at Little America returned to New Zealand in the *Bolling's* hold, and 42 Little Americans therefore had to make do with quarters in-

Winter Quarters for the Ford
The Floyd Bennett *is buried for the Anarctic winter. Before
bringing it out again to fly to the South Pole, the Little Americans
will have to do a great deal of shoveling.*

tended for 25. Until the *Bolling* turned back for the last time the
members of the winter party had been *em*igrants, defined as the
kinds of persons they were by the lands and families and cities
they had left behind. Hereafter, until the sun and the ships came
again, they were *im*migrants; Antarctica was no longer a far
frontier to which one might run off, but a present homeland where
one had to live day by day. More complete geographic isolation
than theirs, the only human inhabitants of a continent as large as
the United States and Mexico combined, could scarcely be
imagined; but "it was a group isolation," Larry Gould later noted.
"Individual isolation was about the most unattainable thing in
Little America." Like an isolated farmhouse in winter on the
Dakota prairie, their quarters were at the same time both intensely
crowded and achingly alone.[2]

The experience may have been more uncomfortable for Richard Byrd than for anyone else. The situation of being shut in with 41 others seems to have been very hard on the "loner" Byrd had been at least since he was twelve, at which age he had travelled by himself around the world. Neither by birth, nor training, nor temperament was he suited for the kind of Babbittish first-names goodfellowship American men expected of each other in the 1920s, and this pleasantly smiling but still essentially humorless man's attempts to relate to the others in the party appear to have been rather awkward. Long barracks association usually has a way of knocking off people's rough edges; not so, apparently, with Byrd. "I found I did not know Commander Byrd any better" after a year together in Little America, Chief Pilot Bernt Balchen afterward testified. "The rest of us were drawn closer by the darkness and the isolation, but he managed always to hold himself apart." This could have been merely the necessary aloofness of leadership, in the ancient tradition of a ship's captain who walks the quarterdeck alone. But a revealing passage in Byrd's *Little America* hints at an attitude toward himself and others that may have made this man's winter sojourn a distressing ordeal indeed: "They are measuring you constantly, some openly, others secretly—there is so little else to do!"[3]

Byrd was the only member of the party to have a separate room of his own. In the administration building with him, hanging their gear on double wooden bunks, were sixteen others; these included Dr. Coman, *Times* man Russell Owen, two of the airplane pilots, the newsreel cameramen, and most of the scientists. Two hundred yards away—for safety, in case of fire (a greater hazard in an Antarctic camp than the cold) or in case a section of the ice shelf on which they were camped should break away—fourteen others bunked along one wall of the mess hall. These included "Blackie" the boxer (and expedition supply officer), chief cook George Tennant and cook's helper Arnold Clarke, machinist Czegka, pilots Smith and June, and ship's mate Strom. Adjoining the mess hall on one side was Czegka's machine shop; and beyond the machine shop was the Norwegian House (or, more ironically, the "Bilt-more"), an eleven-by-fourteen room with double bunks on all four sides, a kerosene heater, and a large box in the center that served for a table. Its ten tenants included aviation mechanic Pete Demas and amateur taxidermist Paul Siple; the unluckiest among them drew the bottom bunks, whose mattresses froze to the slats early and stayed that way.

A few expedition members sought greater privacy. Quin Black-burn, who was down on the roster as "Seaman and Topographer" but who was also making himself indispensable to the party as an expert darner and knitter of socks and sweaters, carved himself out a snow house adjacent to the radio shack. Byrd gave the Yukon veteran Arthur Walden and the Norwegian ski expert Chris Braathen permission to build a house of their own from the crate that had contained the Ford airplane's two outboard engines, pro-vided that in heating it they did not use up any of the expedition's coal. Braathen thereupon seized a sledge hammer and cold chisel and attacked a gasoline drum to convert it into a blubber stove, with comically disastrous results; "the drum finally resembled nothing at all, and he was in a condition to melt it with profanity." But eventually they had their stove, and thus was born "Blub-berheim." Walden and Braathen bunked there at night, and in the daytime Bernt Balchen and Sverre Strom used it as a shop for overhauling and rebuilding the dog sledges.[4]

The same ingenuity that provided additional living quarters also provided the Little Americans with more spaces for work. "Cap" McKinley, the aerial photographer, needed a photo lab and dark-room; "Chips" Gould, the expedition's carpenter—no relation to Larry—"waved his wand and produced it out of scrap lumber." The fuselage crate for the Fairchild monoplane, hauled up from the Bay of Whales by dog teams, became an aviation workshop and flight office; the wing crate from the same plane was used by the radio men as a repair shop. The final structure built at Little America, finished in fact after the sun had gone down for the last time, was Paul Siple's penguin dissection room. It was roofed with a lifeboat taken from the *City of New York* and, like "Blubberheim," it was heated by seal oil. The first time Siple tried to use his own gasoline-drum blubber stove, however, the place promptly caught on fire. After several days of trying to cut up penguins under conditions that ranged swiftly from red-hot overheating to fifty-below chill, with the dogs on one occasion finding and making a useless mess of the half-finished specimens, Siple got permission from the cook, George Tennant, to bring his penguins into the kitchen and hang them from the rafters. In spite of others' protests, Tennant also permitted Siple to take them down and finish the job in the same spot: "He did his butchering on the kitchen table, and he said I might as well do my butchering there too." Even a tough Scout, however, sometimes found it a bit much to take, when after spending the whole day at this unappetizing chore he would find George serving gamy penguin meat for supper!

A network of tunnels and trails—tunnels for inclement weather, and trails if one wanted to go outdoors—linked these and other structures together; weather and magnetism stations, storerooms, and a snowblock-lined gymnasium where some of the hardiest regularly worked out even at fifty below. The dogs had also to be housed. Next to the seal cache the dog drivers built a chopping room, and radiating outward from that hub they dug the dog tunnels, roofing them with strips of wood, chicken wire, canvas, and eventually snow. They set the dog crates into holes carved ten feet apart along the walls, "just far enough so that the dogs on short chains would not tangle but could rub noses." The hardy Greenland huskies seemed unmindful of the cold, preferring not to bed down in the crates but rather to sleep on the ice in front of these roughly built doghouses, "curling up into little balls and melting down into the ice as they slept."

One small room, off to one side of the chopping house, functioned as a maternity ward. Even in the Antarctic ice Nature was

Al Smith
*The runt of a litter born at Little America, and named while the
voice of the New York Governor was booming out on what Smith
called the "raddio," this husky pup grew up to become Larry
Gould's lead dog, as shown here.*

taking its usual course, and the busy Boy Scout soon found himself looking after living puppies as well as dead penguins. Indeed,
the expedition's dogs enjoyed something of a population explo-
sion. On one occasion, when the reverberant voice of Al Smith
was booming forth from the radio, one of the men brought in a
new litter of pups in a bushel basket and dumped them out. Someone, evidently a Republican, pointed to the runt and said, "That
one must be named Al Smith." The scrawny infant may have
somewhat comforted the Democratic partisans in Little America
after their champion's recent downfall at the polls; grown to stately
maturity, Al Smith would be stepping out the following spring as
lead dog for Professor Gould, and Gould still speaks of him with
pride and affection across a span of fifty years.[5]

On April 19, after one last great green, blue, red, and yellow flare, the sun dropped below the skyline and stayed down. For some days there would remain a dim half-light on the northern horizon, "a weird, diffused light in which everything was distinct but faintly veiled," wrote Russell Owen, "like the twilight of the gods in Asgard. One can understand the old Norse legends so much better here." For the next four months the members of the Byrd Antarctic Expedition would be "a family of moles who scuttle through glittering snow tunnels with lanterns and flashlights, live all day by the light of lamps, and only emerge into the dusk of outdoors for a short walk in the bitter cold or for some task which must be done," guided by the electric beacon that was turned on to keep men from becoming lost between the houses, or by the cold moon.

This was the time of the expedition's stay that had worried Byrd the most. "The Antarctic is the last stronghold of inertness," the Commander reflected. "On this continent, whence all life has been driven, save for a very few primitive or microscopic forms, inertia governs a vast empire." For mere survival's sake it was essential that everybody have enough to do to keep from sinking into a fatal torpor. Even Russell Owen, who by his own admission was physically indolent and detested taking his regular turns at "K.P.," saw the basic point that nobody could be allowed to lie abed the whole dark day; "That way lies breakdown and insanity." Antarctica lived by long, slow cycles of light and dark, but Little America lived by the clock.[6]

At seven in the morning the night watchman, clothed in furs, his parka hood still muffling his head, threw some kindling into the long black kitchen stove, lighted it, and put on coal. With the kitchen fire going well he poked chief cook George Tennant in the ribs and then went over to the main building, checked the meteorological instruments, lighted the stove in the bunk room, filled the bucket on the stove with snow for wash water, and at eight waked executive officer Gould. "Larry leap[ed] into his clothes with a speed which would shame a fireman going to a three-alarm fire,"

called the others in that room, and went over to the mess hall.
Shuffling out of the gloom to gather near the pink-glowing iron
stove, the Little Americans pulled on the socks and boots they
couldn't manage inside their sleeping bags, and one by one went
out, "subdued as men are the world over before breakfast."

Over in the mess hall a few early risers were sitting down to eat;
machinist Czegka, pilots Balchen and Smith, and ship's mate
Strom never had to be called. Afterward Gould woke up the crew
in the adjoining "Biltmore," and regularly he had to go back and
rout out the rest of the people in his own building, tasks he accomplished with a loud and joyous verve that earned him the nick-
name "Simon Legree." (Commander Byrd typically did not get
about until a few minutes before the end of the breakfast hour.)
While the second shift ate, the first might be talking over the
previous night's news, intercepted by their radio operators and
posted on the bulletin board. "It must be a tough place to live in,
that world," with its floods and tornadoes and murders, Russell
Owen mused; "not quiet and peaceful like ours." And as the
weeks wore on, the tie with that other world thinned out like fading radio signals. "There was a faint memory of other places and
people where we bathed regularly and always brushed our teeth in
the morning, and put on different clothes, if we had them. But we
had lost all connection with that life, despite the radio."

While Tennant and Arnold Clarke cleared away the breakfast
debris, the others drifted off to their work. The mess table sometimes was so cluttered with gear under repair that Siple was forced
back out into his lifeboat-roofed penguin laboratory. Members of
next spring's sledge parties molded dog pemmican into trail-ration
sizes; others weighed and packed the man-food. Carl Petersen,
earphones over his blond head and long legs under the radio table,
might be trying futilely to raise New Zealand, "cursing under his
breath in Norwegian." On better days, however, he or operator
Howard Mason would be talking with the Graf Zeppelin on its
flight around the world, or with the Russian expedition at Franz

Joseph Land, or with the University of Michigan station in Greenland, or with the Army in the jungles of Panama. From the machine shop next door came the whine of Czegka's lathe, and over
in the other house one could hear the clatter of Owen's typewriter
and the happy whirr of Ronne's sewing machine. Warning the others not to poke up the fires lest smoke ruin their observations, meteorologists "Cyclone" Haines and Henry Harrison launched their
weather balloons, with little paper lanterns attached, containing
short pieces of lighted candle so that they could track them through
the Antarctic dusk.[7]

Even the most simple kinds of operations were enormously
complicated by the cold. At $-55°$ F ($-48°$ C), kerosene lanterns
in the tunnels went out, the fuel having frozen; flashlight batteries
would not work, because the cold stopped the chemical action;
rubber insulation on the telephone wires became brittle and broke.
"Even a book lying against a cold wall steamed like a teakettle
when opened in a slightly warmer atmosphere." If one inadver-
tently breathed on a camera lens, the instrument had to be baked
near the stove before it could be used again. Developing and dry-
ing "Cap" McKinley's hypersensitive aerial photographic film
would have been hard enough in a properly equipped laboratory;
"in the Antarctic," Byrd remarked, "it borders on necromancy."
Snow in a bucket on a red-hot stove reduced eventually to one-
third its bulk in meltwater, and when one set that residue to one
side and placed a second bucket of snow on the stove the first one
promptly froze. If this object lesson in the physics of heat transfer
perplexed the photographers, it exasperated anyone trying simply
to keep clean; Arnold Clarke, recording in his diary the most noteworthy events of his days, set down for May 17 only the laconic
entry "took a bath."[8]

This scorching cold could raise routine activities—physicist
Frank ("Taffy") Davies's bundled-to-the-eyebrows trips out to the
magnetism shacks to read his instruments, for example, or Henry
Harrison's numbing stands at the theodolite while tracking those

Laurence M. Gould and Frank (''Taffy'') Davies
Scientists had some of the coldest jobs at Little America I. Above, Gould, geologist, with rime-covered theodolite; below, Davies, physicist, with magnetometer.

weather balloons—to the level of adventure. But other chores, like fetching in fuel and food, washing pots and pans, tending fires, or shoveling out entrances after a snowstorm, resisted being glamorized. Commander Byrd, striving to emphasize the point that during a long polar night "the hand is quite as important as the brain," undertook at one time to forbid the posting of Owen's *New York Times* stories on the expedition bulletin board, lest some men's names be given high prominence while others, doing more obscure work, received scant mention. If polar exploration served as a moral equivalent of war, perhaps it could also function as a moral equivalent of socialism, evolving at least temporarily an economy "in which no job is meaner or more meritorious than the rest." The hope was clearly unrealistic, and Byrd soon withdrew the ban; Owen's stories were an indirect connection with expedition members' families and friends, and they were entitled to that tie. (Besides, the leader reflected, "Of all the men here I have the least right to talk depreciatively of the value of getting one's name in the newspapers.") How, then, in the absence either of the carrot of fame and fortune or the stick of military-style discipline, did the daily drudge work get done at all? By the force of peer pressure, Paul Siple recalled; "We had a razzing system which made a delinquent the laughing stock of everybody." This was an effective but fragile social solution; many of these men were too worldly-wise, or as the winter wore on simply too tired, to be amenable to scout troop morality alone.[9]

At one o'clock many knocked off for a coffee break and perhaps a snack, and if the weather permitted some went outdoors, to practice on skis or simply to get away from the place for awhile. Commander Byrd missed few opportunities to go for a walk, usually westward down the trail to the Bay of Whales.[10] At four, Little America's work day ended. Supper, like breakfast, had to be served in two shifts; from one of Russell Owen's radio dispatches, *New York Times* readers learned next day how Freddy Crockett "in his best French" had ushered the Little Americans to their seats at the table, verbally camouflaging the main dish of whale stew as *ragout cras de balène*. Half their meat was of Antarctic origin; the captain of the whaler *C. A. Larsen* on the way down had donated some whale meat, which had been hung in the *City of New York's* rigging, beyond reach of the dogs, and cured in the funnel smoke. (Paul Siple found it a savory contrast to their own barreled beef, but Owen thought its taste bore out the popular delusion that a whale is really a fish.) On other nights the menu might be roast pork, or seal flipper, or fricasseed chicken, topped off by George Tennant's excellent pies and cakes; later in the evening there might be popcorn from a frying pan over the stove.

After dinner on May 6, 1929, "Antarctic University" had its opening session. Larry Gould gave the same course in geology that he regularly offered at the University of Michigan: two lectures and two one-hour discussion groups per week. Nearly everyone attended at first, and six weeks later some twenty of them were still clinging to the course and maintaining their interest. "It is rather pleasant," Gould would write on June 11, with an implicit back-of-the-hand swing at the rah-rah Big Ten students back home, to be "teaching people who are entirely sincere in their attitude." In addition, Harold June with the help of Balchen and Smith conducted a ground school on aviation; "Cap" McKinley lectured on aerial surveying; and chief radio operator Malcolm Hanson taught the theory and practice of radio operation and reception—"a most important course," Gould reported, in that it trained two radio operators, Joe de Ganahl and Freddy Crockett, for the sledge journeys that were to take place in the spring.[11]

Many Little Americans during this after-dinner period played cards. Byrd, third-in-command Ashley McKinley, aerologist Henry Harrison, and motion picture photographer Joe Rucker established a bridge foursome that played together throughout the winter; the rest usually indulged in more plebeian pastimes— poker, hearts, or acey-deucey. George Hamilton Black ("Blackie"), after having spent all morning burrowing with a

George Hamilton Black ("Blackie")
"At night he may be found in his element, eyes sparkling, talking like a Coney Island barker as he runs a blackjack game for tobacco, our only valuable commodity." (*From one of Russell Owen's radioed dispatches to the* New York Times.)

flashlight to bring in supplies from the tunnels, "at night may be found in his element, eyes sparkling, talking like a Coney Island barker as he runs a blackjack game for tobacco, our only valuable commodity." At nine o'clock all these games were supposed to cease, and at ten Professor Gould called "Lights out." Men were permitted to read in their bunks, however, using candles allotted for that purpose. Some saved and re-used their tallow in glass jars or tin cans.

In the mess-hall bunkroom, out of earshot from where the leaders slept, the silence that was supposed to prevail after ten o'clock was not always enforced: "just as soon as taps-time comes," Arnold Clarke wrote in his diary toward the end of the winter, "all the debaters assemble to the stove be it hot or cold." [The fire had been allowed to go out at ten.] "Then the exponents of Bacchus and Pan and Darwin and Christ and Atheism and Freud deliver their views on their subjects, which the debate never fails to touch on at some point in its course." Even when such dormitory bull sessions took place, however, frigid Antarctica always got in the last word. Byrd believed that previous polar wintering-over parties had suffered from breathing stale and unreplenished air, and at Little America, therefore, promptly at 11 P.M. the outside door was opened. "A cloud of fog rolls in and tumbles along the floor, marking the advance of the cold air," Owen shiveringly observed, and as it crept from the bottom bunks on upward the flickering candles and homemade kerosene lanterns one by one went out. Some nights the wind sprang up, Gould noticed, "and as it sweeps across our tiny chimneys, which project up above the house, it sets up a sound much like the deep tones of an organ. It is rather restful." [12]

Sunday was "very much like every other day" at Little America, Russell Owen reported to the *Times* on May 12, even though Commander Byrd officially designated it as a day of rest. Many activities (e.g., reading the recording instruments and feeding the dogs) had to go on regardless; "We get up at the same time and have just about as much or as little to do." However, on Sundays hard-working Martin Ronne forsook his sewing machine for the scale model of the *City of New York* that he was building, and generally the pace slowed. Sunday night was movie night; the films had been presented to the expedition by the National Board of Review, which seemed, as Byrd put it, to have been guided in

Martin Ronne with the scale model of the City of New York *upon which he worked during the Antarctic winter night of 1929.*

its selection principles by "a reverent feeling for antiquity." More likely, second-in-command Gould speculated, whoever selected the pictures had simply been avoiding themes which might too poignantly remind the gender-segregated Little Americans that they were sexually deprived.[13]

No attempt was made to organize religious services. With individual members of the expedition professing Catholicism, Lutheranism, Greek Orthodoxy, Judaism, or nothing in particular, it would have been difficult to find common ground. "But there was a great deal of interest in reading the Bible," Gould remembers, "from men of whom one would least have expected it." Reading, of all kinds, was in fact one of the expedition's most effective weapons against the monotony, the crowding, and the oppressive cold. The dour machinist Victor Czegka, for example, who at the age of 49 was still able to lift 650 pounds off the floor, could certainly have held his own in an argument; instead, ''when he was mad at everybody, he used to climb up in his bunk and read Dickens.''[14]

Gould had picked the books for the expedition's library, within the limitation that most of them came as donations; ''I don't think we ever catalogued them.'' Owen arranged them along the north and west walls in the administration building. On the top shelf on both sides sat the classic Everyman editions; then two shelves of novels, ranging from *The Vicar of Wakefield* to Zane Grey; then, on the north side, an extensive selection of the great polar literature such as Nansen's *Farthest North*, Shackleton's *South*, Sir Douglas Mawson's *Home of the Blizzard*, Apsley Cherry-Garrard's *The Worst Journey In the World;* below these, a row of detective stories; and at the bottom Dr. Eliot's Five-Foot Shelf. Under the window on the west wall stood the *Encyclopedia Britannica,* a few books of poetry, and uniform sets of Dickens and Kipling. A round iron stove, comfortable chairs, and adequate lighting attracted the Little Americans, many of whom now sported both luxuriant beards and shaven heads, to the library corner; ''At night,'' Owen wrote, ''one sees a group of youthful-faced but bald men, each holding a book with one hand and meditatively rubbing his cranium with the other like venerable members of a sedate club.''

Altogether absent from that library, so far as Professor Gould can recall, were the writers we usually think of as ''typical'' of the 1920s such as Scott Fitzgerald and Ernest Hemingway. Popular novelists now forgotten, Joseph C. Lincoln and Donn Byrne, were more widely read than any other authors, closely followed by Mark Twain. The classics also had their devotees; ''books from the Everyman's Library are scattered on every bunk.'' Larry Gould that winter got through the entire Forsyte Saga (as far as author John Galsworthy had then carried it) and Romain Rolland's *Jean-Christophe*. Richard Byrd absorbed floods of philosophy, well-leavened by murder mysteries. The single book in greatest demand was W. H. Hudson's *Green Mansions,* possibly because of the extreme contrast between its tropical setting and the Ross Ice Shelf—although people also read extensively in the accounts of earlier polar expeditions. Conrad was read a great deal; Kipling hardly at all.

Reading is of course not everybody's dish of tea. Chris Braathen's model of the *City of New York* "kept him so busy he didn't open a book." Airplane pilot Alton Parker ambitiously set out to read the entire *Encyclopedia Britannica,* starting with Volume I, letter A; he got as far as "ammonium tetrachloride" and threw the tome down in disgust: "The stuff in that damn book is no good for an aviator." On the other hand, men who had never before cracked a book learned a new and rewarding pleasure; ice cream maker and dog driver Jim Feury, with no more than a grade-school education, opened a personal door into the world of reading by way of O. Henry's short stories.[15]

Of the younger members of the expedition, by all odds the most studious was aviation mechanic Epaminondas ("Pete") Demas, who combined the traditional immigrant American dream of upward mobility through education with a desire to know better his own Greek national heritage. In order to get away from the clamorous distractions of the daytime, among people who (in Russell Owen's words) "argued and laughed or yelled each other down," but "had forgotten how to talk," Demas volunteered for the job of night watchman, which up until that time had been rotated alphabetically. The watchman had each half hour to observe the aurora, and frequently check the direction and velocity of the wind; twice each night he had to make the rounds of the houses, trails, and tunnels, as a precaution against fire—the very existence of the colony might depend on the vigilance of this one man. But the rest of the time his post was in the library, and there, fortified by hot coffee in a thermos jug, Demas could study his scientific and technical books or enjoy the classical philosophers and tragedians.

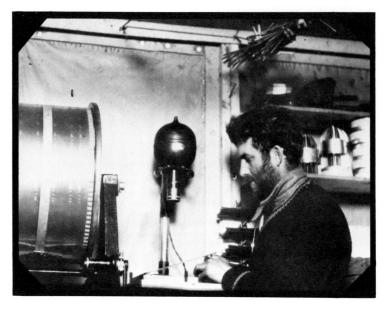

Laurence M. Gould
Shown here in the photo darkroom at Little America, the versatile Professor Gould—construction boss, trail party leader, expedition second-in-command, scholar, lecturer in "Antarctic University"—was in many respects the real backbone of the wintering-over party at Little America I.

Larry Gould, encouraging this bent, gave the young man for his birthday on May 31 a copy of Michael Pupin's *From Immigrant to Inventor;* Demas in response, being worried about his performances in Gould's geology quizzes, asked the professor to write him a letter of evaluation, which the young man then copied verbatim into his journal. After some typical teacher-to-student advice—"Don't let the details obscure the bigger picture. Don't learn anything you do not understand," et cetera—the geologist wound up with an Emersonian flourish: "Find out the thing you like best to do and let nothing stop you from doing it. I believe any man who possesses a soul makes his greatest mistake in life when he turns aside from the thing he likes best to do."[16]

The Scott and Shackleton expeditions, of course, had also had books; copies of *The Secret of the Island,* by Jules Verne, and *Tales of Mystery and Imagination,* by Edgar Allan Poe, left behind by members of Scott's last expedition in 1912, were destined to be found—in reasonably good condition, although they had been out in the open for almost fifty years!—by the American geologist and explorer Robert L. Nichols in 1959, and in due course the National Science Foundation would return them to their surprised and grateful original owners. But Scott and Shackleton had not had radio. More of a break in Little America's winter rountine than its Sundays, in a sense, were the broadcasts from the North American mainland. Each Saturday at 11 P.M. Eastern Standard Time—4 P.M. at the Bay of Whales—radio stations WGY, Schenectady, and KDKA, Pittsburgh, regularly beamed programs directly to the expedition. The Little Americans on their Saturday afternoons heard the voices of political notables such as New York's new governor, Franklin Roosevelt, and of show business figures ranging from the Metropolitan Opera's Lucrezia Bori to the popular crooner Rudy Vallee. Some of the music was spoiled by an echo, as radio waves from New York, coming around the earth from both directions, reached Little America with a very slight interference effect; Fred Allen's comedy routines, however, seem to have come through with all their dry wit intact. More important, the expedition members heard in this manner from their families and friends back home. The catch was that these broadcasts, beamed to Antarctica by shortwave, went out also on standard wavelengths to anyone else who cared to listen in. "One man in particular seemed almost equally popular with two girls who rarely missed a weekly broadcast to remind him of their affection," Professor Gould noted, and the expedition members in high good humor made bets on which young woman would eventually win.[17]

The communications media of that era, much as ours do, self-servingly hinted that their own activity in covering events in the world was really more important than the events themselves. Acknowledging that the Little Americans dwelt in a "world of seem-

ing magic when the boreal lights illume their Southern skies," one
New York Times editorial nevertheless insisted that "the greater
daily miracle" for the expedition members consisted of "the
voices that come out of the North through the long night." So far
as the voices of families and friends are concerned, the point cannot be gainsaid. Apparently, however, it did not occur to the
schoolteacherish *Times* that people might actually prefer watching the shimmering glory of an aurora over listening to Rudy
Vallee sing "As Time Goes By"!

"This afternoon an aurora of auroras," Laurence Gould wrote
in his diary for May 13. "Not the pale electric green which is so
characteristic—but great yet delicate dancing curtains of red, pink,
green, and even purple light—never still—never have I seen an
aurora so full of life." Having written this, Gould at once realized
the inadequacy of language. "That," he admitted, "is a hell of a
figure to describe such a sight"; the aurora "has no parallel—no
counterpart." The human perspective is so small! Such a spectacle
is rather the way one might imagine the scene inside an old-
fashioned glass vacuum tube that has started to go gassy—as seen
from the tiny viewpoint of an animated and sentient electron. Like
any other transcendent visual experience, those fluttering ioniza-
tion discharges out in the semi-vacuum hundreds of miles beyond
the Earth can never really be translated into words, although they
have challenged many gifted writers, notably Nansen, to try.[18]

Professor Gould democratically regretted that the *aurora australis* could not be a gift for everybody: "It isn't fair that but a hand-
ful of us here should be so privileged." Thus was the dilemma of
the frontier-to-civilization cycle manifested once again; for if everybody flocked to Antarctica and set it afire with smog and ablaze
with electric light, then of course nobody would be able to see the
aurora. "This display belongs here," Gould concluded his May 13
diary entry. "Without the bleakness of the all day night and the infinite solitude of the white desert everywhere it would lose some of

its personality. Somehow I just can't imagine such a display over the green fields and the waving trees of my Michigan home. I guess the sky isn't big enough up there anyhow." The silent electrical displays were of course not the only mood of the Antarctic night; there were times, as the same writer noted on June 25, when "the howling wind and the blinding snow combine to give the out of doors an aspect akin to very real terror." [19]

The off-duty hours of the Little Americans were not taken up only with reading, radio, and aurora-watching. Polar expeditions traditionally had paused for parties from time to time, and the Byrd Antarctic Expedition was no exception. "Three days of intermission," Larry Gould wrote in his journal for Sunday, May 12—the same day Russell Owen was telling the world that Sunday in Little America was very much like every other day. On Thursday May 9, the third anniversary of Commander Byrd's North Pole flight, those fourteen of the Little Americans who had also been at Spitsbergen sat down to a turkey dinner at first table, and "for the first time Doc. Coman broke out some liquid refreshment in the way of gin and whatnot." [20]

There were toasts, in the brief course of which one expedition member drank himself under the table. Then the celebration adjourned to Blubberheim, into whose small confines twenty-two Little Americans somehow managed to cram themselves. Comparative peace descended at last around 4 A.M.; it was broken by the clank of a chain and the patter of paws as one of the dogs, which had broken loose, came down the passageway hoping to join in the fun. Not until late Friday morning was everybody in bed, and then they slept all day; some still had hangovers on Saturday. With the return to normalcy on Sunday Laurence Gould, ambivalent toward alcohol like so many in the prohibitionist twenties, wrote: "When I remember my rigid upbringing with regards [to] liquor . . . I wonder why I am not more disturbed." On balance, however, he felt it had been "a grand party—a bit boisterous," but an occasion

for the healthy blowing-off of suppressed steam; "a most delight-
ful atmosphere of conviviality—not a brawl. Our party was not
that." [21]

The routines resumed, from meticulous map-making to casual
K.P.; and so, a few days later, did the drinking. "The boys had
another party last night," Pete Demas reported on May 17. Demas
had been "hit in the mouth several times" by one rampaging Little
American, who had finally cooled off only when another man
conked him on the head with a ski boot. And the following week-
end it happened again. "Liquor is a bad thing to have around!"
Gould exploded, reversing his more mellow judgement on the
polar flight anniversary. "Our party of May 9 was somewhat of a
mistake. There has been considerable drinking since then"—two
ingenious Little Americans had bored a hole through the snow wall
separating the doctor's medical supply room from the general
storehouse, pushed through a rubber tube, siphoned off alcohol
from the big metal drum, and mixed it with bottled fruit juice and
snow—"and now it must stop. I wish the barrel could be emptied
and temptation placed beyond the reach of those who do not know
how to control their appetites." This is *not*, the post-Repeal reader
must realize, just Methodist-style, Prohibition-era moralizing. The
expedition second-in-command knew, realistically, that Antarctica
was no place for the carefree drunk who at home might safely fare
forth well-oiled from a bar in quest of adventure. Patrolling the
houses until 3:30 A.M. with an outside temperature of sixty below,
after an uproarious Fourth of July party which, like the Spitsbergen commemorative affair, had begun as good clean fun, Gould
"feared some of the inebriates might get out of doors and freeze to
death. It would take but a few minutes." Ominously, that Independence Day celebration was also the scene of the first real
fighting they had had in Little America, and Commander Byrd was
afraid there might be more. The responsible burden fell in particular upon Demas, as night watchman, whom Byrd told on July 12

to see to it thereafter that the hard core of incorrigibles were in bed or in the library (near the leaders) after ten P.M.[22]

By that time the harsh lunar topography around the settlement was being softened from time to time by a rosy brightness on the northern horizon from the coming sun. Antarctica still carried in its bag of tricks the potential for cruel practical jokes: on July 28, while sizzling Manhattan had temperatures in the nineties, Little America's thermometer recoiled in the opposite direction, to a truly Martian depth of $-72°$ F ($-58°$ C). But the worst was obviously over, and "with the ever increasing light," Professor Gould wrote on August 9, "the camp seems to bestir itself more each day." The sledging parties worked on trail flags and other preparations for the coming spring journeys; Gould completed the chart which Byrd would use on the actual south polar flight; and— most important of all—"There is an increasingly genial attitude of the various men toward each other. The hardest part of the night is gone." *Times* reporter Russell Owen, who during the long darkness had known periods of depression and disorientation when he had "felt as though I tossed my stories into the air when I handed them to the operator, that they went forever drifting," similarly perked up. "I noticed yesterday how in the increasing light the vision expands," he wrote on August 10:

It comes as a shock that one day the tiny place in which we have lived all winter, this trail of a few feet which has been our narrow existence, should grow and become part of a limitless field. The plain of snow rolls forth, miles of endless desolation, which fade into the indistinct and beckoning horizon. The vastness of it strikes on the mind like a blow; it had been forgotten.

But constrictedness must not be one's final impression of wintertime Antarctica. The silent darkness outside the houses was *not* oppressive, Larry Gould had written shortly after Midwinter Day; "it is an expanding sort of silence. It is the normal state here."

And now that it was over, what the Little Americans remembered from the dark season, Gould believed, were the many quiet hours for reading and the many friendly acquaintances that had ripened into rich friendships they would always cherish, rather than the momentary frictions that would pass with the melting solar rays. "For us the winter is essentially over," Gould wrote on August 21, the day before sunrise, "and it has been a great time."[23]

4

Into the
White
Wilderness

But, after all, it is not what we see that inspires awe, but the knowledge of what lies beyond our view. We see only a few miles of ruffled snow bounded by a vague wavy horizon but we know that beyond that horizon are hundreds and even thousands of miles which can offer no change to the weary eye, while on the vast expanse that one's mind conceives one knows there is neither tree nor shrub, nor any living thing, nor even inanimate rock—nothing but this terrible limitless expanse of snow. It has been so for countless years, and it will be so for countless more. And we, little human insects, have started to crawl over this awful desert, and are now bent on crawling back again. Could anything be more terrible than this silent, wind-swept immensity when one thinks such thoughts?

—Robert Falcon Scott

"The deep shadow of the world" was on the sky to southward, but at the brink of the great Ross Shelf the cliffs were shining in the sun. It was so quiet that from a mile away one could hear the barking of the dogs. Far out on the Bay of Whales, rising from open water, a screen of frost smoke reminded news reporter Russell Owen of the mysterious curtain through which the hero of Edgar Allan Poe's strange *Narrative of A. Gordon Pym* had vanished into the unknown south. "And here was I on the other side of that curtain, the side Poe did not care, with all his imagination, to pierce. It was as fanciful as anything he had ever dreamed."

In its typical fashion Antarctica soon mocked such fancies as Owen's—while confirming some of the darker visions of Poe. A blizzard smote the camp a week before sunrise and raged for two days. But on August 19, 1929, one timid Weddell seal, the white continent's equivalent of spring's first robin or groundhog in milder lands, "poked a brown head out of the thin ice over a blow hole, took one breath of the frigid air, and hastily drew it in again." On the 20th, a few of the Little Americans sneaked a preview of the returning sun by swarming up the radio masts, risking frostbite as they grabbed onto the iron.[1]

"By previous arrangement," Professor Gould still quips, "the sun rose on August 22, my birthday." Both the cosmic and the personal anniversaries were appropriately observed. Expedition members raised the American, British, and Norwegian flags, honoring the Antarctic achievements of those countries, and two Little Americans of Irish descent hoisted aloft also the green banner of the Free State of Eire. "Back indoors," recounted Paul Siple—breaking his usual strict silence concerning Antarctican merrymaking—"we celebrated as only polar explorers could, the return of the sun." "It was a great party and was plenty wet," Larry Gould added. "A football game was started," chimed in Russell Owen, "possibly the only football game ever played in a room filled with bunks, a kitchen stove, tables and general debris."[2]

Night watchman Pete Demas, as in previous such situations, was stuck for the next two weeks with the problem of expedition members who would not stop partying after the party was over. "I gathered the boys up and I gave them a long talk," he finally wrote on September 3, and the talk seems to have been successful. On September 14 Demas stood the night watch for the last time. The four months of kerosene-lit scholarship had greatly benefited his math studies, he felt, but now it was time to go back to work on the airplanes. On the 20th the aviation people cut into the igloo they had built around the front of the Fairchild monoplane. There Russell Owen found them, trying to get the carburetor off at thirty below. Chief Pilot Bernt Balchen worked with bare hands, sometimes taking hold of an engine strut to support himself; when he got a bolt loose he calmly reached up past searing metal to unscrew it and take it out. "Then he would run his hands through the blue flame of the blowtorch once or twice and go back to his cold task."[3]

Out on the bay ice, meanwhile, the seals were basking in the meager sunshine, and on October 5 the first baby Weddell pup was born. Paul Siple and Quin Blackburn tagged his rear flippers, took his measurements, and weighed him in a net tied to a spring balance scale suspended from a bar resting on their shoulders. The mother—all eleven feet and six-hundred-plus pounds of her— angrily disapproved! In the days that followed fifteen or more seals were born in the same area, and Siple and Blackburn, sometimes assisted by Dr. Coman, tried to keep data on ten of them. Weighing only fifty pounds at first, after two weeks on a diet of seal milk the baby seals doubled in weight, and then their mothers began to take them into the water to teach them to swim. At the end of the first month the babies were larger than the two young men. The healthy infants had learned to use their newly cut teeth, and one little fellow embarrassed the Scout by snapping at the seat of his pants. The mothers continued to object to the scientific experiment, but more passively as their children grew older; they lay back at some distance clicking their teeth like castanets, or emitting "great croaking sounds, like bass drums or enormous bull frogs."[4]

The main business of the Byrd Antarctic Expedition, however, was not with the teeming pelagic life in the ice water that lapped against Antarctica's shore, but rather with its vast, biologically empty interior. Far below the southern horizon of Little America lay the Queen Maud Mountains, which Amundsen's men had found rising across their path in 1911 on the way to the pole. The geological structure of those mountains held an important key to the hidden form of Antarctica as a whole, and the glaciers that slashed through them provided access beyond to the high polar plateau. Both Laurence Gould's geological investigations and Richard Byrd's aeronautics must converge, therefore, upon the mighty Queen Maud Range.

On October 13, 1929, five dog teams started south, pulling extra loads. The dog trail that had been so carefully marked out and flagged before the sun went down had been torn to shreds in the night. The bay ice was now a maze of upended blocks and jagged pressure ridges; and the outer edge of the Ross Shelf, where they planned to ascend it, was seamed with menacing blue crevasses. They got their extra sledge loads up onto the Barrier, left them there, and retreated, thwarted by intense cold. Two days later a Supporting Party led by the seasoned New Englander Arthur Walden, with a mission to lay down supply depots every fifty miles for later use by Gould's geological expedition, left Little America in "splendid weather" (a mere 10° F below). Richard Byrd accompanied Walden's group for part of the way, and Paul Siple, driving a team made up of half-grown pups that had been born in the colony, gave Byrd what the Commander afterward described as the wildest ride he had ever had. On October 24 the Ford snowmobile on its caterpillar treads clanked down the slope to Ver-sur-Mer, "obscured in a blizzard of its own making." With the help of a platoon of snow shovelers, bossed by third-in-command "Cap" McKinley, the machine got up onto the shelf the next day. Shooting it across the filled-in crevasses in the style of a First World War tank bridging a trench, its crew—Jim Feury, George Black, and the strongest man in camp, Sverre Strom—scornfully asked if this was indeed the forbidding Barrier of which they had heard so much. Byrd warned them to be careful.[5]

"Radio from supporting party today told of fearful experience with crevassed region at 81° 11' S," Henry Harrison wrote in his diary at Little America on the 29th. "After breaking through time and again they finally retraced their path." In that same entry, however, a few lines down, Harrison jotted down radio news of quite another sort: "Another brief panic on Wall St. . . . . turnover of over 16,000,000 shares. Big financial guns came to the rescue and most stocks were making steady recoveries at the close." Out in the civilized world on September 3, as we now know, the big bull market of the twenties had reached the end of its upward climb, and while Siple was weighing his baby seals and Demas was servicing his aircraft engines Wall Street was lurching toward disaster. Thursday, October 24, the day when the Byrd Antarctic

Dean Smith
While they were all waiting for the South Pole
flight, the stock market crashed—and pilot Smith
watched Chrysler stock "go down with the ther-
mometer." Civilization, by radio, thus extended
its discontents even to the Bay of Whales.

Expedition's snowmobile roared out of camp to shoulder its way through the first pressure ridges, was also "the first of the days which history . . . identifies with the panic of 1929," and Tuesday the 29th, when the dogs and men of the Supporting Party were still struggling through the crevasses in quest of a way south, "was the most devastating day in the history of the New York stock market."[6]

Its whiplash was felt even on the far Antarctic frontier. Airplane pilot Dean Smith, who had taken a flier in an automobile stock just before the expedition sailed, "watched Chrysler go down with the thermometer, while he unhappily directed his broker from the Bay of Whales."

"Did it hit you hard?" Smith was asked, after his stock had tumbled ninety points.

"Hard? It ruined me," he said with a grin, "and I thought I was going to have such a good time with that money when I got home."[7]

On Wednesday, October 30, the outlook from both Wall Street and Little America at least momentarily brightened. U. S. Steel and American Can declared extra dividends; John D. Rockefeller, Senior, "believing that fundamental conditions of the country are sound," came out of seclusion to announce that he and his son had "for some days been purchasing sound common stocks;" and although there had still been no word from the snowmobile Henry Harrison was able to write: "Supporting party after several reconnoiters finds passage through crevassed region." Two days later the Supporting Party reached its destination, 190 miles out from Little America, and laid down its last depot. It would start homeward the next morning, its job well done.

After breakfast on Monday, November 4, some twenty of the Little Americans turned to at digging a runway to bring out the Ford trimotor airplane. To free its skis, which were ten feet below the surface, they cut out and hauled away forty tons of snow. ("Why not leave the blocks here and just move the barrier?" physicist Frank Davies joked.) As men pulled their loads up to the surface and dumped them 200 feet away, *Times* man Owen was reminded of Egyptian slaves quarrying out building blocks for the pyramids. At ten degrees above zero it was warm work; aerologist Harrison "experienced the paradoxical combination of perspiration streaming down my face and blinding my eyes while my ears actually became slightly frostbitten." Even bare-headed, Harrison's "hair became [w]ringing wet and later turned to a solid mass of frost."[8]

That same afternoon at 1:30, "amid scenes of eager, nervous dogs, goodbyes and luck wishing, and movie taking," the Geological Party—Larry Gould, Norman Vaughan, Freddy Crockett, G. N. Thorne, Jack O'Brien, and Ed Goodale—left camp on its long trek south. Fifteen miles out they came upon a large khaki tent, and inside it they surprised Feury, Black, and Strom, who "were unshaved and unwashed and had very evidently been working hard." The snowmobile had broken down the week before in soft snow about 75 miles out from Little America, and its crew had been hiking back ever since. "They were in great good spirits," Gould wrote in his log that evening after his own party had camped for the night five miles further on, "and well they should be for they are due to get a lot of kidding when they get back to Little America." Next day, November 5, the snowmobilers man-hauled their sledges the rest of the way home. "A great burlesque reception awaited them," complete with "welcome home" signs, streamers of confetti, and machinist Victor Czegka solemnly turning the crank of a dummy newsreel camera. "The rear end snapped completely," Henry Harrison explained the vehicle's accident afterward in his diary. "Another Antarctic automobile gone wrong!"—or perhaps, a present-day mechanic might add, it was only another case of a typical Ford rear end.[9]

Two days later Gould's party came upon the snowmobile itself, and took from it some soup, two ice axes, six pairs of crampons, and a little gasoline to cache at the next supply depot. "Dogs were especially full of pep to-day—very encouraging," Gould wrote in his log that night. "They seem to be feeling better all the time." Gould personally was rather glad that the ideal mechanical vehicle for crossing the Antarctic had not yet been invented, and that the loss of the plane in the Rockefeller Mountains had made it necessary for him to go into the field this second summer with the dogs. "I'm glad I was born when I was," he would tell his geology students at the University of Arizona half a century later. "I'm sorry that you will probably never have the opportunity to drive sledge dogs." At the moment on the trail, however, such a sense of pleasure would have been premature. On November 8 the party lost its way and had to retrace. On the 10th, after stopping at their second supply depot to redistribute the burdens, "our heavy work started," and it was a harder day, Gould confessed at its end, "for us amateurs on skiis than for the dogs with their heavy loads. My 'dogs' are pretty sore tonight." The husky pups, he wistfully noted the next evening, "end the day with all kinds of reserve energy—the teams never stop but that they are barking to continue;" for their human companions, however, "it is a damsite harder than anyone who has not tried it can possibly imagine."

They got up at six each morning, but it was always nine or later before they were able to break camp and get away. Breakfast was oatmeal, cooked in a big vacuum jug the night before; "No matter

(above) The Geological Party gets ready to leave Little America on its 1400-mile trek (opposite: top) Ed Goodale with loaded sledge. Little America radio mast in background; (opposite: bottom) Commander Byrd and Chris Braathen.

whether it was 15 degrees above zero or 30 below, we always had steaming hot oatmeal for breakfast.'' While the camp cooker Victor Czegka had designed for them was still hot they brewed up for the trail a jug full of tea, thereby sparing themselves the chore of unlashing a loaded sledge and putting up a cook tent when they stopped at noontime. The rest of their lunch on the trail consisted of biscuits, chocolate, and cold pemmican (the tea was always well laced with lemon powder, an anti-scorbutic). At suppertime Gould, who listed himself on their roster as ''Leader Navigator and Cook,'' made more of their pemmican into a hot stew or ''hoosh,'' adding soup meal sausages and topping the meal off with thick slices of bacon. The dogs, of course, had been staked out first; they each got a pound and a half of dog food a day, and they curled up for the night quite comfortably in the coldest weather. (It was *warm* weather, when their fur got wet, that made them miserable.) Sometimes on a windy night, when the men had carefully to whisk-broom the sifting snow away from the tent floors and from their reindeer-skin sleeping bags, the dogs would be snowed over completely, until only their ears and noses showed over the drift.[10]

A heavy fall of frost on snow the night of November 12 made sledging and skiing very hard the next day. The sledge party started out against a bitter breeze from the south at fifteen below. One hundred and fifty miles away at Little America, however, ''it was a beautiful day—cloudless and with excellent visibility affording fine scenic effects from the air.'' The big Ford airplane, which had ''suffered many indignities and hard knocks since it left New York was well groomed up this morning,'' Henry Harrison wrote, and at 3:08 P.M. it took off for the first trimotored flight in Antarctic history. During the two days that followed, while the Geological Party was picking its way through the treacherous region of wide, snow-covered crevasses and chasms that had been pioneered by Walden's Supporting Party, the aviation gang toiled over the *Floyd Bennett* airplane. Mechanic Pete Demas, who had until that time faithfully kept up his diaries, jotted down for November 15 only the words "too damn busy."

Russell Owen, however, whose commission was to capture in words just such historic moments, had time to wander out and watch Bernt Balchen, with his face framed by the yellow light of the midnight sun through the cockpit windows as the Chief Pilot tested the left wing motor: "He was watching the tachometer and oil pressure and heat gauges," Owen wrote, "his sharp blue eyes fastened on them as he ran the speed up and down. We could tell how the engine was functioning by the expression on his face, for when at high speed it hummed rhythmically, a fleeting look of satisfaction came into his eyes, and when it began to spit at lower speeds, he became grimly intent on studying its eccentricities." The skills by which people had survived on other frontiers were subtly changing, but they were still recognizably human, even artistic, skills; we were a long way yet from the situation of the bedeviled astronaut who reports any malfunction to a far-off, computer-equipped Mission Control which must take ponderous inventory before notifying him what is wrong.[11]

On November 17 the trimotored plane received its crucially important load-ceiling test—crucial because the polar plateau, one must remember, stands at 10,000 feet above sea level, and therefore scrapes pretty close to a maximum altitude for the kinds of aircraft that were available in 1929. On a second flight that day the Fairchild *Stars and Stripes* flew alongside the Ford so that the Paramount cameramen Rucker and Van der Veer could take movies. Down on the ground, meanwhile, the sledge party was encountering much snow with little crust, "hard going for dogs and heavy skiing for men." The day's march of 12 ½ miles brought them to the last outpost of the Supporting Party that had preceded them, Depot #4; "from here we do our own navigating over new territory," Gould wrote. From that cache they had to take on another 500 pounds of dog food, a sudden increase in the loads which, combined with the necessity of picking out a route across unknown

terrain, would make the next few days "much open to question."
These forebodings, Gould wrote in his log the evening of the 18th,
had been justified. Even though Thorne had backpacked fifty
pounds of dog food and others had helped by manhauling the
sledges, "it was too much and the dogs have barely been able to
struggle along."

At noon that day the *Floyd Bennett* had flown over them (with
the thwarted financier Dean Smith at the controls), en route to es-
tablishing its own supply base at the foot of the Queen Maud
Mountains. "We hope they landed some dog food and supplies for
us so we can lighten our loads," Gould wistfully wrote. From the
air the sledging party's plight had been apparent; "some of the
men were in harness, pulling with the dogs," Byrd observed,
"and the sight of their bending backs, the separation of the
sledges, the very, very slow progress told everything."

"Must be cold down there," aerial photographer "Cap"
McKinley yelled. "They have their parkas up—can't hear the
engines."

"Don't cheer, boys," cautioned copilot and radioman Harold
June, repeating Admiral Dewey's famous remark at the Battle of
Manila Bay, "the poor devils are dying."

The trimotored plane swooped down to 300 feet, dropped a
sackful of letters and miscellaneous equipment, and flew on. "If
ever a conclusive contrast was struck between the new and the old
methods of polar travelling," Byrd summed up, "it was then." [12]

Back at Little America it had been "an eventful day full of action and drama." They had seen the big ship off at 9:37 A.M. and
listened afterward for the radio messages that came back from
Harold June. The *Floyd Bennett* had flown over the ill-fated snowmobile; it had landed at the mountains 450 miles away and laid
down its refueling depot for the polar flight; it was homeward
bound. At 7 P.M. came June's report "We have just passed Chasm
Pass and are following trail——" and then an abrupt silence. "All
ears here were strained southward after 7:30 in the hope that she

might still be OK but it finally became apparent that the Ford had come down.''

When the plane was two hours overdue, Bill Haines—in command at camp, now that Byrd and McKinley were with the plane and Gould far out on the trail—told Balchen to warm up the Fairchild. At 10 P.M. the blond Norwegian took off with an emergency load of gas, bringing Pete Demas along as radio operator, and began to follow the dog trail south. Everyone else then rushed back inside to stand by the radio. At eleven, Demas sent back the messages "We see the Ford ahead on the snow"—"we are gliding to a landing nearby." However, "following this," recounted Henry Harrison, "a dead silence reigned in the air"— with the Fairchild on the ground, its radio transmitter was of course not active—"and a note of suspense and tension here at the camp which continued unbroken until two in the morning." At two they heard the welcome carrier-wave come back on the air as the Fairchild took off, and then the words everyone had been waiting for: "Good news!" and, a minute later, "All hands and ship OK." [13]

Roaring ahead at ninety or more miles an hour while the sledge men were mushing along at less than twenty per day "had the advantages of swiftness and comfort," Richard Byrd later reflected, "but we had as well an enlarged fallibility." An hour out from Little America on the way to the Queen Mauds Harold June had found a fairly fast leak underneath the pilot seat near the hand fuel pump. He had applied the Model T era's favorite home remedy: heavy tape over a wad of chewing gum! It had not held, and when he sounded the fuel tanks on the return trip June had had to inform the Commander that they were running dangerously low. Byrd, who had counted on at least seven more hours of flying time and had had his heart set on some further exploration on the way home, was taken aback: "There was nothing to do but turn back at once. We should have to run for it, as it was." They had, and they had not quite made it, by a hundred miles.

Balchen flew out again on the 19th with more gas, climbed into the *Floyd Bennett's* cockpit, got its three motors going, and waited until the Ford was in the air before starting his own engine. (Pete Demas had to break the Fairchild's skis free from the snow and jump in after the smaller aircraft had started to move.) The big ship came in about midnight, traveling fast, and landed. "What a bedraggled looking bunch they were," Russell Owen exclaimed— "oil all over their furs from emptying the engines and filling them again." During all the excitement, lead dog Holly—the only dog allowed inside the houses except Byrd's own pet, Igloo—selected the Commander's room as a maternity ward and had a litter of nine puppies on Byrd's bunk. They were given names commemorative of the aerial adventure, such as Dick, Hal, Dean, Ashley, Bernt, Pete, Ford, and Fairchild, but upon the leader's return the new family was ousted to the library.[14]

At about the same time along the trail, a less happy event was transpiring. At 4 A.M. on November 19 one of the Geological Party's dogs gave birth to a pup; at 7 came two more, which the mother ate. "She stood up in harness and pulled hard," Gould reported in his journal, but during the day she dropped a total of seven—all of which had to be killed. "This is cruelty to animals but this is a hard land and there is no other way." Three days later, on the 22nd, the sledging party established its first new cache for the return journey, at latitude 81°35' South. Here they could abandon two heavy sledges, but here they "must also kill four dogs that have served us well." That hard land provided no local humane society where a cherished pet could be, as people say, "put to sleep" and then not seen again; the carcasses would have to be cut and cached as dog food for the return. "It is the hardest part of our work," the party's leader admitted. "But in making such a long sledge journey as this no dog could carry his own food and still deliver any pay load for us."

Back at camp that day the Ford was warmed up for action, but the weather thickened and snow began to fall. Ominously, Sir

Hubert Wilkins was now back in Antarctica. "The Wilkins buga-
boo persists in the back of everyone's mind," Henry Harrison reported, "the Commander's included, I think—and a strong impression prevails that priority at the Pole by Sir Hubert would
mean utter ruination for us." Delay after exasperating delay followed as they waited for the weather to turn; either weatherman
Haines at Little America or Gould by radio from the southward
trail, many miles nearer to the South Pole, said "NO." Nobody
was able to work, Arnold Clarke wrote in his diary on November
26: "The anticipation of the flight has almost destroyed the morale
and routine of the camp." Doc Coman helped the morale a little
by breaking out a dozen phonograph records he had kept stored
away during the winter. "They have had," wrote Harrison, "a
most refreshing effect."[15]

Hand-cranking their portable radio transmitter's generator, the
Geological Party at noon on November 28 sent at last the welcome
word "Unchanged. Perfect visibility. No clouds anywhere."
Three hundred miles away at Little America the sky was hazy, and
Byrd still hesitated. Meterorologist Haines told him that if they
didn't go now they might never have another chance this good.
The South Pole flight was on.

A bucket brigade passed five-gallon gasoline cans up to men
standing on the wing. Another line of men passed gear—tents,
sleeping bags, food, clothing, and much else—into the aircraft.
"Blackie," the supply officer, weighed each item before it went
aboard; the loaded plane totaled up to 15,000 pounds. Every
pound had previously been debated and grudgingly allowed like a
miser yielding up coins from his hoard. For months during the
long night the leaders had argued over whether it would be possible to fly the plane up to the plateau without leaving their mapping
camera behind. They needed it, if the scientific investment in the
flight were to be justified; however, neither Bernt Balchen, nor
Harold June, nor Byrd had the competence to operate it, aerial surveying being at that time a new and highly specialized art. But the

Ready for the South Pole
*Commander Byrd, in the library at Little
America, ties an American flag to a stone from
the grave of Floyd Bennett, whose name was
also given to the Ford Trimotor airplane chosen
to make the polar flight. The stone was dropped
from the air as the plane passed over the Pole.*

camera, "Cap" McKinley, and McKinley's three months' supply
of food and equipment added up to 600 pounds—cutting down by
a thousand feet the highest altitude at which they could fly. This
was going to be a very close business indeed.[16]

The pre-flight tension Harrison and Clarke had noticed among
the Little Americans was not visible in the men who were going to

fly the *Floyd Bennett*. "I'm going to lie down for a nap," said Bernt Balchen; "you can start warming up [the engines] about one thirty and I'll be out to see them get started about three o'clock." Harold June with his radio helmet "waited non-chalantly," according to Arnold Clarke's report; "for all the outward excitement he expressed you would more likely think he was just waiting for an elevator in a Hotel." A last-minute decision was made to take on board an additional hundred gallons of gasoline; it added to the weight, but if they ran into heavy winds it might spell the difference between failure and success. Commander Byrd went into his office and picked up an American flag, weighted with a stone from Floyd Bennett's grave, to drop over the South Pole, and shook hands all around.

At 3:29 P.M. under a cloudy sky with a fresh east wind the Ford began to move. The plane taxied to the end of the snow runway and turned about, the engines "burst into a crescendo of sound," and after a run of only 27 seconds the skis were in the air. Forty-five minutes later—a little after 11 P.M., New York time—the next day's *New York Times* was on the streets with Owen's takeoff story. The Times reporter, as he watched the *Floyd Bennett* go through its paces, gave himself up to fantasy: "It is hard to believe, as it wheels in graceful curves with long-sweeping dips of its wings, that it is not a conscious entity," Owen wrote. "One never tires of watching it. Is it because it is so out of place here, or because in this lost land it becomes a prehistoric denizen of the air, this its natural abiding place which by accident we have discovered?" [17]

The course of the flight was laid along the meridian of the southward dog trail. The party flew as sightseers over the crevassed area through which men and dogs had struggled for days. A strong southeasterly breeze blew the sky clear but forced them to compensate against wind drift, "and so the plane crabbed along toward the south with its nose pointed well to the left of the trail." For the first few hours they had time to look around at the great glaciers flowing into the Shelf and at alpine peaks glistening with reflected sunfire, like great volcanoes in eruption. At 8:15 P.M., 305 statute miles due south of Little America, they sighted the Geological Party, "a cluster of little beetles about two dark topped tents." No arduous sledge work today; standing by for the polar flight, Gould and his men could afford to let the dogs rest.

The plane dropped to 750 feet, and "Cap" McKinley put overboard a bag containing radio messages from home, letters from friends at Little America, cigarettes, and the photographs McKinley had taken of the Queen Maud range during the base-laying flight. The parachute fluttered open and two or three members of the ground party rushed out to catch it. Balchen, reflecting that the *Floyd Bennett* had just flown the first Antarctican air mail, opened the engines to full throttle; their throbbing tone became fuller and more high-pitched, and the Ford commenced its long climb.

They had been headed straight south toward the Axel Heiberg Glacier, where Amundsen's dogs and men in 1911 had found a way through the mountains to the polar plateau. Roald Amundsen had reported that the highest point of the pass was at 10,500 feet, and that it was narrow. The peaks boxing it in on either side rose well above the maximum altitude of the heavily loaded plane. If they should be grabbed at or shoved by treacherous air currents in that cramped space, there would be no room for maneuver at all. Drawing nearer, the plane edged thirty degrees west of south, bringing into view not only Axel Heiberg but also Liv's Glacier, named after Dr. Nansen's daughter, which Amundsen had seen and christened but had not personally investigated. The pass at its summit appeared wider than the Axel Heiberg. Beyond it, however, unseen, might lie undiscovered mountains over which they could not fly.

Balchen pointed to fog vapor rising from the black foothills of Mount Fridtjof Nansen, a further complication. If the clouds that capped Axel Heiberg Glacier and partially obscured the Liv were the fringe of a vaporous mass up on the plateau, the flight was already in trouble. They could not pause for very long to make up their minds what to do next; "minutes stood for gasoline, and gasoline was precious." If they made the wrong choice and had to backtrack to find another pass, they would not have enough gas left to fly to the Pole; if the walls ahead closed in far enough, they might not be able to get the plane turned around to get out at all. As between the two great glaciers it seemed the flip of a coin; a choice between an unknown and a dangerous known. They decided to take their chances with Liv, the unknown.

"Everywhere we looked," Byrd thought, "was some formation no living thing had ever before seen." But there was little time for such reflection; the plane, in contrast to its lifeless surroundings, was a busy place. Panting from effort in the rarefied air, "Cap" McKinley snapped picture after picture with his great camera. Harold June cut open the last of the fuel cans, poured the gas into the wing tanks, and dropped the empty cans through the trapdoor; they weighed barely a pound each, but at a plane's critical ceiling pounds are precious. He figured for a moment on a pad and, with a smile, handed Byrd the result. Owing to head winds they had taken longer to reach the Queen Maud Mountains than expected, but the extra fuel taken on just before they left Little America had absorbed the balance. If they made it over the mountains they could reach the Pole, and return.

At 9:15 P.M., they flew past the chosen glacier's eastern portal, behind which bulked the horizon-filling glory of Mount Nansen. On the right the ramparts of Fisher Mountain made almost as great a mass against the sky. Balchen settled into his work. The Liv Glacier was a long one, and its floor rose in terraces and icefalls, some of which were well above the nose of the plane. The air became rougher; the great wing shivered. The plane swung left toward Mount Nansen, away from the turbulence. But that brought it into a down-drafting area that damped their rate of climb. The altimeter showed 10,000 feet;[18] their weight was a little over 13,000 pounds. Tantalizing, the great polar plateau suddenly loomed through the clouds—but the wheel turned loosely in Balchen's hands as the ailerons failed to respond. They were not yet high enough to make the pass.

Balchen yelled in Byrd's ear over the roar of the engines: "We must drop 200 pounds immediately or go back." June stood by the dump valve of the fuselage tank, prepared to let go 600 gallons of gasoline.[19] But if they dumped the gas, they might as well give it up; they would not have enough left to reach the Pole and still make it back to their supply base at the foot of the mountains. The only other item they could throw overboard, except for McKinley's precious camera, was food; and to dump food was to take a risk of another, more protracted kind. If the plane should have to come down on the polar plateau, there was no way this time that the small Fairchild could go after them—and not another plane with the Ford's range and power could be found within thousands of miles. North polar fliers, landing at sea level if they were forced down, could subsist if they had to on the bounty of the Arctic Ocean, but on the Antarctic tableland it was absolutely impossible to live off the country. The solitary gull that might, rarely, wing its way to that high wasteland would not have gone very far, divided four ways!

McKinley had already dragged one of the 125-pound food bags over by the trapdoor. "Shall I do it, Commander?" he shouted. Byrd nodded. The brown bag went overboard. Chief Pilot Balchen looked around and grinned, for even the loss of that little weight had had an immediate effect. A plane, hovering near its absolute ceiling, acted like a balloon; a few pounds overboard would make it shoot upward. "Things were better now," Byrd observed, "but I was not sure it was fair to those fellows to dump food."

Still they were not high enough. The plane lurched and shuddered in the great down-drafts from Mount Nansen. The Chief Pilot eased over to the right, where—another touch of Byrd luck—the lowest part of the pass was clear of clouds. "Flying shrewdly," Bernt maintained sufficient distance below the abso-

lute ceiling of the plane to keep maneuverability enough to make
him its master. But the head of the pass was still at the same level
as their line of flight. "More," Balchen shouted. "Another bag."

McKinley pushed a second food bag through the trapdoor. This
time they saw it hit the glacier; 250 pounds of food, enough to
feed four men for a month, exploded over the wasteland. The
plane leaped upward; the engines dug in; and Balchen shouted for
joy as he saw that there were no hidden mountains blocking their
way. Flying brilliantly, he took advantage of one last gusting
updraft, and cleared the pass with five hundred feet to spare. They
emerged over the great plateau and rode their engines downhill—
literally, for toward the Pole the plateau descends gently from the
mountain ramparts that define its edge.

Byrd looked over to the right and spied a whole new mountain
range; a new bit of land to add to the map of the world; "one of
those kicks that pull a man away from civilization, which repay
him for his efforts." Most of the remainder of the South Pole
flight, however, was anticlimax. All the mountains drew away
from view as the Ford neared its goal, for the Pole itself lies in the
midst of a vast, blank white plain. At 12:38 A.M. under midnight
sun conditions Byrd succeeded in taking a sun shot. Astronomy
and dead reckoning agreed that they were but 55 miles from their
destination. "So the Pole, the mysterious objective, was actually
in sight. But I could not yet spare it so much as a glance. Chrono-
meters, drift indicators and compasses are hard taskmasters." At
1:14 A.M., November 29, Little America Time (1:14 P.M., November 29, GMT), their calculations showed them to be over the
South Pole. Byrd handed June a message to that effect "to radio to
our comrades at Little America." An alert radio operator *in New
York* picked it out of the air, and the message was then transmitted
by loudspeaker to the jammed streets (it was the height of the
morning rush hour) leading into Times Square. Next morning,
November 30, it also appeared in a box on the *New York Times's*
front page. This was a far cry from the handwritten note for King

Haakon of Norway that Amundsen had left in the tent he pitched at the South Pole in 1911—a note found by Scott, who months later would no doubt have delivered it had he not perished on the homeward trail from hunger and cold. For once, media self-congratulation was justified; to have rendered the people of the United States "able almost to live the life of an explorer in the field" over a distance of 11,000 miles, noted W. L. G. Joerg, was truly "a feat of communication which we shall hardly see surpassed unless we establish contact with worlds outside our own."

The explorers turned, turned again, recrossed the pole, dropped their flags—those of Britain, France, Norway, and the American flag weighted with the stone from Floyd Bennett's grave—and headed for home. Storm clouds were gathering and they wasted no time; Balchen took them upward to get the boost of the stiff following wind. They hit the pass over Axel Heiberg Glacier ahead of the clouds, but they had a wild ride down the gorge; the eddies, Balchen later declared, tossed the big plane around "like a cork in a washtub." They emerged from the glacier around 4:00, and at 4:40 Harold June, who had been with the base-laying party and knew the terrain, set them down on the ice-hard sastrugi at their little refueling base. They put aboard 200 gallons of gas and left 350 pounds of food, 10 gallons of gas, 10 gallons of oil, and a gasoline stove for Larry Gould's party, whose most important work had not yet begun. After an hour's work the *Floyd Bennett* roared into the air again, and at 10:00 they sighted the radio spires of Little America. At 10:38 A.M. the plane touched down; the mechanics stood and beckoned to Balchen and June in the cockpit, steering them in. The plane slid into its hole, and man's first flight to the South Pole was history. It had taken eighteen and a half hours; Amundsen, walking, had taken three months. The fliers had given their engines "a laboratory test which could not have been arranged in any other way," gathering "performance data which no amount of work on test blocks and experiments can duplicate," the vice-president of the Wright Aeronautical Corporation, which had manufactured one of these engines, somewhat anticlimactically commented. Skipping the automotive phase for the time being, travel to the South Pole had jumped directly from the dogsled age to the air age.

"What was the Pole like?" Paul Siple asked after it was all over—little suspecting that he himself would one day go and live there. "A white desolation and solitude," Byrd replied. Bernt Balchen put it rather more pungently: "I was glad to leave. Somehow our very purpose here seem insignificant, a symbol of man's vanity, an intrusion on this eternal white world. The sound of our engines profane[d] the silence as we head[ed] back to Little America." In the midst of the victory uproar Balchen slipped quietly out of the mess hall and put on his skis. With Chris Braathen and Sverre Strom he spent a couple of hours on the white, silent snow.[20]

Little America's postponed Thanksgiving dinner was served at five the next afternoon (November 30), right after the regular Saturday broadcast from WGY. Two impromptu skits, "The Snowmobile Party" and "The Polar Flight," highlighted an evening of hilarious good fellowship fueled by a concoction that was labeled "Compass Fluid." Some men tried walking on a barrel; others wrestled in the snow. The six members of the Geological Party, however, did no celebrating that day. As soon as the plane was safely home they had resumed their onward slog, and presently an optical illusion led them into what Larry Gould described in his sledge diary as "the toughest going we have ever had." One of the photographs of the Queen Maud Mountains, taken by Ashley McKinley on the base-laying flight and dropped to the men on the ground from the *Floyd Bennett* on its way to the Pole, showed "a system of crevasses so regular," Gould later wrote, "that we all thought this particular print had been made with a celluloid grid with parallel lines scratched on it overlying the negative. Surely there could be no such regularly spaced system of crevasses anywhere!" As they came up toward the foot of Liv Glacier, therefore, instead of altering their course to avoid this morass as much as possible, the dog drivers plunged at once into "the most frightfully uncertain and hazardous traveling that we encountered all summer." They had trusted an abstraction; and in this instance modern technology, far from easing their tasks, had lured them into greater hardship and peril.

Some fifteen or twenty miles out from the upper end of the Ross Shelf the Geological Party encountered great gentle rolls in the ice surface—so gentle that at first Gould did not realize the party was no longer on level terrain, until he began to see dog teams disappearing in the hollows and reappearing on the crests. Soon these became great wrinkles in the ice, punctuated by seemingly bottomless snow-bridged gulfs. The men were able to slide over these crevasses on their skis, but the dogs kept breaking through the thin snow roofs, sometimes falling in and dangling in their harness

Geological Party camps on the trail

until hauled out by the rest of the team's forward surge. There was no going around this frozen inferno; nor could they camp in its midst for the night. They did not find a patch of snow suitable for staking out the dogs and anchoring their tents until 9:30 that evening, by which time the sledge meter had registered for the day's run a grueling 34.9 miles. "The dogs fell in their tracks and were practically asleep before they hit the snow," and in the cook tent one of the men dropped off to sleep with a spoonful of hot hoosh halfway to his mouth. Less swiftly than the Ford plane's three engines, but as surely, aching feet and paws had brought the Geological Party to its goal. After a year of living and working and traveling on top of the sheet of ice that floats on the great Ross Sea, next day they would set foot upon land.[21]

Dog teams at foot of Queen Maud Mountains near Liv Glacier
The bicycle wheel behind the last sledge is for measuring trail mileage.

5

"I'd Go
Back
Tomorrow"

All experience is an arch wherethrough
Gleams that untravelled world whose margin fades
Forever and forever when I move.
How dull it is to pause!

       —*Tennyson,* Ulysses

"Most often to my inward eye comes the vision of Mount Nansen," Laurence Gould would write in retrospect, "with its cap of ice and shoulders of bare black looking rock as it is lighted by the long skeletal rays of the low morning sun." In sight of their goal, and thus no longer dependent on dead reckoning, the Geological Party for several days beforehand had been steering visually across the ice toward the mountain's vast, silent bulk. Their heavily packed sledges were puny beneath its dark-colored outlying buttresses and crags. In the clear Antarctic air the the gray and yellow flat strata at its 13,700-foot crest seemed deceptively near.

On December 1, 1929, thinking it would be possible to climb up Liv Glacier to an exposed mass of those flat-capped rocks, Gould, Jack O'Brien, and Mike Thorne fastened crampons onto their ski boots, roped together, and started climbing the glacier. After the first mile they got into soft snow which camouflaged any gaps that might lurk beneath their feet. Sure enough, Larry Gould stepped onto a thin snow roof and it gave way. Catching the far wall with his arms he got a dizzying glimpse into blue-black depths. Thereafter, he and Thorne resolved, it would be better if they wore skis! Meanwhile, it was clear that any quick solution of Antarctica's geological mysteries, such as they had just attempted, "was hopeless." Accordingly on December 3 the party broke camp, moving in to the foot of a smaller glacier on Mount Nansen's northwest slope.

Here, in Latitude 85°7'S and Longitude 163°45'W, the explorers established their base for field operations. They named it Strom Camp, after the powerful Norwegian sailor who during the winter had helped so much in their preparations, most notably by working (together with Bernt Balchen) to whittle down and reshape their trail sledges into light, strong, flexible creations of functional beauty. Here also they faced their most unpleasant necessity. They had set forth with 46 dogs, but by the grim arithmetic of trail food consumption they must return with no more than 21. These sledge dogs were highly individualized personalities, who had served the expedition faithfully and well; it would have been in vain to rationalize that farm families after all had had to deal with favorite livestock pets from time immemorial in the same unkind way. "This has been our 'butcher shop,' " Gould sadly wrote on December 5 in his sledge log. "It has been a most depressing day."[1]

At the other end of the Ross Ice Shelf December 5 was a day not for depression but for exultation. The Little Americans had not really expected much more excitement now that the flight to the South Pole was over; aviation mechanic Pete Demas in fact had already packed his sea bag, even though the ships were not due in for another month. But then, quite unexpectedly, "the delicately balanced weather which precedes the Summer, arriving when the warm winds come in from the north," which had been clinging to a fogbound Little America for days, broke and cleared. Without the ponderous planning that usually preceded one of Byrd's actions, almost on impulse, the Commander took off in the *Floyd Bennett* once more to probe the unknown lands to the east. Harold June again operated the radio, "Cap" McKinley once more positioned his great aerial camera, and Marine Corps pilot Alton Parker, so pleased at the chance at last to fly a major exploratory mission that he put on his red and black checked lumberman's pants for the occasion, was at the controls.[2]

They flew high above the jutting coastline of the great ice shelf.

"The Ross Sea as far as the eye could see was jammed with pack ice," June afterward recalled:

No ship in the world could have gotten through that stuff. It had stopped every ship that ever attempted a passage. . . .

Then ahead of us there slowly lifted, running north and south to the horizon, the frosted tops of a magnificent range. . . . Deep glacial rivers ran between black rock. The peaks were upwards of fifteen thousand feet high. And behind these great shoulders of rock we saw—or thought we saw—the white dome of a plateau—similar to the polar plateau—rolling to the east.[3]

True to form, Byrd named the newfound chain the Edsel Ford Range. "It is much more than I ever expected to find," he said upon returning to Little America. The press inevitably neglected this last discovery as an anticlimax, even though Harold June was later to call it "more thrilling than the polar flight." Scientists, however, geographers in particular, recognized the significance of the Edsel Ford discovery at once. Back in the era of Robert Falcon Scott's tragic Antarctic success, Britons and other Commonwealth people had thoroughly mapped and defined the west shore of the Ross Sea and of the great Ice Shelf. Roald Amundsen, trudging toward his own polar goal, had found and named the mountain range that bounded the Shelf on the south. To the east, however, on 1929 maps of Antarctica the Ross Coast was no more than a conventionalized dotted line. But now, as a result of this find, the vast area Richard Byrd had glimpsed the previous season and named Marie Byrd Land was firmly anchored to a known shore.

On December 7 the American Geographical Society's director, Isaiah Bowman, reacting in New York to the news from Antarctica, saw in addition to the scientific gains from the latest flight certain far-reaching political implications. The Byrd Antarctic Expedition had settled within a region long claimed for the British Commonwealth, and technically the Little Americans were guests of New Zealand. Some of their own new discoveries, notably the

Rockefeller Mountains, lay well within the area staked out under
the Union Jack and/or the Southern Cross. Marie Byrd Land, however, lay well beyond that imperial claim; and now, Bowman
pointed out, by connecting his previous discoveries with the sea at
a point about which there could be no argument, Byrd had put the
United States in position to lay claim to 35,000 square miles of
territory along the hitherto unknown coastline.[4]

The American geographer thus publicly raised an issue that the
Little American pioneers—and the United States State Department—theretofore had tactfully ducked. The formal U.S. position
on Antarctica, set forth in 1924 by Secretary of State Charles
Evans Hughes, was that nowadays no mere act of discovery, without the prospect in so harsh a land of following it up by permanent
settlement, entitled the discoverer to establish any national territorial claim. Therefore, without compromising possible rights of its
own in Antarctica, the United States declined to recognize anyone
else's. While the expedition was enroute toward Antarctica in
1928 Sir Esmé Howard, the British Ambassador in Washington,
had informed the State Department that his own government
would, if desired, "send instructions to the appropriate authorities
in the Falkland and Ross Dependencies to give every possible assistance to Commander Byrd while he was in their territories."
Following Hughes's 1924 guideline State Department legal
officers had hesitated to reply, stodgily fearful that even a polite
acknowledgement might constitute tacit acceptance of Britain's
definition of the Antarctic claims as set forth at a Commonwealth
conference in 1926. All through the settling of Little America, the
first flights, and the wintering over, the hesitation had continued.
Indeed, the ultra-punctilious State Department did not reply to Sir
Esmé's note until November 15, 1929, nearly a whole year since
the overture from His Majesty's Government and barely two
weeks before the South Pole flight itself. Lamely and belatedly the
United States government now expressed "regret over its uninten-
tional oversight in responding" to the British note (of November

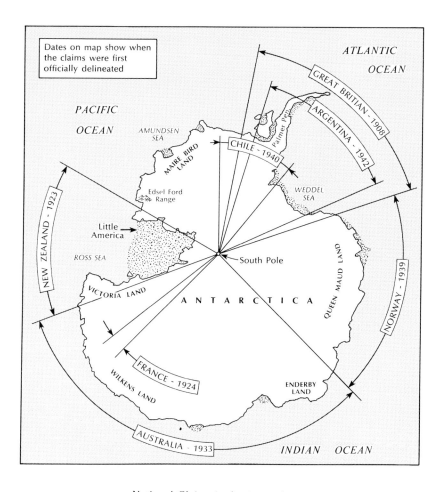

National Claims in the Antarctic.

17, 1928!), and thanked the British for their offer of assistance to Byrd.[5]

For most of 1929, therefore, Little America had existed in a political and diplomatic limbo. Commander Byrd as expedition leader had been in an awkward international situation, and he had scrupulously played the role of gracious guest. On April 15, 1929—four days before the sun set at Little America for the last time—he had sent a message to the London *Evening Standard* for "our friends in Great Britain," assuring them "that we approach our problems with respect for those who have preceded us." Scott, Shackleton, and Mawson had been "more the pioneers than we who follow." The Little Americans now knew "from first hand, as we could not have visualized from their modest records, the frightful hardships they endured." By those hardships, the American explorer implied, his heroic predecessors had learned their national title. "Even if international law, vague as to Antarctica, may not be satisfied with their claims of discovery, international courtesy acknowledges them," Byrd asserted, in tacit disagreement with Secretary Hughes. "Sportsmanship is more important here than the strict letter of a rule."[6]

However, could either Byrd or Hughes speak for burgeoning, entrepreneurial America as a whole? The *Dunedin Star,* published in the Little Americans' hospitable New Zealand home port, had speculated on May 22, 1929, that the Byrd discoveries might tempt the United States to make a formal bid for Wilkes Land, which the U.S. Navy's Charles Wilkes had first sighted as long ago as 1840 but which in 1929 was generally regarded as the property of Australia. "With American economic standards now at their peak from prosperity that arises from the possession of half the visible gold supply of the world," the Star had editorialized five months before the Crash, "and the millions owing by the principal European powers, America and Americans are determined that their presence will be acknowledged more and more outside their territorial boundaries." (It is a view strikingly at variance with the traditional "isolationist" picture of America in the 1920s, but it is not at all out of phase with the picture of 1920s America that has been drawn in recent years by younger historians, inclined to see American activities overseas in the twenties as having been marked by a good deal of informal imperialism.) "Their claims to the Antarctic," the Dunedin newspaper had concluded, "must be considered in the light of this world encircling ambition."[7]

However that may have been, the latest flight of discovery on December 5 clearly changed the claims situation in the Americans' favor. Between the meridian of 150° West, where New Zealand's Ross Dependency ended, and 80° West, where Britain's Falkland Islands Dependencies began (or 90° West, if one accepted the boundary of Chile's partially overlapping claim), stretched an immense *terra incognita* that was, by diplomatic custom, up for grabs. By the traditional rules of the game the Americans were welcome to help themselves. On February 18 the Byrd Antarctic Expedition had sighted and named Marie Byrd Land; on December 5 it had established the eastern hinterland's relationship to the coast. However, nobody had yet set foot on that terrain and planted, rather than air-dropped, a flag. If Gould's Geological Party, then happily engaged in scrambling over the rocks in search of specimens, could trek eastward far enough to pass the edge of the Ross Dependency, its scientific mission could become political as well.[8]

At the moment, however, science was front-and-center. On December 7, having moved their camp still nearer to the mountain's exposed shoulder, Gould, Mike Thorne, Freddy Crockett, and Ed Goodale roped together and herringboned up around a difficult icefall to a saddle, from which they were able to traverse past a 300-foot chasm or *bergschrund* at the head of the glacier and come at last to the coveted outcrop. Larry Gould, the moment he picked up a small chunk of rock half the size of his hand, knew that it "told us a story of such amazing interest as to make the whole trip worth the effort"—much as Neil Armstrong's moon rocks would

Dog teams at foot of Queen Maud Mountains

seem, to a later generation of scientists, worth the effort of cross-ing the gulf of space. As Gould later radioed Byrd, "No sym-phony I have ever heard, no work of art before which I have stood in awe ever gave me quite the thrill that I had when I reached out after that strenuous climb"—they had ascended 6500 feet, a re-spectable effort at any latitude—"and picked up a piece of rock to find it sandstone. It was just the rock I had come all the way to Antarctica to find. Eddie[,] Mike and Freddie who were with me will tell you that I even forgot to cuss."[9]

What was the story this little scrap of yellowish-gray sandstone told these men, as they caught their breath in the thin upland air? Over on the west side of the Ross Sea, in Victoria Land, Scott's scientists had seen and described a great plateau bounded by upthrust fault-block mountains, capped by horizontally disposed layers—the Beacon formation, as they named it—that had been

The Geological Party camps at the foot of the Queen Maud Mountains
December 1929.

laid down over a span ranging from the time of the great armored fishes to the age of the dinosaurs. The sandstones and interbedded volcanics the Little Americans had found were "at least lithologically equivalent to Farrar's Beacon sandstone," Gould would tell the scientific community in 1931; and in 1933, more boldly, "the structure of the Queen Maud Range is an exact duplicate of that of South Victoria Land north of Beardmore Glacier" (the polar route of Shackleton and Scott) "and possesses the same stratigraphic relationships." This meant that the terrain where Scott had struggled and died, and the realm where Amundsen had marched and prevailed, were geologically one—"the most stupendous fault block mountain system in all the world."

But there was yet more. Rocks similar to those exposed in the midst of the Antarctic snow exist in India, South Africa, Australia, and South America. The outlines of those continents and Antarctica, when one looks at them on a polar-projection map, eerily fit together like a giant jigsaw puzzle. One savant, Henry Fairfield Osborne of the American Museum of Natural History, drew the obvious conclusion. "One of the most important problems is [Antarctica's] relation to South America on the one hand and Australia on the other," said Osborne, in response to the first news of Gould's discoveries. "I am a strong believer in the theory that the Antarctic Continent will be found to be linked with both, and this expedition more than any other undertaking should throw light upon that theory." Forty years later that theory would be convincingly vindicated, and the clinching evidence, like the initial clue, would come from Antarctica.[10]

But that was for the future to disclose. At the moment of discovery there was little time for speculation. "In the midst of our rock cracking we were quite suddenly engulfed in clouds," Gould's sledge log narrative continues. "We hastened to our skiis hoping that we would be able to retrace our steps. Then it began to snow and we began to get a bit nervous," thinking of that great crevasse they could now no longer see gaping beside their return trail. Luckily the snow did not completely cover their tracks. At the saddle they unroped. Thorne, who for all the Antarctic irrelevance of his Yale degree in forestry was superb on skis, led the way down the slope toward their camp; Crockett successfully followed; but Gould and Goodale, after an attempt to sidehill properly, "finally sat down on our skiis and disgracefully slid down hill on them." The keen-eyed Goodale brought home some trophies of his own: bits of gray lichens he had plucked from the rocks, at a spot farther south than any form of life had ever before been found.

The next day, undaunted, they moved camp farther up the glacier, driving the dog teams much closer to the rocks. (The Little American-born pups, who had seen no surface in their lives except ice and snow, licked at the strange substance curiously.) Above the camp, cutting steps into the steep, slick glacial surface with an ice axe, Gould and Thorne got "all the climbing thrills we wanted." Then, from a band of material darker than the sand-stone, Thorne brought back some hard, shiny fragments that "burned reluctantly when a match was applied." Found little more than three hundred miles from the South Pole, it was coal, and it turned out to be sufficiently coextensive with the Beacon sandstone "to enable us to state rather definitely that the Antarctic has coal reserves second only to those of the United States." Half a century later, showing a slide of the Beacon formation to his geology class, Gould called that coal "inaccessible—not a resource"; and perhaps it is just as well. It is hardly inspiring to imagine those crystal-clean heights on Mount Nansen obscured by coal dust or ravaged by strip mines.[11]

The explorers backtracked to their base camp, where after sup-per three days later they found a macabre sign of animation on the dead land: a lone scavenging skua "feeding on the bits of dog meat left from our slaughter of some days ago." On December 12 Gould and Goodale traveled nearly thirty miles in search of the cache laid down by the Ford trimotor weeks earlier at the outlet of Liv Glacier. Finding it at last—no easy task on that crinkled land-scape—they brought back 250 pounds of food and five gallons of stove gas; now, with three weeks' supplies, the sledges would be able to head eastward and try to make good the American claim to Marie Byrd Land. The next day was Friday the 13th, "but time is too precious for us to be superstitious," the leader wrote in his sledge log that evening after a trek of nearly seventeen miles, "so we are on our way again." Superstition might have said "I told you so," inasmuch as they were snowbound for the next several days. Philosophically the party waited out the weather playing bridge and hearts, with chocolate for stakes.

In the early Antarctic summer it was comparatively warm, and therefore wet. At $+26°F$ ($-3°C$) their sleeping bags seemed suf-focating; at $35°F$ ($1°C$) the clinging snow melted on anything it touched. "Hope your roofs do not leak like our tents," Gould

radioed Byrd. At Little America, muffled most days since the one
lucky moment of the Edsel Ford flight by fog on the Ice Shelf or
low clouds over the sun, it was equally damp; on one day, as Russell Owen informed the *Times*, "it actually rained, a thin drizzling
mist."[12] Morale in the little Antarctic town was not high. Marking
time, "doing nothing but wait for our mail," most of the Little
Americans had settled into the kind of grousing that is inevitable
once a great collective effort is over. At least the Geological Party
still had something important left to do.[13]

Meanwhile, in Washington, the Congress elected with Hoover
in 1928 had convened for its regular annual session. On December
18, 1929, the most dramatic news on the Hill was made by Oscar
DePriest, a freshman Republican from southside Chicago, whose
maiden speech in the House of Representatives that day was the
first address by a black member of Congress in twenty-eight years.
"Word that DePriest was on his feet spread through the Capitol,"
the *Washington Post* reported, "and the Chamber and the galleries
filled rapidly." At about the same time in the Senate one of
DePriest's white southern colleagues and adversaries, Claude
Swanson of Virginia, introduced a bill to promote Commander
Byrd to the rank of Rear Admiral—jumping him over the grade of
Captain, an action which in the United States Navy was most un-
usual. Byrd's great predecessor in Antarctic exploration, Charles
Wilkes, the *New York Times* pointed out, had remained a lieu-
tenant till he died.

Senator Swanson, destined a few years later to become, technically, Byrd's employer as FDR's Secretary of the Navy, urged
his colleagues to rush the bill through before their Christmas ad-
journment as a present to Byrd. On Friday, December 20, while
Wall Street stocks dropped to their lowest for the month,
S. 2740—"in recognition of his extensive scientific investigations
and extraordinary aerial explorations of the Antarctic Continent,
and of the first mapping of the South Pole and Polar Plateau by
air"—passed the Senate without roll call or debate, as Swanson

Geological Party at the foot of the Queen Maud Mountains (*see chapter 5*).

wished. The House completed action next day amid applause, and shortly a scratch of Herbert Hoover's pen made Richard Byrd the youngest admiral on the Navy's retired list by seventeen years. His salary went up from $3300 a year to $4500, a striking reminder to us of the comparative modesty of America's military establishment in those days.[14]

The sledging party's radio operator, Freddy Crockett, out on the surface of a great glacier that the Geological Party had just discovered and named after Mike Thorne, received the good news from Washington (as relayed from Little America) on December 19. On the 20th, camped on a site they named for Dr. Coman, at 85°25'17" South and 147°55' West—well east of the New Zealanders' farthest claim—and not having sighted the "Carmen Land" Roald Amundsen imagined he had seen lying in the direction toward which they had been heading, the Geological Party concluded that they were the first human beings ever to set foot upon Marie Byrd Land. "Tomorrow we shall raise our tiny American flag with appropriate ceremony if that is OK with you," Gould radioed Byrd. Next morning after oatmeal they doffed their caps and planted their flag; then—leaving, as always, one member in camp to keep an eye on the dogs—they climbed the nearest accessible peak, which they named "Supporting Party Mountain" after Arthur Walden's stalwart team that had pioneered their route from Little America and laid down the indispensable supply depots. Constructing a rock cairn, the explorers left inside it a tin can enclosing a page torn from Gould's notebook and signed with all their names. "This note indicates the furthest east point reached by the Geological Party of the Bryd Antarctic Expedition," the leader wrote. "We are beyond or east of the 150th meridian and therefore in the name of Commander Richard Evelyn Byrd claim this as a part of Marie Byrd Land, a dependency or possession of the United States." [15]

It was a keenly felt moment; yet for Larry Gould and his men this was still not the high point of the summer. That came four days later on their return journey, on Christmas Day. Camped near Mount Betty, and still a day's journey out from Camp Strom (or rather a night's; on the backtrack they were traveling at "night," when the sun was nearer the horizon, and sleeping by "day," to avoid as much as possible the perpetual solar glare), they "decided as a last hope to look at a curious pile of rock far down on a low ridge from the main mountain," Gould explained in a radio message to Byrd. It turned out to be the long-sought landmark built by Roald Amundsen and his men eighteen years before. "As though it were a sacred relic we removed just enough to see what was in the cache," Gould's narrative continued. "It contained a 5 gallon can of kerosene in excellent condition two small packages of matches and a tin can." "Gosh," Freddy Crockett interjected irreverently, "he didn't leave any grub."

Under the can lid was a message in Amundsen's own handwriting. Crockett copied it (another hand, probably Bernt Balchen's, later corrected his Norwegian accent marks and spelling), and Gould wrote and left a brief note describing the Geological Party. Afterward they carefully rebuilt the cairn to look just as it had when they found it and just as Amundsen had left it eighteen years before. "Each man was allowed to take some little bits of rock from it but not enough to disturb it in any way"; the preservationist mentality of the museum was already curbing the careless ways of the Antarctic frontier. The most important exception to this implicit rule against plundering for souvenirs was made on behalf of Amundsen's aged companion Martin Ronne back at Little America. "Tell Martin I will bring him some matches from Amundsen's cache," Gould advised Byrd by radio. "I had already taken the liberty of keeping Amundsen's note. It is almost as precious to me as my rock collections."

It was high time they were heading for home. Goodale and Vaughan spent a snowbound day in camp making sails, with the idea of boosting themselves along faster on their skis. "We start northward for Little America tonight," the party's leader notified Admiral Byrd on December 29. "We are [a] disreputable looking outfit right now for no one has washed or shaved since we left Little America." At Little America Byrd's men could not only wash and shave, reported Russell Owen, but even sun-bathe, stretched out on an engine crate "drowsing in the grateful warmth" or idly looking out over the Bay of Whales, upon which "pressure ridges rise, topple and form lagoons where seals bask and whales roll." On the Geological Party's homeward trail, conditions were even more pastoral; Norman Vaughan spent the afternoon of January 7, 1930, "travelling with neither shirt nor pants and no underwear—as naked as a track man at home except for his ski boots." The sledgers' chief hardship now was sleeplessness, even in the tents, under the never-ending summer sun.[16]

But appearances, as so often in the great south, were highly

Geological Party stopping for lunch
Mount Nansen in background.

deceptive. This season, whalers which ordinarily crossed the pack
in December had been unable to get through; according to navy
lieutenant Harry Adams of the Byrd Expedition, "It was the worst
ice year known in the Antarctic." The whales themselves, he asserted, had not been able to make it past the ice into the Ross Sea
that year! While the Geological Party's tired huskies were waddling homeward through soft or pie-crust snow and their masters
were worrying lest the pemmican in the depots ahead have been
spoiled by the thawing sunshine, the *City of New York*—"the
pseudo flag ship," as *Bolling* partisan Arnold Clarke still insisted
on calling it—put out to sea from New Zealand's Port Chalmers.
Early on January 6, still only a short way out from land, Captain
Melville radioed Byrd that he was hove-to under sail after an all-
night southwest gale with "squalls of hurricane force. Rain, hail

The City of New York in pack ice
Even today the pack can be a formidable adversary, calling for skills that predate the age of technology. In 1930 the City *at sea coped with hazards far greater than what was then happening at Little America.*

and a very high sea." In classic understatement he added: "At present moderation indicated." At 8 that morning Melville notified the admiral that he was under way again, his ship laboring heavily in high seas; by the 10th of January the ancient craft was logging a more respectable hundred miles in one day. "That's the way to do it," commented Byrd. But the first storm had been a harbinger of worse things to come.

The passage into the pack itself was somewhat easier than the *City's* crew had expected. South of the ice, however, they encountered not the usual relatively calm summer waters of the open Ross Sea but another terrific gale. "The ice suddenly began to heave under long swells as we approached the edge of the pack," Adams reported, and when they reached the open sea, with their elderly engine going full speed ahead, they found themselves "drifting backward several knots through the half-darkness." Any one of the great ice cakes that were heaving up on both sides of the ship could have slid down onto the deck and wrecked them. Captain Melville took the only possible course of action: he ordered the ship worked around until it was before the wind, and headed straight into the pack, forcing a way through that roaring, plunging ice-mass to comparative calm and safety.[17]

Byrd, who had already given the order to start breaking camp, now faced the possibility that the Little Americans might have to winter over for a second year. There was still enough dehydrated food, if they had to (it was left over from the First World War). Professor Gould, still out on the trail, cautioned his academic department back at the University of Michigan by radiogram that he could "not give definite answer about summer school until end of month when I am back in Little America"—hinting that next term he might still be in Antarctica! However, only the scientists and Scout Siple really looked forward to such a prospect. While the *City of New York* waited for the wind to abate, and the faster *Eleanor Bolling* was putting out from Dunedin, Byrd canvassed the possibility of having Little America evacuated by whalers. As he soon learned, however, it would cost the financially stretched Byrd Antarctic Expedition another half million dollars—the largest fraction of which would be the cost of the insurance—to bring a whaling factory ship into the Bay of Whales.[18]

In a spasmodic fashion, even while the dog teams hauled supplies down into the bay where many of the men were living in tents, the scientific work at Little America still went on. Paul

Siple, for one, had his hands full looking after a penguin farm. Since mid-December the Scout had had a dozen Emperors and half that many Adélies confined, more or less, in the pit where one of the Ford wing tips had formerly rested; the plan was to escort them eventually northward to various zoos. In the absence of proper fishing gear to catch food for them, and without the freshly frozen fish the long-overdue ships had been expected to bring in, Siple and his friend Jack Bursey had to force-feed their charges with whatever was on hand—frankfurters, canned meat, cut-up strips of seal blubber, or sardines. But that was not the worst of it. Penguins, Siple remarked, seemed to be not very bright as they stood idly about "like huge bottles," but when unobserved they could be diabolically clever at engineering jailbreaks. Again and again they cut steps with their beaks in the snow and lit out for the Bay of Whales. Fences of inwardly slanting bamboo sticks, even barriers of upended gasoline drums, failed to deter them; they simply climbed on one another's shoulders in a pyramid and so got out. It thus became necessary to add to the expedition's duty roster the new job of penguin watch—and the big birds retaliated by stationing a lookout of their own! If the human watchman should sneak up on them as they worked away on the wall, their own sentry, facing toward the houses, "would let out a rasping squawk which would cause his prison associates to turn about sharply and start walking away in a very innocent manner, for all the world like little boys making their exit from a room after being caught with their hands in the cooky jar." [19]

From this frustrating task Siple was distracted by the return of the Geological Party, which trudged into camp on the morning of January 19, 1930, after a triumphant trek of fifteen hundred miles. In this otherwise happy reunion there was a tinge of bitterness for Paul Siple. The dog team the Scout had so conscientiously trained the previous season had been taken from him in November for the sledging expedition's use—and as the teams now came barking joyously into Little America Siple realized that his own had been

Geological Party with erratic on Ross Ice Shelf
December 27, 1929, en route from Amundsen Glacier.

among the dogs killed on the trail. For the Geological Party, it had
been "a great trip—filled with romance and achievement," which
"aptly combined . . . the glamor and adventure of exploration
with the opportunities for sound scientific research"; for Paul
Siple, the time of their return was "my unhappiest day at Little
America."[20]

Larry Gould, back in town as second-in-command amid all the
clutter and confusion of breaking camp and the uncertainty as to
whether the ships would be able to take them out that year, admitted to a feeling of letdown. "We had been on the trail so long
that it seemed the natural way of living," the geologist confided to
his diary, "and it is hard to get used to this place and the deaden-
ing lethargy that pervades the atmosphere." Having little to do, he
acknowledged, "I am at once restless and yet dead." Perhaps his
restlessness was a function of the shortness of Little America's

span of history. In the endless recycling of human events, the Ant-arctic frontier was no longer on the Bay of Whales; it was away, at a windswept cairn near the frosty summits of the Queen Maud Range.[21]

Out on the high seas, meanwhile, the crew of the *City of New York* could not spare time for the lethargy that pervaded Little America. Heading southward again for another rescue attempt the ship got through the pack safely and into the open Ross Sea; but now it turned intensely cold, and the bitter spray that dashed over the ship froze at once into ice. Furiously, hour after hour and then day after day, with fire axes, knives, or any other instrument that came to hand, the *City's* men hacked away at the ice and threw it into the sea. They could not go onto the forecastle head for fear that as the heavily iced bow dipped deep it would wash them over-board. The ice on the martingale—the vertical spar under the bowsprit used in guying the stays—was as thick as a barrel, and before their ordeal was done this five-hundred-ton vessel, decks nearly awash, was groaning under two hundred tons of ice.

Suddenly on the night of February 15, as all hands were at the point of exhaustion, the clouds opened. Through the break, ice pilot Bendik Johansen descried the great smoking plume of Mount Erebus and the bleak shores of Ross Island. The gales had driven them more than three hundred miles off course! Captain Melville worked his ship in under the lee of the Shelf and radioed Little America that he was proceeding eastward, with the crew still chopping away. The *City of New York* arrived in the Bay of Whales on the evening of February 18, its topmasts showing first above the sea smoke, its hull and rigging still festooned with ice. The struggle to reach Little America had consumed forty-four days. Everything in camp had by that time been moved to dock-side; loading began at once, and the entire job was done in about twelve hours. As they cast off, around 9:30 A.M. on February 19, 1930, the ice around the ship was beginning to freeze in small floes.[22]

"Winter cannot be far off," Byrd had written two days earlier.

"We shall get out just in time. And yet, with the end so near, I am
rather sorry that it is over." Paul Siple felt much the same way.
Standing in line on deck to get his mail, Siple caught his last
glimpse of the great Ross Ice Shelf that loomed over the fast disappearing bay, and it gave the Scout a strange "feeling of home-
sickness for that bleak continent"—a much stronger sense of loss
than he had known when he had sailed away from his actual home
out of New York Harbor a year and a half before. "So I swal-
lowed hard to keep down my emotions and looked away from the
ice to the bundle of mail in my arms." For Larry Gould the
wrench was equally great: "I must confess," he wrote in his diary
that day, "that it was with a heavy heavy heart that I saw my last
of the Bay of Whales."[23]

Not all the Little Americans shared such longings. "We'll be
back, Bill," Admiral Byrd said to meteorologist "Cyclone"
Haines as they watched the barrier cliffs recede. "Not me,"
Haines replied, "once is enough." Wryly, Pete Demas wrote in
his diary: "I forgot one thing when I left the states and that was to
stay there." As they passed the capes the young aviation mechanic
"looked back at the Bay full of sea smoke desolate deserted and
gloomy," and thought "how dismal it would be to be standing on
that Bay looking at the ship disappearing and to have another Antarctic winter to face." Demas reserved his nostalgia not for the
empty land but for the airplanes he and the other mechanics had
buried two weeks before. "I felt a peculiar feeling after we had
taken the elevators and rudders off of them and piled snow around
them," Demas wrote, personifying the Fairchild and the Ford in
the way Americans so often do with their favorite machines:

> There they were sitting, probably never to move again and they had
> done there duty with out a single mechanical or other failer and had
> made the success of the expedition. We stopped for a minute and gazed
> at them as we started down the hill and complemented them. Everyone
> of us wished they could go back with us.[24]

Prosperous futures awaited such men back in the states; good marriages, college scholarships, rewarding careers (even in the face of the Great Depression), and honors. Yet a substantial fraction of them would remain under lifelong enchantment by the great white south—including some, like Demas and Haines, whose reaction at the actual moment of departure had been "Never again!"

"How did it feel to come back?" I asked Professor Gould, upon first meeting him nearly five decades later. Noting that his own feelings at that time had been "colored by romance"—like a number of other Little Americans, Gould was married soon after the expedition's return—the 81-year-old scientist added that he also remembered, from the time when the old *City of New York* came into the harbor of Dunedin, the taste of the fresh fruits and how green everything was: "You forget about all that, you know." Then in the next breath the veteran explorer, whose intervening years as educator and statesman had been filled with constructive national and international accomplishments, added: "But I'd go back to Antarctica tomorrow."[25]

6

A Ghost
Town Returns
to Life

And a bird flew up out of the turret,
Above the Traveller's head:
And he smote upon the door again a second time;
"Is there anybody there?" he said. . . .

But only a host of phantom listeners
That dwelt in the lone house then
Stood listening in the quiet of the moonlight
To that voice from the world of men.
—Walter de la Mare, "The Listeners"

The wind roared unhindered past the sheltered hollow at the edge of the Ross Ice Shelf. Above the abandoned village which huddled in that basin, only the tops of smokestacks and ventilators and the radio mast jutted from the otherwise unbroken snow. The carrier waves with their clucking Morse-coded burdens had long since ceased to disturb the primal stillness; for the past four years the only electronic activity over the Bay of Whales had been the lovely, insensate natural flickering of the aurora. And then, on January 8, 1934, the breathless silence yielded, subtly, to the sound of wood sliding on snow. For the second time in his life Bernt Balchen was skiing into the deserted site of Little America.

The Norwegian-born flier was an American citizen now—no thanks to the United States Immigration Service, which in its humorless bureaucratic fashion had ruled that Balchen's previous sojourn in the Antarctic in 1929, by interrupting his continuous American residence for more than six months, had made his first papers invalid. In the midst of the triumphant uproar surrounding the Byrd Antarctic Expedition's return to the states in 1930, the immigration authorities in all seriousness had tried to deport Balchen to Norway—a fate averted only when feisty New York Con-

Christoffer Braathen
*One of eight Norwegians in the wintering-over
party at Little America I, Braathen, shown here
with a snowy petrel, revisited the camp in 1934.*

gressman Fiorello LaGuardia, abetted by several powerful Mid-
western Senators of Scandinavian ancestry, had introduced a
special bill making Bernt Balchen a citizen. In a rare victory of
representative government at its best over administrative government at its worst, LaGuardia's bill had raced through a properly
embarrassed Congress and become law.

All such matters receded to the background of consciousness
now, as Balchen and his fellow Little America veteran Christoffer

Braathen, surrounded by a cheering section of penguins that clapped their flippers together like delighted children, strode across the sastrugi toward the cherished airplanes they had buried four years before. While his companion checked out the Fairchild *Stars and Stripes,* Bernt Balchen crawled through the escape hatch into the Ford and settled his big frame into the cockpit. As his hands closed on the tri-motored *Floyd Bennett's* ice-locked controls, in imagination the pilot was again fighting the heavily loaded plane up Liv Glacier: ''The snow-packed windshield is a solid wall of ice looming ahead, and a gust of wind that shakes the exposed tail is the sudden updraft that boosts us the last few feet.'' As the wind at Little America died away, reminding him of the infinite silence of the South Pole, the burly blond flier's eye caught sight of the slide rule he had used both on the trans-Atlantic crossing with Byrd and on the polar flight. Balchen had often wondered what had become of it; now he picked it up and slipped it back into his pocket.[1]

Bernt Balchen and Chris Braathen were not working for Richard Byrd this time. Their employer in 1934 was Lincoln Ellsworth, who had been co-leader of Amundsen's dirigible venture at Spitsbergen in 1926, and was now planning a trans-Antarctic flight. Twelve miles away their ship, the *Wyatt Earp*—named after the legendary Arizona frontier lawman, whose original cartridge belt hung over Ellsworth's bunk—awaited their report from Little America. Hundreds of miles to the northeast, aboard the *Jacob Ruppert,* an oilburning outcast from the Pacific lumber trade, Admiral Byrd's Second Antarctic Expedition was then making its way through a damp, berg-infested, fog-haunted region lately christened the Devil's Graveyard. Heartened by Bernt Balchen's report as relayed by radio from Ellsworth that all seemed well with Little America, Byrd and ship's captain Hjalmar F. Gjertsen (who, years before, had sailed with Amundsen on the *Fram*), now anxiously scanned the ice-choked ocean for an open lead that would let them thorough to the Bay of Whales.[2]

With Richard Byrd on the *Ruppert* were other First Little Americans, such as Quin Blackburn and radio operator Carl Petersen; Paul Siple, who had rushed through three years of college in two so that he could come a second time to Antarctica; "Cyclone" Haines, on unpaid leave from the U.S. Weather Bureau, who was again matching his meteorological wits against the treacherous Antarctic skies; Harold June, who had already flown several seaplane sorties form the *Ruppert* in search of the unknown north coast of Marie Byrd Land; Pete Demas, who this time would be applying his mechanical skills not to aircraft but to ground transportation (when not standing iceberg watches during the long voyage down he had spent much of his time assembling tractor sleds); and Victor Czegka, on loan from the Marine Corps, who when they got to the Bay of Whales would be in charge of unloading. Before that cruise began Czegka had also been responsible for drawing up the blueprints of a structure which Siple and skilled cabinetmaker Ivor Tinglof had built in secrecy in a Boston loft. Now it lay in "cunningly contrived knock-down sections" deep in the *Ruppert's* hold, and "except for Haines, the builders, and myself," Byrd affirmed, "nobody else had more than a dim suspicion" of its purpose. Unpacked and assembled, it would become the focus for one of the most dramatic stories ever acted out in Antarctica.[3]

Not all the members of the first Byrd Antarctic Expedition had volunteered for the second. Several of them, however, had helped to speed it on its way. Although Dr. Coman during the next Antarctic summer season would be on the *Wyatt Earp* with Ellsworth and Balchen, he had also given his former shipmates a hand; while Byrd's other ship, the *Bear of Oakland,* was in drydock at Newport News, the Johns Hopkins medical professor had come down to do some heavy stevedoring. Norman Vaughan, of Larry Gould's 1929 Geological Party, had taken a six month's leave of absence from his business to recruit and organize the second Expedition's dogs. There were other continuities. Since the first Expedition old Martin Ronne had died, but his son Finn was on board the *Ruppert*. Arthur Walden had also passed on, but first Expedition ships' company member Alan Innes-Taylor had replaced him as master of the sledge dogs. Arnold Clarke, who had finished up his education at MIT and launched a career in oceanography at Woods Hole, was not returning to the Antarctic. Clarke, however—loyal as always to the *Eleanor Bolling!*—had married the sister of his *Bolling* crewmate Leland Barter, and Barter was now chief engineer aboard the Second Expedition's ice ship, the *Bear of Oakland*. The *Bear*, a wooden sailing vessel built in 1874 (and thus even older than the *City of New York*, which after its last Ross Sea ordeal had had to be honorably retired), had made it safely to New Zealand and was expected soon to fare forth from Dunedin, shouldering through ice cakes such as the thin steel-sided *Jacob Ruppert* must avoid with care, and join the *Ruppert* beside Little America.[4]

As compared with the leisured millionaire Lincoln Ellsworth's expeditions, financed in large part from a family fortune, Richard Byrd's 1934 operation was a bargain-basement affair. For the *Bear of Oakland* Byrd had paid $1050, outbidding a junk dealer by fifty dollars; for the *Jacob Ruppert* he was paying the United States Shipping Board rent of a dollar a year. It was just as well the the *Ruppert* and the *Bear* had come so cheap. The expedition as a whole, with an elaborate scientific and aeronautic investigation program projected and with no spectacular South Pole stunt planned to sweeten the pot, was costing more than a million dollars, and the times were no longer the Golden Twenties. The second Byrd Antarctic Expedition had been expected to get under way in the fall of 1932; the delay since that time was the result of financial undernourishment.

Byrd, to be sure, had the benefit of the immense favorable publicity Little America had already received. The whirlwind of praise that had swept around the Little Americans upon their return in 1930 had at times gone to embarrassing lengths, as when one *New*

York Times reader proposed to name a whole newly discovered *planet* after Byrd. (The astronomers, more conservatively, had fallen back on Greco-Roman mythology as usual and called it Pluto.) The poignant climax had come in 1931 when National Geographic Society president Gilbert Grosvenor had presented Byrd with ten bound volumes containing five thousand letters from American school children. They ranged from a Seattle lad, who declared that a place where "you only had to wash your face and hands once while you were down there" would be a fine place to live if only it weren't so cold, to a more serious-minded high school student in New Hampshire who wrote that the public recognition accorded to people like Byrd was "tremendously important to us—the youth of America." Lindbergh-style idolization had not, after all, come to an end with the stock market crash.[5]

But the idealistic youth of America, alas, did not write the checks. Raising money in 1932 and 1933 had been even more heartbreaking than in 1928. These were the early months of the New Deal, when businessmen had more pressing—and, from their point of view, gloomier—matters on their minds than Antarctic exploration. Victor Czegka, the canny machinist whose expert metalwork had at times literally pinned the first Expedition together, functioned on the second as its business manager, and part of his job had included writing donation-begging letters—30,000 of them!—to American business firms. Most of those overtures had been unsuccessful; 127 requests to suppliers of denim, for example, had provoked not a single offer to provide the second Little Americans with overalls.

Perhaps the most discouraging letter of all in Czegka's files was a polite refusal on behalf of Edsel Ford, whose namesake mountains the second Expedition intended to explore. "In response to your letter of July 21st to Mr. Edsel B. Ford, I am obliged to say it is not possible to offer any financial backing for Admiral Byrd's proposed second expedition to the Antarctic," the motor executive's secretary had written to Czegka on August 3, 1933. "The depression has created increasing demands and Mr. Ford is unable to reconsider his decision.'' But Mr. Ford evidently did reconsider (or overruled his subordinate); he became one of the second expedition's major sponsors, and in due course Byrd's book *Discovery,* detailing the achievements of that expedition, would be dedicated to Edsel Ford. Other capitalists—the malted-milk king William Horlick, the computer pioneer Thomas J. Watson, and the beer entrepreneur Jacob Ruppert—had also come through, and $100,000 worth of expensive scientific equipment was on loan from colleges, foundations, and government agencies. Equally crucial, from a fiscal standpoint, had been sales to the communications media: newspaper rights, newsreel rights, and—something technologically new in the world—broadcasting rights *from* Little America. Criticized, in the anti-business climate of the early 1930s, for the huckstering aspects of his venture, Byrd shrugged: "Even Columbus worked on a percentage basis." The main thing, in 1934 as in 1929, was to get to Antarctica.[6]

The expedition leader himself was not happy with at least one of his sponsors. The manufacturer of a tractor he counted on using had sent the expedition the wrong cabin for it, and during the voyage Pete Demas and his crew had had to fit the vehicle somehow to the one they had. Then Byrd learned that other needed accessories shipped by the same company were not going to reach New Zealand in time to be picked up by the *Bear.* "The Admiral is quite sore over it," Demas wrote. It was a sobering situation for the young Greek-American. Byrd, as usual delaying announcement of his top leadership choices until the last possible moment, at Czegka's and Haines's urging was about to place Demas in charge of the second Byrd Antarctic Expedition's entire tractor fleet. Much—including, as it turned out, human life—was going to depend on those machines.

Pete Demas had also been worrying about the expedition's morale in general. "The spirit on the ship at the present as I see it is quite poor," states his diary entry for December 29, 1933.

"There are very few men on board who real[l]y have the spirit of the expedition or who understand its seriousness." Did these words reflect a subtle "generation gap" between the little corps of old Antarctica hands and the newcomers to polar exploration? Earlier in the *Jacob Ruppert's* shakedown cruise Paul Siple had given a far more optimistic assessment: "During the past few months of preparing I saw a new ideal," he had written on October 30, two weeks out of New York. "I felt sure that this Expedition was going to be a thousand percent improvement over the last." Perhaps the sag Pete Demas reported shortly before New Year's was only the result of having languished for many days in the dark, dripping environs of the Devil's Graveyard, for as they headed westward to look for their passage into Little America the spirit of the men seemed to Demas to have greatly improved.[7]

On January 12 a pleasant social note found its way into the young mechanic's diary: "It will be great to see old Bernt," Demas wrote. "He is one of the most interesting persons that I know. A great fellow." Regrettably the reunion was not to happen. That same day, terrifyingly, heavy swells—possibly generated by an earthquake over by Mount Erebus—rolled out from underneath the Ross Shelf, breaking the bay ice where the plane that Bernt Balchen was to have flown for Ellsworth was parked. Only its wings, falling upon opposite sides of a new crevasse, saved the aircraft from dropping into the bay. "I am certainly sorry to hear it," Demas wrote, adding that the accident should make more of Byrd's men on board the *Ruppert* aware of "how quickly disaster can happen." The only place where repairs could be made, Balchen reported by radio, was the factory that had built the airplane. Lincoln Ellsworth, declining all offers of assistance, gave it up for the season and sailed away to the north. The *Wyatt Earp* and the *Jacob Ruppert* passed each other on the Ross Sea, unseen.[8]

The Byrd expedition, meanwhile, was enjoying a stroke of Byrd's proverbial good luck. Nobody had ever tried to come down into the Ross Sea from their present direction before; Cook himself had turned back, baffled, in the inhospitable waters they had just traversed, and during Antarctica's Heroic Age a passage along the meridian of 178° W. had come to be considered relatively fast and safe. Yet Ellsworth recently had been caught in heavy pack along that traditional line—heavier, at any rate, than was good for the thin-shelled *Jacob Ruppert*. Byrd accordingly gambled on discovering a new back route into Little America. On January 14, 1934, the *Ruppert* found it, in Longitude 169° W.—an absolutely clear track containing no ice at all. "We have evidently sneaked around the pack," Pete Demas wrote, and on the 17th they sighted the great Ross Ice Shelf and came to a stop five hundred yards away. "A vast sense of pleasure came over me," Siple afterward recalled, "at the familiar sight of the sheer 100-foot cliffs of this frozen sea."[9]

The ship's motor sailboat put a landing party ashore about three miles north of Little America. As usual after a long sea voyage the dogs went happily crazy. "In no time the place was a shambles of broken harnesses, overturned sledges, slithering huskies and exceedingly wrathful drivers." Leaving the dog drivers to corral their teams, Byrd, Haines, Carl Petersen, and George Noville (who had not been with the First Expedition, but was a veteran of Byrd's Arctic and trans-Atlantic flights) trudged up the gentle incline that rose from the low front of the bay ice, sinking knee-deep at every step. Before them as they topped the ridge lay the buried town, "with its slender upperworks rising darkly against the snow." "It looks as if we left it only yesterday," Petersen exclaimed. Soon they stood above the old Administration Building. Alongside its ventilators, stove pipe, and cleated anemometer pole a broom, "an irrelevant suggestion of domestic felicity," stuck out of a drift.

As soon as the dog teams arrived with the snow shovels, Haines and Byrd paced off the distance from the stove pipe, trying to recall the number of steps between the stove and the old tunnels, and Little America's first archeological dig began. So quickly on a new frontier—compare the mining ghost towns of the American West—a freshly abandoned place takes on an atmosphere of antiquity! As Bill Haines broke through a shell of hard blue ice three or four feet down and crawled headfirst into his old balloon station, he might have been breaching King Tut's tomb. "At first the place was black as the inside of a derby hat," Byrd reported later by radio, "but the ice packed against the windows shone with a ghostly blue refraction. We used lighted pieces of paper as torches. Then I found a fruit jar filled with kerosene which used to be my reading lamp. It burned slowly."

The dim light fell on 1929 calendars with the days crossed off, hanging on the ice-filmed walls. Long icicles glittered from the ceiling. Broken beams lay across the upper bunks; the roof had sagged under its burden of ice, and it would have to be jacked up and re-braced before the building could again be used. The floor was strewn with items scattered during a hasty departure—unmatched mukluks, torn parkas, dirty underwear, and the rubber ball with which Byrd's pet dog Igloo had used to play. On the table were the pot of coffee and the slab of roast beef on which Dr. Coman had been lunching while he waited for the last sledge to come back for a man stricken with appendicitis. Then the homecomers became aware that Finn Ronne was standing silently in front of his father's bunk. The young Norwegian beckoned to Byrd and held his light near the wall. Old Martin, just before he packed up, had written his son's name there. "The old man must have known I'd come down." [10]

In the meantime another party had been digging down into the Mess Hall two hundred yards away. They broke through the roof of "Cap" McKinley's photo lab. "It was just as you left it, Mac," Byrd said in a broadcast a few days later. "As usual, you forgot to shut the door." Thanks to its sturdier construction the Mess Hall was in better shape than the other building; except for a little cleaning up, the group that shortly moved in as residents "just threw our sleeping bags into the empty bunks and called it home."[11]

Truly this was a place where neither moth nor rust could corrupt. In the old aviation cache the second Expedition's airmen would find a better supply of tools than the ones they had brought with them. The seal and whale meat and beef in the tunnels outside were all perfectly preserved. Cans of baked beans, meats, coffee, cocoa, and powdered milk were neatly racked behind the galley stove, where Al Carbone would soon be cooking as George Tennant had before him. On top of the stove were half-filled pots of food, frozen solid. There was coal in the scuttle, so Byrd's exploratory party made a fire and warmed up the four-year-old leftovers. On the mess table Tennant had left a big pork roast, for "whoever might come back here—you can't ever tell." So Tutankhamun's mourners in about 1325 B.C. had brought their young king's belongings to the sepulcher, devoutly expecting that in the afterlife those things would be used.

A pair of boxing gloves hung from a nail. A girl's picture was on the wall. In Sverre Strom's bunk they found the accordion on which he had often played Norwegian folk melodies. The phonograph was on the long mess table, and somebody cranked it up. "It broke into a tune forty-two men will never forget"—*The Bells of St. Mary's,* which Quin Blackburn on the previous expedition had played, maddeningly, over and over again for fourteen months. Haines, Petersen, and Byrd broke into helpless laughter. ("Wait a moment," said Blackburn, standing nearby. "Don't tell me—I'll remember it in a second.") The clock was wound, and ran; the lights went on, dimly, when Petersen flicked the switch; the telephone rang. (George Noville raised his eyebrows when he heard it: "Did somebody miss the boat?") "For a moment," Byrd summed up, "I had the feeling that time had rolled back and the old gang would fill the place with shouting."

Admiral Byrd returned to the ship at ten that evening, leaving Chief Scientist Thomas Poulter, the expedition's second-in-com-

Pressure ridge, Bay of Whales
Formed where two ice floes are forced together,
such terrain can compel the use of ice axe and
rope, as shown here.

mand, in charge of reclaiming Little America. The nostalgic holiday was over. It was the 17th of January, and the *Jacob Ruppert*, low on fuel after her extensive cruise through the Devil's Graveyard, had to be emptied and sent back to New Zealand by February 5. Four hundred tons of supplies must be flown, tractored, dog-sledged, or man-hauled to Little America. But Ver-sur-Mer Inlet, where the First Expedition had unloaded in 1929, was now choked from end to end with pressure ice, shoved and heaved into irregular blocks and thirty-foot ridges and "mighty bulges, like arrested waves." The choice before the second Expedition was either to carve out a long, roundabout route southward along the Bay, eastward across some lighter pressure ice, up onto the Ross Shelf near Framheim, and northward at last to Little America—twenty miles of trail in order to reach an objective less than three miles away!—or else to risk tying up and unloading directly onto the Shelf.[12]

The Bay of Whales to the beholder's eye seemed solid and enduring. Like any other permanent-looking geological structure it was actually subject to change and decay. On the maps made by Scott in 1902, Shackleton in 1908, Amundsen in 1911, and Byrd in 1929 the Bay's boundaries had shifted substantially; Commodore Gjertsen, who had sailed in to the Bay with Amundsen, now found it "changed so much as to be almost unrecognizable." Cliffs of ice erode more rapidly than most other kinds. "The persistence of the Barrier as a fresh fracture cliff," Larry Gould warned in a paper he would be reading before the Geological Society of America some months thereafter, "is sufficient evidence to anyone who has wintered on the Shelf Ice that it is a transient feature. Such fresh clean faces are short lived; they indicate places where portions of shelf ice have recently broken off." Byrd, as the *Jacob Ruppert* stood in close to the Shelf on the morning of January 18, 1934, of course knew this; nevertheless, the risk seemed worth taking in order to avoid the back-breaking alternative.

"Cyclone" Haines was standing on the bridge next to Byrd. They were watching a smooth thirty-foot wall, behind which rose the Barrier, seemingly as solid as masonry. "Staunchness was deceptively written in every gothic line," the Admiral later recalled. "But delicacy was there, too . . . the delicacy of an avalanche poised for the final overbalancing ounce."

"What do you think of that place, Bill?" the expedition leader asked. "Does it look good to you?"

"Before he could answer," as Byrd afterward told the story,

''something happened. No eye was fast enough to catch it all. A slither of snow, a dark line running, and for a quarter of a mile that fine barrier cliff, seemingly so staunch, melted into a tempestuous white waterfall. A sharp, rending crack, prolonged as the break gathered length came to the ship, then the clatter of small bergs hitting the water. The ship creaked to the sudden surge. . . .

''Bill Haines got out his answer. 'Admiral,' he said, 'I don't think I should care to tie up there.' ''[13]

Nature, transcendent and uncaring, had decided the question for them. The *Jacob Ruppert* returned to its former mooring place, and that afternoon the nightmare began, along a track that quickly became known as Misery Trail. Without successfully functioning tractors, such as the First Expedition had lacked, the job could not have been done at all; even so, half the loads were pulled by dogs and men.

First, three intermediate supply dumps had to be established: Pressure Camp, three miles from the water's edge—a safety margin which suddenly vanished when the bay ice went out; West Barrier Cache, reached by a road they hacked and bridged across the ridges and crevasses until they reached a gentle slope up onto the Ross Ice Shelf west of the Bay of Whales; and East Barrier Cache, on the heights east of the Bay about three miles south of Little America. Relays of men, dogs, and machines wrestled the cargoes from the *Ruppert*'s holds to the sledges through the successive depots, and on to Little America—endlessly, relentlessly, to the edge of fatigue and beyond, often for thirty-six hours without a break, or interrupted by blizzards or heavy fog that wore people down as much as the work itself. ''Exhausted men were found,'' Siple recalled, ''who could not remember what they were supposed to be doing, let alone guess what time of day it was in the unending Antarctic summer daylight.'' Byrd himself later admitted that perhaps at times he might have cracked the whip too hard.

Dog team in pressure ridges
This picture was taken on the First Expedition; this tortured landscape was even worse; the route carved out from the ships to the site of Little America II was quickly dubbed "Misery Trail."

At the end of the month the *Bear of Oakland* sailed in, to be greeted by three welcoming whistle blasts from the *Jacob Ruppert*. The reinforcements, especially the additional little red tractor which the *Ruppert*'s forward boom presently plucked from the *Bear*'s deck and lowered onto the ice, engine already running, were a tonic for morale. ("Stay away from the edge of the ice," Demas told his newly recruited tractor driver J. H. Von der Wall, "and keep her rolling.") At two o'clock in the morning on the first of February, the most serious obstacle on the trail through the pressure ice was overcome. With stinging drift in their faces at fifteen below, Harold June and his crew pounded the last nails into a sturdy contrivance of hatch covers and telephone poles that bridged a 40-foot crevasse. At 3:15 A.M. that same morning a heavily loaded tractor rolled over this "Bridge of Sighs," as they named it, carrying the electric generator for Little America's radio station. That afternoon engineer John Dyer was on the air with Buenos Aires and New York for voice tests, and two days later radio station KFZ—for which the expedition had solemnly secured an assigned frequency and a formal license from the FCC—was ready to go on the air.[14]

KFZ was only six miles in a direct line from KJTY, over which they had been broadcasting from shipboard on the voyage down, with a recording of the *Jacob Ruppert*'s whistle as their program signature. Temporarily the transmitter for KFZ reposed inside a tent on top of the snows that covered Little America. A westerly wind buffeted the tent and dusted its interior with drift. Outside the tent, oblivious to the blizzard, the power plant chugged away. Down in the old mess hall, fifteen feet beneath the surface, the Little Americans awaited their first cue from New York. It came, and Dyer put on Record No. 1—the call letters KFZ, repeated slowly three times, and then the sound of sledge dogs in full cry.

Guy Hutcheson, on the monitor board, cued the announcer, Charles J. V. Murphy—not one of the expedition's volunteers who served for their room and board, but a polished media professional whose salary was being paid by CBS. "Hello, America," Murphy said into the microphone. "Byrd Expedition calling. . . . You have just heard the call letters of station KFZ—Little America—inaugurating the first broadcast from the Antarctic continent." By the light of kerosene lanterns, expedition members read their scripts and spoke their lines. Byrd, when he had heard the first Morse signals go chattering out from Little America five years before, had had deeply mixed feelings about the experiment, and a like ambivalence came over him now. On the one hand he admired the "cool competence" of modern young technicians like Dyer and Hutcheson; such men, "springing full-fledged from great scientific universities, . . . arrive while still in their early twenties with a confidence and security no other profession seems able to impart."

However, as he thought of the contrast between Captain Scott and his men twenty-two years before, silently dying of hunger only 160 miles from the members of their base party, and his own expedition as it described "our prosaic doings" to a large anonymous audience ten thousand miles away, Byrd was seized for a moment by misgivings. Perhaps the Admiral had in mind the ranting oratory that lately had swept over the world from Berlin and Nuremberg as he wrote in his diary: "When too much talk seems to be the cause of much of the grief in the world, no man could break the isolation of the Last Continent of Silence without a twinge of remorse." [15]

Next day, February 4, 1934, the *Jacob Ruppert* had to leave. A skeleton crew would take the ship out; the rest would stay to help the wintering-over party in its continuing struggle to move the stores to Little America. Victor Czegka, who had been ailing for some time, regretfully would have to go back with the *Ruppert* while the process of unloading that he had initiated was at its madcap height. An even greater blow was the resignation of the winter party's only doctor. His reason, Admiral Byrd rather blandly explained in the official narrative of the expedition, was high blood pressure. (Reminiscing with Byrd twenty years later, Paul Siple gave a strikingly different account: expedition second-in-command Tom Poulter had confiscated thirty cases of liquor the enterprising physician had smuggled in, and poured their contents out upon the snow, whereupon the doctor had demanded to be sent home.) This was a cruel blow, but once again Byrd luck intervened. The British exploring vessel *Discovery II* happened to be fitting out in New Zealand for an Antarctic cruise. Advertising in the local press, the Byrd Expedition secured the services of Dr. Louis Potaka, a highly recommended graduate of Otago University in Dunedin. Swiftly cutting the requisite red tape, the British and New Zealand governments arranged for the new recruit to ship south aboard the *Discovery II,* and Byrd sent the *Bear of Oakland* out through the ice pack to get him. On February 21 the two ships made a hair-raising rendezvous in a snowstorm. "I dare say no doctor ever received a stranger hurry-call," Potaka told Little America's radio audience over KFZ two weeks later. A patient they had meanwhile been trying to doctor on radioed instructions from New York, he reported, was "much improved." [16]

The gangplank to civilization was lifted on February 26 when the *Bear of Oakland,* having set Dr. Potaka and some additional food and gasoline ashore, sailed away through the sea smoke in the Bay of Whales. Fifty-six men, the largest ice party in Antarctic history, prepared to winter over. They had, however, certain creature comforts all their predecessors had lacked. Ten new flat-topped buildings, arranged in a double row east of the old mess hall, gave them much more space in which to move around. Abundant electricity, deriving from a wind-driven generator on top of one of the radio towers, powered saws and drills, sewing machines, coffee and meat grinders, and George Noville's shaver. Rugs (manufacturers' end pieces) broke the bleakness of the floors, and luxurious mattresses covered the bunks. Three cows yielded them forty quarts of milk a day—"or did," Charlie Murphy observed, "until the yield diminished according to the workings of an inexorable natural law which the cowherd, [E. S.] Cox, tried in vain to explain to the simple souls of Little America." (The Little Americans had already taken a bit of kidding from the crew of the *Bear of Oakland* when the ship came in, after having sighted an ice floe on which was floating a bale of hay.)

They were still building and digging on April 19 when the sun went down, and they were a month into the Antarctic night before they finished shoveling out and shoring up the last structure, a ramshackle tractor garage. Like others who had preceded them into the great white south, the second Little Americans now faced the ordeal of wintering over—an ordeal whose rigors, CBS's Charles J. V. Murphy insisted, had become somewhat exaggerated in the polar literature. "Through the narratives of the British expeditions on this same continent runs a certain note of tragedy and spiritual enrichment," Murphy acknowledged. On this second Byrd Antarctic Expedition, however, that note was overcome by "the good-natured tolerance, the easy-going, the what-the-hell-of-it attitude which is peculiarly American." The British explorers' mystique of rank and place also took a beating from their irreverent colonial cousins. Admiral Byrd, to be sure, anticipating his own long absence from the base (to be described in chapter 7), had worked out an elaborate departmental structure and chain of command, within which the leaders were supposed to bombard one another with bureaucratic Navy-style written memoranda, duly signed and titled. "But this looked pretty silly," Charlie Murphy later observed. "The fellow to whom you were addressing a formal communication was quite likely sitting in the bunk overhead, in the same sort of sleazy gray underwear, trying to compose one in the right severity of style to you." Anyhow they had no place to file such things. Radio engineer John Dyer welcomed these memos, however; they were handy for starting a fire in the morning.

By far the most comfortable building in the second Little America, double-walled and insulated with wool shearing, was the radio shack, although it had the clutter to which men typically revert when they are neither in a home environment nor under military discipline. The corner set apart for the weekly broadcasts over CBS "became a studio by the hurried acts of brushing the chessmen from the monitor board, advising [Clay] Bailey please to pipe down on his snoring, plucking the reindeer hairs from the collapsible organ . . . , and carefully conveying from the vicinity of the microphone all coal bags, coal scuttles, pokers, stray pups, water buckets, etc., over which the agitated performers were likely to stumble." KFZ itself was a symbol of how much less austere a business Antarctic exploration had become since the first Expedition. The introduction of regularly scheduled network voice broadcasting, complete with commercials (for General Foods), subtly but strongly shifted the balance between Antarctica and civilization. Voice broadcasting *to* Little America on the First Expedition had diverted and encouraged the members of a remote outpost somewhat in the manner of a traveling USO troupe during a war. With KFZ's weekly programs *from* Little America, however, the outpost in turn was diverting and encouraging the parent society.[17]

Inevitably this introduced a note of distortion and artificiality, as happens when anyone consciously plays to an audio pickup or a TV camera. The Second Little Americans not only had to *be* explorers, they had to *act* the part as well. (Byrd had anticipated this theatricality during the first Expedition, by sometimes having people dress up in furs for the cameras when it was not really necessary.) Sometimes they found themselves doing documentary "reenactments," as when KFZ broadcast a meeting in which the expedition members discussed whether to move out of their comfortable quarters to a "Retreat Camp" because the ice barrier had begun to crack under Little America itself—an exciting moment, but synthetic, because the real debate and vote which Byrd, Poulter, Haines, Blackburn, and Alton Wade read from their radio scripts on March 10 had actually taken place the week before!

Anchored in New York by the smoothly turned radio announcer phrasing of Harry Von Zell, CBS's Little America station had to compete for attention with whatever else was on the air. That meant it had to be entertaining, at all costs. Talent emerged in unexpected places. Chief Cook Al Carbone advertised himself as the world's greatest harmonica player, and challenged anyone back in the States to do as well. A men's chorus was recruited by seismologist E. C. Morgan, and went on the air as "Dr. Morgan's Knights of the Gray Underwear," singing a college glee club number about sitting cozily by a fire while "a great white cold walks abroad." Murphy and meteorologist Haines joked about Antarctic temperatures in much the same way that the joyboys on TV nowadays report the weather on the local evening news. Geologist F. Alton Wade, counting the many days that yet must pass before the expedition could return, imitated the sinister chuckle of that renowned radio crimefighter "The Shadow." (At times, reading these scripts, I was reminded of Thoreau's rejoinder to the great news that a telegraph line was being built from Maine to Texas: "But Maine and Texas, it may be, have nothing important to communicate.")

Occasionally the station sounded a didactic note, as when Paul Siple told any Boy Scouts who might be listening in that Scouting had prepared many of the expedition members for daily Antarctican emergencies: "We lash the loads to our sledges with tenderfoot knots." And sometimes announcer Murphy became more reflective. "The uniqueness of this place is that since Genesis it has lain outside the universal flow of things," he remarked on May 30, Memorial Day:

> Here no wars have ever been fought. There were no vast feeding places and natural resources to contend for. Throughout the rise and fall of whirling empires and spinning civilizations Antarctica has known only peace. Here, removed from the distractions of civilization, you come to see things with a steady simplicity; and you wonder at the tragic unrest behind the news items in the radio press that Petersen distributes in the morning.

Then George Noville spoke on behalf of Little America's war veterans, Morgan's Knights sang the Battle Hymn of the Republic, and KFZ signed off. Antarctica was beginning—just barely beginning—to find a voice with which to criticize the world from which its settlers had come, to hint that from its frosty silences humanity could learn a better way. But such thoughtful moments on the program were rare. More often Charlie Murphy tempted his listeners quite frankly into escapism. "And now, America," he announced on June 27, the week after Midwinter Day in the great south, "forget the summer heat, forget drought—and strikes—and economic difficulties—draw your chairs up closer —and we shall tell you how a superb adventure is planned."[18]

7

To
Walden Pond
with Gasoline
Engines

Columbus discovered no isle or key so lonely as himself . . .
Such is the tragic necessity which strict science finds underneath our domestic and neighborly life, irresistibly driving each adult soul as with whips into the desert, and making our warm covenants sentimental and momentary. . . . But this banishment to the rocks and echoes no metaphysics can make right or tolerable. . . .
Solitude is impracticable, and society fatal. We must keep our head in the one and our hands in the other.
—*Ralph Waldo Emerson,* Society and Solitude

The second Little Americans posted a record of solid scientific accomplishment. With hydrophones immersed in a tank of seawater and antifreeze, the *Bear of Oakland* on its way to Little America listened to fathometer pulses at 525 cycles (close to treble "C" on a piano keyboard) and drew a bathymetric map of the bottom of the Ross Sea. Paul Siple and Alton A. Lindsey studied birds, both in the Antarctic ice pack—"a purgatory for the navigator but a paradise for the observer of bird and mammal life"—and on the side of Mount Helen Washington in King Edward VII Land, where they found a petrel rookery, the only known bird breeding ground within four hundred miles of the Bay of Whales. (Its inhabitants, the young scientists wryly reported, "defended their nests with the customary marksmanship.") Another sledging party made directly for Supporting Party Mountain in the Queen Mauds, where Gould's group in 1929 had left off, then backtracked over to Thorne Glacier, finding fossils—leaves, branches, whole tree trunks—and twenty seams of coal. New names appeared on the Antarctic map, expressive of the spirit of the 1930s: Darryl Zanuck Mountain, Mount Saltonstall, Mount Louis McHenry Howe; the front of the Edsel Ford Range and the hinterland of the Queen Mauds became far better known. Out of all these investigations came a harvest of scientific papers. Many of them were written with a charm one does not expect to find in scholarship's dry realm; Lindsey, for example, writing on the Weddell seals in the Bay of Whales, struggled in vain to maintain monographic "objectivity" as he described how mother seals playfully ducked their pups' heads under the icy Antarctic waters as they taught them how to swim. The biological papers, in particular, were the first such monographs to be published by any Americans since James Eights had come back from the Antarctic one hundred years before.[1]

Except among Antarctica specialists, however, these activities were (and remain) generally unknown. What seizes the public mind is drama. The first Byrd Antarctic Expedition had not made headlines for its scientific discoveries (except, of course, in the all-inclusive *Times*), but rather for the struggle of the *Floyd Bennett* as it clawed its way up Liv Glacier toward the polar plateau. So with the second; what would live in legend afterward was the tale of how Richard Byrd had spent four months alone in a shack under the freezing Antarctic night.

When Eleanor Bolling Byrd had greeted her son in 1930 after the First Expedition's return, she had affectionately told him: "Next time you start on any expeditions some one is going to chloroform you." Her feelings upon learning that this second time he would be all alone at a weather station more than a hundred miles from his companions at Little America—a station he named "Bolling Advance Weather Base," after her—can well be imagined. In this episode the tradition of the lone American wanderer, braving prairie blizzards or hostile Indians, reached to the ultimate edge. Schoolbooks have continued to perpetuate and canonize the episode. One typical literature anthology lately used in junior high schools, with such a book's usual "discussion questions" and definitions of all the hard words, concluded its unit on biography (other examples: Edison, Jefferson, Mark Twain on the Mississippi) with an excerpt from Byrd's own account of his ordeal in solitude. The textbook's editors invited the youthful reader to "imagine yourself, if you can, in a tiny wooden hut. . . ."[2]

Why did Byrd do it? Was he talked into it (as has been conjectured) merely as a publicity stunt, to make up for the lack in the second Expedition of any built-in "spectacular" comparable to the First Expedition's flight to the south pole? Byrd insisted he was forced into his decision by circumstances beyond anyone's control. Advance Base, the Admiral explained, had originally been in-

Ice anticline, Bay of Whales
One more hurdle for the hard-working dog teams.

tended as a three-man operation, not as a solo ordeal. He had
hoped to place it even farther from Little America, at the foot of
the Queen Maud Mountains if not on the polar plateau itself. Its
function would be meteorological research, gathering data through
the Antarctic night at a spot whose temperature extremes could be
expected to be far greater than at the edge of the Ross Sea; for that
purpose, the farther inland the better. However, a succession of
unforeseen delays made it impossible within the available time to
lay down enough supply depots, and the plan had to be drastically
curtailed.

The unexpected hardships along Misery Trail, and the false
alarms—which could just as well have been true warnings—that
Little America was about to break loose from the Shelf, delayed
any attention to Advance Base until March of 1934, two months
after the expedition's ships entered the Bay of Whales. Alan Innes-
Taylor's Southern Sledging Party, pioneering a way through the
crevasses and laying down depots for the scientific parties that
would move out the following spring, took the pick of the sledge
dogs, and Advance Base would therefore have to be supplied by
tractors, not nearly so well seasoned in polar travel as the dogs.
This was to be the first serious attempt at Antarctic automotive
transportation; the humiliating failure of the Ford Snowmobile on
the first Expedition was still vividly remembered, and Misery Trail
had shown that the second Expedition's machines were under-
powered for day in, day out travel over the Barrier. As the Antarctic twilight stretched over the land, it raised the forbidding prospect of a four-hundred-mile return journey from the Queen Mauds
in the dark. "We might go a hundred miles inland," Paul Siple
told Admiral Byrd, "but it would be dangerous to venture beyond
that point." Disappointed, Byrd agreed.

Even at the lesser distance it proved impossible to transport and
cache enough supplies to support three men. As Charlie Murphy
remembered the key conversation, Byrd said: "It's got to be two
men or one, so it's got to be one."

"Why so?" I asked.

"It just wouldn't work with two men. Three men could live like human beings. But two? No, it's too risky. . . .

"Put two men out there, and you invite a tragedy. Anybody who knows arctic history knows this. A third man in a crowded shack is always an equalizing force, a neutral point of [view], a court of appeal, the man outside the quarrel. After a couple of months two men might be at each other's throats."

"So you want to have a go at it alone?"

"Yes. I want to."

On the face of it, Byrd's explanation of how his solo sojourn at Advance Base came to be is quite logical. However, his conclusion that one man, or three, may succeed in an operation in which two must fail is by no means inescapable. The United States on cold-war alert staffed its missile sites, surely as psychologically stressful an environment as Antarctica, with two men rather than with one or three; and nineteenth-century fur traders, missionary priests, and prospectors quite commonly had roamed across the Great American Desert in pairs. At any rate, for a person who was being compelled against his will to make a choice, the Admiral seemed not merely resigned to the necessity but eager to undergo the ordeal.

In addition, the secrecy with which Byrd had instructed Czegka and Tinglof and Siple to design, build, and stow away Advance Base for shipment to Little America is hard to account for unless he had foreseen the possibility of something unusual in the way it was going to be used. Indeed, it strongly suggests that Byrd had intended all along to spend the winter in solitude. The operative words in that conversation with Charles J. V. Murphy may well be the simple statement "I want to go," and Murphy, browsing through Byrd's diary later on to work up a magazine article on the Admiral's experience, concluded as much: "I believe he welcomed the chance." By early March of 1934, as if scorning the comparative comforts of the new Little America buildings, Byrd

was already living in the shack which would later be moved out to
Advance Base.[3]

"For ten years I've lived a crowded life—one expedition after
another," Byrd told Murphy just before his departure from Little
America. "I've had no time for leisure or contemplation. But out
there I can live in utter simplicity, can sit still and think things
over. I'd like to see the world from a different angle, and take
stock, perhaps, of the things we live and die for." In his book
Alone, published four years afterward, Byrd elaborated this argument. "You might think that a man whose life carries him into
remote places would have no special need for quietude," he explained. "Whoever thinks that has little knowledge of expeditions.
Most of the time they move in fearful congestion and uproar, and
always under the lash of time." Even on the far Little American
frontier, then, one could feel a necessity to get away from it all!
Scotching some of the more scurrilous and absurd rumors that had
sprung up as to why he had gone off to Advance Base, Byrd maintained that basically he "wanted to sink roots into some replenish-
ing philosophy."[4]

To put it that way was to place himself in a time-honored tradition of American cross-grainedness. "Dick Byrd, the Virginian,
Dick Byrd, the American, is also inseparably Don Quixote and
Parsifal," one reviewer of *Alone* exclaimed. "To Ford his peace
ship; to Byrd his ice barrier." Nevertheless certain pointed questions were asked, and are still asked, about that personal quest.
Could an expedition leader properly go off into the unknown for
spiritual renewal, or whatever, leaving fifty-five people leaderless
on the ice? And if he got into trouble at his solitary outpost, could
he legitimately ask others to risk their own lives to get him out?
Expedition second-in-command Tom Poulter deftly fielded the first
question. "You may wonder how this camp functions in the absence of Admiral Byrd," Poulter told the host of phantom listeners
to KFZ two months after the leader's departure. "The answer to
that is: we function exactly as if he were here." To the second

question Byrd himself responded—in a round-about way—with a note penciled on scrap paper which he handed to Murphy just before he left. "I hope that no one will make anything of what I am about to do," the Admiral had written. It was no sacrifice, but rather something he was personally "anxious to do." He was no radio operator, Byrd admitted, so the radio at Advance Base would "probably fail. This should be no cause for concern." By implication, if Richard Byrd at Advance Base fell into peril unknown to his companions at Little America, the problem would be his, not theirs.[5]

On the evening of March 16, 1934, nine men left Little America

Dogs made the difference
(*This one's name was Shackleton.*) *Not until the Second Byrd Antarctic Expedition (1933–35) was motorized ground transport able to compete with sledge dogs—and anyhow, "divertingly maddening as dogs can be, they offer certain compensations not possessed by internal combustion engines"* (Appalachia, *June 15, 1958, p. 135*).

in four tractors, pulling sledges loaded with the "Mountain House" and the other equipment that Admiral Byrd would need to establish himself at Bolling Advance Weather Base, plus survival gear for themselves should the caravan break down on the way. "Limousine exploring," the dog sledgers scoffingly called it, but it had its own brand of hardship. Spending four hours with a blowtorch to thaw out the tough, rubbery stuff into which crankcase and transmission oil congealed at fifty below, or cleaning out a plugged gas line with "the cold gasoline all over the hands and handling cold metal barehanded," were surely miseries comparable with unsnarling fractious huskies' tangled lines. It was, moreover, an experience with which homebodies back in the States could emotionally identify. Few Americans at that time had even ridden in, let alone flown, an airplane; fewer still had driven sledge dogs. But most inhabitants of the region north of what would some day be called the Sun Belt had some notion at least of what it was like to struggle with a stalled car on a dark winter morning on the way to work.

On the largest of the tractors, which was intended to pull 50 percent of the payload—about 16,000 pounds—Pete Demas had rigged an ingenious safety device: 60 foot lines attached to the right and left steering levers and to the clutch, then let out through small holes at the rear of the cab. On dubious terrain the driver could thus walk well behind his vehicle and operate it by "remote control." At 9 A.M. the next morning, after an all-night drive, as they entered the heavily crevassed area that Innes-Taylor's dog sledgers had earlier found and marked, Demas got a chance to test his invention. "We were going along approaching the markings of the crevasses," he wrote in his diary for March 17, "when all of a sudden I felt the rear end of the Cletrac drop 2 ft. from under us." Stopping the tractor with its engine running, Demas got out with Tinglof to find the three loaded 12 foot sledges poised at the edge of a 3 foot crevasse; "the light disappeared in its black depths."

The driver went back to his machine, threw the clutch out with the lever he had made for that purpose, and shifted into high. Tinglof held the clutch out for him while Demas dismounted from the tractor, took over the ropes to the steering levers, and loosened the clutch rope. "The governor opened the throttle, the engine roared with an even powerful beat and the machine and sleds started moving forward. The sleds dipped their front end[s] down and then up again on the opposite bank. We drove with the remote control until we were across the bad area," breaking through two other such crevasses, and without further incident caught up with the advance party at Fifty-Mile Depot at dark, just in time for a hot pemmican hoosh. So far, so good. Next day, however, the lead tractor—a Citroën driven by Harold June—hit another crevasse and broke through, heeling over at an angle of 45°. The following day (the 19th) at midnight the rest of the party caught up with the Citroën and camped in a 40-mile per hour gale. "I didn't dare stop the Cletrac due to the crank not operating," Demas noted, so they let that tractor's engine idle all night. At 8 A.M., as they made ready to move out, "I went to give it the gas," he reported, and the big Cletrac promptly gave up the ghost.[6]

Half their carrying power was thus knocked out at one stroke. That fact settled where Advance Base had to be placed: no farther south than 100-Mile Depot, 123 statute miles from Little America at Latitude 80° 8' South, Longitude 163° 57' West. With the sledges rearranged so that the portable shack sections would get there first, the remaining three tractors moved on, leaving the less essential part of the load to be relayed later. Drivers Pete Demas and Joe Hill stayed with the broken-down Cletrac, still doggedly tinkering. After two days of hard labor and ingenious improvisation they got the Cletrac's engine to run for a few seconds. "Encouraged by its firing we cranked until we could not turn it over any more," Demas wrote in his diary on the night of March 21. "We were all in." Afterward, aggravatingly, they could not get a decent night's rest. In a bag that had been wet and iced since they left Fifty-Mile Depot, sleep was only to be had in short spells,

Demas later wrote, and "Every morning I would take a fistful of ice from under the zippers of my sleeping bag."

Meanwhile the rest of the tractor party reached the site chosen for Advance Base, where they pitched their tents. They were joined there by Alan Innes-Taylor's Southern Sledging Party, stopping on its homeward way toward Little America. On the morning of the 22nd all hands "set to work in frozen boots and ice-covered parkas," hollowing out a foundation in the Ice Shelf surface to hold the house that Ivor Tinglof and Paul Siple had constructed back in Boston. After several hours of strenuous digging the men heard an airplane engine's drone. "A few minutes later Byrd comfortably stepped onto the barrier, after an hour's flight from Little America," and asked Siple how the shack was coming. "Slowly," the frostbitten former Scout replied.

Impatient to take off lest the intense cold stop his engine, airplane pilot W. H. Bowlin was soon airborne again. The plane flew back over the broken-down Cletrac; Pete Demas, still hoping to get it started, was out of sight underneath his machine. More slowly, Harold June with two of the tractors and five men were rolling in the same direction, to fetch in the rest of the load. That left Siple, Tinglof, and Carl Petersen, together with Innes-Taylor's dog sledgers and Admiral Byrd, to set about bolting and spiking together the prenumbered sections of the shack itself—not an especially complicated job, had they not had to do it at sixty-one below. The shack was still unroofed when the early autumn night rushed over them at 5 P.M. Pressure lanterns died as the kerosene in them froze; flashlights faded away as their batteries stopped working. At 1 A.M., by the feeble light of two gasoline torches, the workers finally got a roof over their heads.

Next morning, the 23rd, the beep of the tractor horns awakened them. Demas and June were back with the rest of the supplies. Now that fourteen people were crowded into its 7' x 9' x 13' confines, not to mention the howling sledge dogs who were staked outside, Bolling Advance Weather Base was a more populous

place than it would ever be again. However, the festive farewell
dinner these men had hoped to have with the Admiral before leaving him to his lonely vigil turned out to be a somewhat dispirited
occasion. "The kerosene in the stove had frozen, and the meat
was so rigid we had to thaw it out with blow torches," Alan Innes-
Taylor reported afterward. "We tried to make it lively, but
couldn't quite pull it off." Byrd told them not to worry; once the
frost was out of the Kapok-insulated walls, he insisted, the place
would be warm and comfortable. Innes-Taylor, who until the last
moment before his departure had been watching Paul Siple tinker
with the stove, was not so sure. A coal stove, such as the great
ship-supplied British expeditions had used, would have been ideal,
but to transport enough of that bulky fuel out across the Ice Shelf
to Bolling would have been impossible. Alarmingly, the oil burner
brought from the States for use at Advance Base had proved defec-
tive; it had made two men ill. At the last minute, in one of his
unexpected impulsive decisions, Byrd had had an ordinary coal-
burning caboose stove converted for oil. "Mark my words,"
Innes-Taylor prophetically observed, "that stove is going to give
him trouble."[7]

On Sunday, March 25, Innes-Taylor's dogs got off for Little
America. Later that day "after a fine seal pilaf" Demas, Hill, and
Bernard Skinner left in one of the Citroëns, heading north to work
on the Cletrac again. On Monday, in the middle of a stand-up
lunch, Harold June suggested that it was time for the rest of Byrd's
boarders to be shoving off. As Paul Siple remembered it Admiral
Byrd "stretched out our departure until it was embarrassing,"
calling after them "Good-by and good-by and good-by." Then,
anticlimactically, one mile out from Advance Base, June's radiator
froze. Hearing the sound of their tractor treads returning so soon
"gave me a nasty turn," Byrd recalled in his book *Alone,* "because I was desperately anxious to have them on their way to Little
America." This was on the face of it a statesmanlike worry; the
big Cletrac's breakdown had demonstrated how vulnerable to the

Antarctic climate the tractors really were, and the last sunset before the months-long winter night covered Little America was now less than a month away. From Siple's account, however, one might infer that a more personal motive was mixed with the leader's concern. "By the time we pulled out the next day," Siple wrote, "flashes of annoyance crossed his face that we were still there, and his farewell to us was more perfunctory." Those flashes might be read as a sign that by that time Richard Byrd had become anxious to have the Little Americans out of *his* way; that he was eager to begin his adventure alone.

Byrd's diary entry for March 28, 1934, the date on which the roaring, pollution-spewing motor vehicles finally went away, gives an impression of snug contentment. "The tractors are off at last; and at 12:10 noon I commenced my isolation. For more than 200 days I shall see no living thing." The data gathering which was Advance Base's formal *raison d'être* had already begun; "topside on the pole the anemometer cups are gently turning." Within this little world, which four strides would cover in one direction and three in the other, the Admiral affirmed, "the means of a secure and profound existence were all handy." On the same evening in which Byrd was taking that first comfortable inventory Pete Demas and his companions at their trail camp finally and reluctantly gave up on the Cletrac, "due to the lateness of the season and the life of 10 men," and headed for home. Arriving at Little America on March 29, Demas slept late and took it easy next day (Good Friday), and then in his usual methodical fashion wrote up a report on the trip, concluding with a summary of all that had gone wrong with the Citroëns. "They will all be remedied," he vowed, "before the tractors head out for the trail again."[8]

On Saturday, March 31, over KFZ, Paul Siple described the shack he had just helped to assemble for Admiral Byrd. "Is there any danger from carbon monoxide?" asked announcer Murphy, functioning as an interviewer. "That, too, has been prepared for," Siple replied:

A ventilating shaft sticking up in the snow is carried down the side of the building, passing under foot, and arises in the center of the room to within a foot of the ceiling. That keeps a continuous flow of cold air in the room. Admiral Byrd will put out the fire every night before he turns in.

MURPHY: By the way, Paul, is he a good cook?

SIPLE: I wouldn't call him a good one; but you don't have to be down here. All you need is a fire and a can-opener.

The isolation itself was no cause for alarm, Murphy smoothly explained. With his books, music, writing, and meteorology, Byrd did not think his stay on the Barrier would be "the empty life people imagine it to be." Moreover, the leader "was interested in the psychological problems involved in solitude as complete as this. He comes from a family line of solitary men."

Next day, Easter Sunday, Byrd had to make his first radio schedule with Little America. Two hours beforehand he lugged in the gasoline-driven generator from its niche in the food tunnel (it could not be run in the shack because of the fumes), and set it down beside the stove to thaw. Then he filled it with a gasoline and oil mixture, carried it back to its alcove, rope-cranked it like an outboard motor, and ran back to his desk. Promptly at 10 A.M. as he put on his headphone the Admiral heard John Dyer speaking on the agreed wavelength, 100 meters: "KFZ calling KFY." Byrd responded, slowly, in Morse code (his equipment could not send voice), and at the end of that first 20 minute contact Charlie Murphy told him: "Dyer rates you D minus on your debut." The schedules continued, and Byrd learned to write out his longer messages beforehand, vertically down the page "Chinese fashion" with each letter opposite its dot-and-dash equivalent. "It's really comforting to talk this way with Little America," he wrote on April 15, "and yet in my heart I wish very much that I didn't have to have the radio. It connects me with places where speeches are made and with the importunities of the outer world." When he wavered from this proud stand against civilization Byrd immediately regretted it. "Curiosity tempted me to ask Little America for the stock market quotations," he confided to his diary on May 6. "It was a ghastly mistake."[9]

"I was the inspector of snowstorms and the aurora, the night watchman, and father confessor to myself." The words are cribbed from Thoreau, and the flavor of *Alone*—before Byrd's near-fatal accident—is that of *Walden*. However, the relatively mild setting of the limpid pond next to Henry David Thoreau's hovel did not begin to compare with the starkness which surrounded that little house on the Ross Ice Shelf. Thoreau when the going got rough could hike a few miles into Concord for a home-cooked meal, and if he got tired of the whole Walden experiment he could simply quit. Richard Byrd, tied to civilization only by the tenuous link of radio, was stuck where he was. Furthermore, no addition could be made through any effort of his own to the supplies the tractor crews had so casually dumped in his snow tunnels. The Admiral could not cut a hole in the ice to go fishing (nobody succeeded in drilling all the way through the Ross Shelf until the Antarctic summer of 1978!), nor could he walk out into the woods to dig for roots and gather berries. The cozy relationship with uncorrupted nature that is celebrated in the Thoreau tradition assumes a *biological* congruence between the person and the environment—and that, at Latitude 80° 8′ S., Longitude 163° 57′ W., would have been an illusion.

Actually, Richard Byrd in his shack was no more "back to nature" than is an astronaut in his space capsule. The glass-enclosed meteorological register that revolved near the foot of Admiral Byrd's bunk, and the radio transmitter and receiver across the room, were the fine spearpoints of a massive, intricate technological culture which Byrd himself admitted he did not understand very well even though he had been flying its airplanes for years: "the fact that I knew none too much about them," he said of his various electronic devices, "only intensified my humility." The complexity of that culture was social as well as technological. It is ironic that Byrd's contemporary and rival Charles Lindbergh, when first he wrote about his own solitary exploit, produced a book titled *We;* whereas Byrd, even after two lengthy residences in Antarctica amongst a variety of interesting and, in their way, sophisticated people, summed up his Antarctic experience most definitively in a book titled *Alone.*

Regularly for more than two months Richard Byrd took his weather observations, re-inked his recording devices, read his books, played his phonograph, took his walks (weather permitting), and philosophized. Here, he decided one afternoon as he "paused to listen to the silence" at $-57°$ F $(-49°$ C) were "the imponderable forces of the cosmos functioning gently, harmoniously, soundlessly." At other times, however, the stillness concealed a potential for terror: "Sometimes it seems to have that curious, fatal quality of the silence that grips you when an airplane engine suddenly cuts out and in a breathless calm you swing over for a dive with a dead stick." Those gently functioning cosmic forces could effortlessly sweep life away; "this," Byrd acknowledged as he watched the sun sinking into the Antarctic night, "is the way the world will look to the last man when it dies."

The blow fell on May 31, a Thursday. Byrd was talking with Little America on their regular radio schedule. Out in the snow tunnel the engine started skipping. "Wait," he signalled to Dyer. Twenty minutes later, by Murphy's account, "we heard him call and slowly spell out: 'See you Sunday.' And he signed off." In the interim he had unhooked the lantern, gone into the tunnel, bent over the generator engine's carburetor to tinker with the needle valve, straightened up—and dropped unconscious, felled by carbon monoxide. Revived by the cold and the cleaner air near the floor he had drowsily crawled back into the shack and managed to sign off.[10]

What he did next he did not remember for certain. "The notes which I jotted down a few days afterward insist this stranger reeling in the dark acted with the utmost deliberation. Perhaps so."

He staggered back to the tunnel and shut the poison-breathing motor off, then got into his sleeping bag against the creeping cold. He could not stay there; the stove was out and Thursday was the day when the tank had to be filled. Somehow he accomplished the task, without which all was lost; somehow—incredibly—he kept the meteorological instruments going. He brewed up a thermos of hot water and condensed milk and managed to keep some of it down. Through the fog of pain and disorientation he became aware that the stove itself must be emitting invisible fumes, in which case Byrd was damned if he did, damned if he didn't; if he ran the stove enough to warm his shack, he would suffocate, but if he shut it off very long he would freeze. As he closed the valve on the fuel tank the Admiral blacked out again. Waking up on the floor he gave way for a moment to self-pitying despair—a mood this man, brought up to believe "that sickness was somehow humiliating, something to be kept hidden," and that a Virginia gentleman "never gives way to his feelings," would remember afterward with shame. That mood, however, did not last long. Out of those psychic reserves that are there for life's deepest emergencies Byrd pulled himself together and wrote letters to his wife, his mother, his children, and his associates at Little America. For the first time he understood, more than intellectually, Scott's final diary entry "For God's sake look after our people." In his own journal after three eloquently blank pages the Admiral wrote on June 2 "I'm afraid it is the end."

On June 3, however, he kept his regular radio schedule with Little America. Keeping it was "nearly fatal," he confessed next day. "It drained my last bit of reserve." Unable to carry the forty-pound engine in to thaw he dragged it along the tunnel floor, inch by inch, moving on his hands and knees. When Dyer's crisp voice came in it would have been simple enough for Byrd to send out an SOS—but he did not. Instead he sent some weather data that he had written out before the disaster, and answered his colleagues' current queries with "yes," "no," and "will think over."

"Thank God, it takes only the pressure of a finger to operate the key," he confided to his diary. "Code won't betray me." He would not involve the Little Americans in his downfall by asking them to risk a rescue mission in the Antarctic night.[11]

On May 30, one day before the accident, Paul Siple had been telling the world over KFZ that Byrd was "pretty well equipped for contending with almost anything." Conceding that "his stove is the weakest point in his defense against cold," Siple had optimistically reassured the listeners: "You can be sure nothing will happen to it." Unaware of the bleak real-life drama running its course 123 miles to the south, therefore, KFZ continued to serve up a mixture of entertainment and schmaltz. While Morgan's Knights in the background hummed "Yes, Sir, That's My Baby," on the June 6 broadcast, Navy aerial photographer J. S. Pelter declared: "I was sure glad to hear that my kid won first prize at a baby show. It goes to show that you can't beat the Navy." Meanwhile, across the Ross Ice Shelf that same day, Byrd in his sleeping bag was writing by candlelight in his journal "This is a ghastly way to go out. . . . It is human to want to live." If he were to give "just a hint back there at Little America, they'd move heaven and earth to get out here," the expedition leader was aware. "But I know better." He acknowledged a feeling of remorse for putting his own family through this, when they eventually learned his fate. "But life makes you pay in heavy risk for a rare experience."

Carefully the stricken Admiral nursed himself along, leaving the sleeping bag on brief forays to fetch in food and fuel from the tunnel. With the stove turned off for fourteen hours each day to minimize the monoxide fumes, the awesome polar cold hunched in closer. "Drift has sealed the skylights," Byrd wrote on June 8, "and a film of ice is creeping across the one nearest the bunk." Having extinguished the pressure lamps, which he thought might also be polluting the air, Byrd was now in darkness almost all the time; "no medieval dungeon could be more dismal." On June 10 he summoned the strength to go out and climb the anemometer pole, to clear the cups of accumulated ice; that noon he serviced his recording instruments, inked the pens, changed and dated the sheets, regulated and set the clocks. "How pitilessly resolute and faithful they are," he wrote; "clicking day and night, demanding a replenishment I cannot give myself." In the cold stillness they seemed to be saying "If we stop, you stop; if you stop, we stop." [12]

The June 14 radio schedule brought a flash of hope, although Byrd did not realize its implications at the time. Thomas Poulter, delighted with the throngs of meteors he was able to count in the clear Antarctic atmosphere, wanted to send a meteor party thirty or forty miles out along the southward trail. Only once before had anybody undertaken a major journey in Antarctica during the midwinter night: the penguin egg hunt chronicled by Apsley Cherry-Garrard of the Scott expedition—and Cherry-Garrard without exaggeration had titled his account of that venture *The Worst Journey in the World*. Such a trip in 1934, however, need not be so bad. Pete Demas had been overhauling the tractors, replacing their canvas tops with stout wooden bodies and equipping them with bunks and stoves. (Wood, in treeless Little America, was of course in short supply; Charlie Murphy one day saw Demas and J. H. Von der Wall sneaking through the radio shack with one large piece "which I was horrified to identify as the door—the only door—to our only toilet. An hour later, crescent moon and all, it was being nailed into the sides of Tractor No. 3.") "Why not push through to Advance Base?" Murphy suggested to Poulter. The meteor watchers would have shelter there, as well as a longer baseline for their observations, "and—well, you might also learn how the Admiral is making out. He isn't very communicative these days."

They outlined the project to Byrd on the June 28 schedule. Tractor Number One had just made a successful trial run through Amundsen Arm and up onto the Barrier. If a tractor party left Little America during the first clear spell between July 23 and 28 there would be a full moon dead ahead to the South, augmented around noon by some twilight glow behind them from the sunken sun. "Well, what do you think of it?" Poulter asked Byrd. The Admiral's hand hesitated on the key. "They want to come here on their own account," he told himself, "and you need have no shame." Yet ultimately, Byrd, knew, he *was* responsible. Finally the Admiral asked Poulter "if he were making [the trip] for science alone," and on that basis granted tentative approval, pending further trial runs. "Yet, even as I said this," the leader admitted afterward, "I knew deep in my heart that I should never have the will to refuse him. I had been through too much to cast aside any straw." Byrd's calorie intake, by his own count, had lately been averaging a scant 1200 a day. In Antarctica that was nowhere near enough to sustain the flame.[13]

Far from Advance Base and from Little America the complexly interlocked world of finance and public relations continued to make its mundane demands. On the last day of June, which Byrd confessed had been "the longest month I have ever known," Charlie Murphy read a message from the Admiral to the National Education Association, then assembled at Washington, D.C. for its annual convention. "It gives me real pleasure to greet the teachers of America from this solitary outpost on the Ross Ice Barrier," declared Byrd—or Murphy, who may well have written these lines himself. "Even in my isolation I am not unaware of the many problems that confront you," the message went on, with never a hint of the Admiral's physical and moral torment. "Bits of news trickle in from the outside. I know what a difficult task it has been to maintain the schools . . . during a period when the full resources of the nation are required to keep its head above waters." Then, no doubt also largely for the benefit of NEA, Station KFZ broadcast sample classroom moments from "Antarctic University" in Little America's mess hall; for example, Alan Innes-Taylor lecturing a class on trail operations:

Never travel over a snow bridge along the length of a crevasse. This is a most dangerous position. Speed and absolute control of your dogs are then essential. To save your team you must be ready to throw your sled in a diagonal position with a moment's notice, and then throw yourself onto firm surface.

Then the broadcast switched over to Amory Waite's class for radio operators:

The important thing is to send clearly. Speed doesn't count. Be sure to start those hand-generators half a minute before you start sending. Give your tubes time to warm up.

Then KFZ cut to Kennett L. Rawson's course on navigation:

On account of the proximity of the Magnetic Pole, the compass is extremely sluggish and reluctant to settle down to point in a fixed direction. . . . Therefore the trail navigator must watch his compass like a hawk.

Vicarious thrills, these, for armchair explorers beside their radios whose own lives did not depend on knowing how to manage sledge dogs or send Morse code or lay a compass course. But there was nothing vicarious in what was going on out at Advance base. "From the first part of July," Murphy was to write later, "every time I sat beside Radio Engineer Dyer and started to call KFY Advance Base on 100 meters, it was with a foreboding of disaster"— and with good reason. On July 5 Byrd's radio generator broke down, and he had to resort to hand-cranking the emergency transmitter—which he barely had strength to do. On the next radio schedule it suddenly struck Murphy "that Byrd was sending awfully slowly, even for him. The sending was ragged. The messages filtered in in groups of three or four words. In between Byrd would spell: 'Wait.' We'd wait five minutes for him to come on the air again." Byrd's heart was thumping; his head had turned dizzy; his arms were giving out. When he finally signed off he slumped over the generator head.

For a week he struggled to keep up those tyrannous schedules—
and for that week nobody at Little America was able to hear him.
On July 15 the anxious listeners at last picked him up in mid-mes-
sage. Byrd was foot-cranking by that time, but he kept up the pre-
tense that all was well; and on their side his colleagues concealed
their own growing anxiety. "The whole business sounds fantas-
tic," Byrd admitted four years later in his book *Alone*. "I was
lying, because there was nothing else for me to do. But at Little
America they were lying, too. The difference was that *they* were
coming to suspect that I was lying and even as they divined that I
was concocting a fiction to mislead them, so *they* in turn concocted
their own brand to mislead me." Their fiction, according to Byrd,
was their insistence that Poulter and his men were coming to Advance Base purely for its convenience in carrying out their astronomical mission. Had they presented it to Byrd frankly as a rescue
journey, they reasoned, he would have felt he had to veto it! "No
man is an island, entire of itself," but Richard E. Byrd—even
after all he had gone through—was still striving to be just such an
island.[14]

"At 2:20 of the afternoon of July 20th," according to Murphy's
account, "No. 1 tractor, a grotesque, misshapen monstrosity, rum-
bled out of the camp, its exhaust drooling plumes of vapor," and
pointed toward the south. "The headlights made deep furrows into
the night, and Poulter, looking like a Mongol in a yellow face
mask, sat astride the hood, playing a searchlight over the trail."
The temperature, sagging toward the winter's low, touched
$-75°F(-59°C)$, and at Fifty-Mile Depot the trail through the crevasses was blown over and invisible. Poulter turned back. On
August 4 they tried again with tractor #2, but the clutch slipped
when they were 23 miles out. A radio schedule with Advance Base
took place while they were making ready for a third attempt, and
in it the elaborate game Byrd and his officers had been playing
with each other began to break down. "Listen, Dick, we don't
believe you any more," Murphy snapped. "Are you ill, or hurt?"

Sastrugi
These wave-like ridges of hard snow formed by the wind, are one of the distinctive features of ski travel (on foot or by airplane) in Antarctica.

"Please don't ask me to crank any more," the Admiral responded. "I'm okay, Charlie."

On August 8, at 1:20 A.M., tractor #3 got under way; and on the 9th the lone explorer out on the ice at last admitted his common humanity and called for help. Bill Haines, in charge at Little America as third-in-command, promptly sent a radiogram off to the leader of the trail party:

> Byrd today said quote Bill, get them here fast unquote I'm afraid he can't hold out much longer stop make all possible haste even if it means taking chances stop other tractor repaired and standing by and available if you require it stop delay now may have grievous consequences.
>
> Haines

On August 10 second-in-command Tom Poulter, sitting on the tractor cab roof with the compass on his lap, saw the blue glare of a magnesium flare; hours later he picked up a tiny light winking a point off his port bow, and at the last rise before Advance Base came "a livid burst of gasoline" from a whole bucketfull ignited by Byrd. The tractor stopped its forward crunch. "Into the head-light's glare a figure in furs walked very slowly. 'Come on down, fellows,' Byrd said. 'I have a bowl of hot soup waiting for you.' As Poulter jumped off to shake his hand, Byrd stumbled and collapsed." Shortly Little America heard Byrd's hand-cranked transmitter come on the air. "The fumes from the stove got REB down about June first," Poulter reported from the shack. "Please don't publish as it would be hard on his wife."

"Bill we cannot realize what REB has been thru," Poulter radioed from Advance Base two days later. "He has stuck to his ideals of the polar code and has played the game gallantly. . . . I cannot yet tell how long it will be before REB is able to travel but it will be several months before he is strong again." The sacrificial gallantry was undeniable, even though the ideals of a polar code might well have prompted another kind of leader to decide before-hand, in the interest of the mission and of its other members, not to play such a game at all. The hard question of whether Byrd *should* have gone alone to Advance Base—a question which his-torically must still be asked—was drowned at the time in a wave of sentiment. Piecing the story together and airing it on August 15 over KFZ, Charlie Murphy closed the program with praise for any-one who would do what Byrd and his rescuers had just done, "in these troubled times when old loyalties are in disgrace . . . when thinking men feel that it is bother enough just to live." Under Murphy's words Morgan's Knights had been humming "Carry Me Back to Old Virginny;" as he finished speaking they swelled up and bridged into "Auld Lang Syne."[15]

8

New Dealers and
Cold Warriors
in the Great
White South

*The discovery of lands unknown to civilization, even when
coupled with the formal taking of possession, does not support
a valid claim of sovereignty unless the discovery is followed
by actual settlement of the discovered country.*
　　　　　　　　　　　　　　　—*Charles Evans Hughes*

*Men cannot fight each other in the Antarctic because the one
universal enemy is the cold.*
　　　　　　　　　　　　　　　—*Richard E. Byrd*

"The snow picked up by the mumbling wind fled in level,
blinding lines across the face of the buried camp. If a man stepped
out of the tunnels that connected each of the camp buildings beneath the surface, he'd be lost in ten paces. Out there, the slim,
black finger of the radio mast lifted 300 feet into the air, and at its
peak was the clear night sky . . . under the licking, curling man-
tle of the aurora." Indoors, the odors of melted seal blubber,
musty wet furs, harness dressing, machine oil, "and the animal,
not-unpleasant smell of dogs, diluted by time, hung in the air."
　　The descriptive language resembles that of Russell Owen or
Larry Gould. The sounds—"the muted whoosh of the pressure
lamp," "the mingled gargles and bugle calls of a dozen men
sleeping," "the occasional rustle of falling coal in the copper-
bellied stove"—are authentically those of an Antarctic wintering-
over. The names—Connant, Van Wall, a New Englander named
Caldwell, a sledge man named Ralsen—have unmistakable echoes
from Little America I and II. Even the homely tale of the theft of a
crescent-moon door, to build into the wall of a tractor-cab, is told
again. But this is a work of the imagination, "Who Goes There?",

by John W. Campbell, Jr., and it first appeared in the August 1938 issue of *Astounding Science-Fiction*. Campbell's imagined explorers have found, buried in the Antarctic ice, a creature from outer space that was quick-frozen when its spaceship crashed near the South Magnetic Pole long ago. Thawed out, it revives, and promptly shows a horrifying ability to pass itself off as an exact duplicate of any human being in the camp, down to the details of how a person lights a pipe or turns a phrase. Is that entity sitting on the bunk across from you your dearest friend or your deadliest enemy? *Who goes there?* [1]

In the late 1930s this was a question metaphorically well worth the asking. Admiral Byrd's Second Antarctic Expedition had left for Little America in 1933, at the bottom of the Depression; it returned in 1935 to find ''the fear of wings over the world.'' Nations on our shrinking planet, Byrd wrote in 1937, were ''like so many families crowded into a small apartment house,'' and one of them starting a fire could burn all of them down. Not even icy Antarctica was immune from territorial urges far more sinister than the sporting, and basically harmless, national competitions that had formerly made a mountain range Norwegian, a glacier British, or a penguin species French. ''Who goes there?'' Explorers, unrolling the farthest edges of Earth's maps and planting flags to mark for others what they had found? Or conquerors, staking down No Trespassing signs at the outer limits of empires? Scientists, wresting secrets for the benefit of all from the cold, dark land? Or soldiers, learning from their harsh Antarctic environment the techniques they might need for fighting each other in future wars over the poles?

On December 17, 1938, six weeks after the conclusion of the Munich crisis, Dr. Alfred Ritscher departed by ship from Hamburg ''to secure for Germany her share in the approaching division of the Antarctic among world powers.'' Germans had been in the Antarctic before, and maps of the southernmost continent remembered those earlier visits in names like the Filchner Ice Shelf and

Kaiser Wilhelm Land. But this was a new Germany. The four cata-pult-launched seaplanes which roared out from Dr. Ritscher's superbly equipped ship toward the ice-cliffed Princess Astrid and Crown Princess Martha Coasts in Queen Maud Land between January 19 and February 15, 1939, pioneered in photogrammetric mapping, which has since become a basic and invaluable technique in polar exploration. But the planes also dropped long, pointed metal shafts, stabilized with fins bearing the national insignia. The heroic Nazi nightmare thus reached literally to the ends of the earth, in a scene straight out of the propaganda film *Triumph of the Will:* spears falling like meteorites out of the sky to plant themselves in the ice, each with its swastika waving in the chill Antarctic wind. To ensure the claim, a party went ashore to raise the flag. They greeted one curious penguin with a "Heil Hitler!"—which, as one of the shore party afterward admitted, "did not make much of an impression."[2]

King Haakon VII, the long-lived (1872–1957) sovereign under whose flag Amundsen had marched to the pole, tried to forestall the intrusion by formally proclaiming (January 14, 1939) that that part of Antarctica belonged to Norway. Ignoring the old king—whose homeland was destined the following year to be overrun by Hitler's legions—the Germans named the area New Swabia (Neu-Schwabenland). It would be developed, the expedition's formal report declared, in accordance with "the economic interests of Greater Germany, . . . unhindered by the rights of sovereignty of other nations." The Soviet Russians, hitherto silent on such matters, also took exception to the Norse monarch's claim because it included Peter I Island, which had been discovered 118 years earlier by Faddei Bellingshausen under the banner of the Tsar. Suddenly America's "open door" policy toward Antarctica, set forth by Secretary of State Charles Evans Hughes in 1924, seemed outdated by the rush of events.[3]

Even before the Ritscher Antarctic venture, the United States government had begun to edge away from its former hands-off policy. Lincoln Ellsworth, who had briefly revisited Little America after Byrd's departure in 1935—locating a stovepipe and letting himself in through a skylight, after a successful trans-Antarctic flight which had had to land, out of gas, twelve miles short of the Ross Shelf's edge—set off again for the Antarctic shortly before the German expedition got underway. On August 30, 1938, Secretary of State Cordell Hull cabled to Ellsworth through the U.S. consulate in Capetown some advice as to how the millionaire explorer's new expedition to Antarctica could assert American claims to territories theretofore undiscovered and unexplored. Lincoln Ellsworth, flying on January 11, 1939, over what later was to become known as the American Highland, with due formality dropped a brass cylinder which contained a message claiming the area "for my country, so far as this act allows."

Meanwhile in Washington, at FDR's instigation, the State Department had been working on an Antarctic policy study. Roosevelt approved it on January 7, 1939, just a few days before Ellsworth's flight and just a few days before the German expedition slipped through the ice pack. Adopting a suggestion initially made by Richard Black, who had been with Byrd's second expedition, Secretary Hull—after consulting, in the government's usual ponderous inter-agency fashion, with people from Interior, Treasury, Navy, and War—recommended on February 13 that the United States establish and maintain permanent, year-round settlements in Antarctica. On July 7, 1939, the President created an executive committee for a brand-new government agency, the United States Antarctic Service.[4]

Congress, although at that time a bit balky toward nonmilitary federal spending, came through with $350,000—the first tangible support (aside from the nominal cost of striking a few medals) that it had given to Antarctic exploration since the great Wilkes Expedition of one hundred years before. "Because the proper people were not consulted at the time the budget for the expedition was set up," however—in the opinion of geologist and senior scientist

Laurence M. Gould at Geological Party cairn *December 21, 1929. "We are beyond or east of the 150th meridian and therefore in the name of Commander Richard Evelyn Byrd claim this as a part of Marie Byrd Land, a dependency or possession of the United States." Between 1929 and 1939 the U.S. Government had a change of heart concerning the validity of such claims, and during the opening months of World War II it actively encouraged them.*

F. Alton Wade—"a woefully inadequate sum of money was set aside for scientific equipment and for the expenses of the scientific department." From lack of funds the entire field of oceanography, for example—crucial for understanding Antarctica—had to be abandoned. Government bureaus, scientific foundations, and businessmen pitched in to help close the gap. The War Department contributed $100,000 worth of supplies and equipment, the Navy $200,000; private individuals in Milwaukee and Chicago provided a seaplane. Richard Byrd, who had been fund-raising for a proposed privately sponsored third Antarctic Expedition, brought in $240,000 for the new government undertaking. By November of 1939, while the first magnetic mines to be used in World War II were wreaking destruction upon Allied and neutral shipping in northern seas, two ships—the oil-burning wooden ice ship *North Star,* on loan from the Interior Department's Alaska run, and Admiral Byrd's ancient *Bear of Oakland,* newly equipped with a diesel engine and commissioned in the Navy under the more terse name U.S.S. *Bear*—were on their way to Antarctica.[5]

It is reported that when this enterprise was first proposed President Roosevelt said: "Fine, but let's get Byrd to run the program." As was typical of that President, the decision was not as offhand as it sounded. Franklin Roosevelt had been on familiar terms with Richard Byrd for quite some while. When he was governor of New York in 1929, FDR had sent a chatty message to Commander Byrd on one of the regular Saturday night broadcasts to Little America over Schenectady's radio station WGY: "Had some nice talks with your brother Harry [at that time governor of Virginia]. He is one of the best, and we need more people like him in public life." As President in 1934, at the time of the Advance Base vigil, Roosevelt had told the lone explorer by radio that he hoped "the night was not too cold or the wind too strong for an occasional promenade in the dark." In 1935, when the Second Expedition returned, FDR had been on hand at the Washington Navy Yard to be photographed shaking the Admiral's hand.[6]

More recently the presiding genius of the New Deal had had his differences with the Admiral's staunchly conservative brother. Harry Flood Byrd, as a Senator from Virginia, in 1937 had vigorously opposed the administration's plan to pack the Supreme

Court, and such political disagreements were fated to continue. Harry Byrd's name would in fact be placed in nomination at the Democratic National Convention of 1944, against Roosevelt's—an act tantamount in those days to *lèse-majesté*. Divergencies of this kind, however, do not appear to have carried over from the banks of the Potomac to the shores of the Bay of Whales. In his formal instructions to the commanding officer of the United States Antarctic Service on November 25, 1939, Roosevelt was generous; he was naming Admiral Byrd to this command, the President explained, "because of your experience and brilliant achievements in polar exploration and because of the confidence which the people of the United States have in you and in your qualities of leadership." That word "confidence" may be the key to the Roosevelt–Byrd relationship. Just as Franklin Roosevelt had dramatized for Americans the struggle against economic depression, so Richard Byrd had dramatized for them the struggle against Antarctic darkness and cold.

The Rooseveltian rhetoric in those instructions, however, was much diluted with Bureaucratese. Sprinkled with "you wills" and "it is desireds," the document compares in tone with the minutely niggling orders the intrepid Admiral Bellingshausen received in 1818 from the Imperial Russian Admiralty. Byrd himself was told to return to the United States in the spring (Antarctic autumn) of 1940, as soon as possible after the American bases had been established, because his presence at home was "essential for other duties in connection with the administration of The United States Antarctic Service." No more wintering-over parties for him; this expedition was going to be run from Washington. "The free and easy days of the first two Byrd expeditions" to Antarctica, as Paul Siple remembered them, were over.

This development was not without precedent on the nineteenth-century North American frontier. The cowboy on the long drive had often been grubstaked by outside investors; the free-wandering fur trader had generally functioned in fact as an employee of John

Jacob Astor or the Hudson's Bay Company. The important difference was that the stockholders' ultimate clout had rarely been *personally* felt by the man in the saddle or on the trail. For Byrd's tractor operators and dog drivers this was no longer the case; under radio supervision from the homeland, expedition members who at Little America I or II would have been considered doughty explorers had descended to the status of civil servants.

Particularly galling to the civilian scientists of the new expedition, most of whom were being paid no more than $10 a month (an army draftee's base pay in 1940 was $21!), was Roosevelt's order that Byrd at the end of the expedition "require from every person under your command the surrender of all journals, diaries, memoranda, remarks, writings, charts, drawings, sketches, paintings, photographs, films, plates, as well as all specimens of every kind." These people were making considerable sacrifices in order to go to Antarctica, and upon their return to the States they expected to "publish," as academicians say. When Admiral Byrd flew out to the Canal Zone to join the *North Star,* on November 30, 1939, carrying this controversial order, it provoked an uproar; "for a while," Paul Siple later recalled, "I expected a full-scale mutiny over this unfair and stupid ruling." Exactly the same ruling had beset and divided the Wilkes Antarctic Expedition—a melancholy sign that governments, even in a century's time, find it hard to learn anything.[7]

The plan was to establish one of the American settlements, East Base, on one of the islands or bays of the Antarctic Peninsula (on the white continent's Western Hemisphere side) and the other, West Base, on terrain more familiar to Little Americans—the eastern shore of the Ross Sea. From these outposts exploring parties would fly or sledge out to yet unknown or unclaimed regions, where they were encouraged to "take any appropriate steps such as dropping written claims from airplanes, depositing such writing in cairns, et cetera, which might assist in supporting a sovereignty claim by the United States Government."

A third party was intended to rove independently on board a

Snow Cruiser, built at the Pullman shops near Chicago with the cooperation of 70 manufacturing firms. This was a mighty machine 55 feet long, 20 feet wide, and 15 feet high, atop whose separately powered 10-foot, 3-ton wheels would ride sleeping quarters, a kitchen, darkroom, radio room, laboratory, and machine shop. It would carry enough food for a year, enough diesel fuel for 5000 miles, and 1000 gallons of aviation gasoline for the small Beechcraft airplane which would ride on its roof on skis. Rumbling across Antarctica like something Frank R. Paul might have painted for the cover of a 1930s-era science fiction magazine (on descending slopes it could even retract its wheels and toboggan downhill!) the Snow Cruiser was expected to crunch its way to the South Pole and winter there. Alas for human ambition. The vehicle sank into the snow under its own thirty tons (approximately the weight of one brontosaurus) and had to be parked at West Base for the duration of the expedition's stay.

The very location of West Base had been dictated by the Snow Cruiser's supposed needs. Byrd and Siple had checked out other possible sites, at Kainan Bay and Okuma Bay, places originally discovered and named by a Japanese expedition under Lieutenant Choku Shirase that had been in Antarctica back in the time of Amundsen and Scott. Both sites had lacked suitable bay ice for unloading the Snow Cruiser, however, and the *North Star* had instead docked at the Bay of Whales. Happily, no "Misery Trail" faced the immigrant Antarcticans this time; West Base—Little America III—was built only two miles from the ship over a comparatively easy access route. Twenty-nine men, plus the four (led by Alton Wade) who were to have roved across the Antarctic wilds aboard the Snow Cruiser, wintered over at West Base under Paul Siple's command. Twenty-six more, among them Richard Black as base commander and Finn Ronne as transportation engineer, went on to found East Base at Stonington Island, nearer to South America, in the region where Nat Palmer and Faddei Bellingshausen had once ranged.

Little America III stood half a dozen miles north of Little

America I and II, whose larger buildings had caved in too badly to be used again. Living over double floors, between which circulated heat from the galley so that one's feet in the early mornings struck boards that were blessedly ice-free, the third Little Americans dwelt in physical comfort unprecedented in Antarctica. "Wish you could see this camp," Paul Siple radioed to First Little American Victor Czegka back in the States on July 9, 1940. "I know you would enjoy yourself even tho it is a little to[o] civilized x Some men take daily bathes." Although Siple spoke of enjoyment in this radiogram to an old friend, a later memoir suggests that the young leader of West Base was finding his third expedition—despite its greater comfort—much less pleasant than his first two. "Disgusted with many half-thought-out orders dispatched to us from Washington," and "harassed by the amount of paperwork required" for an enterprise that had turned from a private romp into a public institution, the Scout-turned-administrator was not having as much fun at Little America as he had had during its pioneer days.[8]

Despite their limited budget, the third Little Americans pressed forward with a program of science and exploration. The meteorologist at West Base, Arnold Court, made the first radio-balloon soundings of Antarctica's upper air. An International Harvester tractor and an Army tank braved the polar night to get photographs of the aurora, time-synchronized with pictures taken at West Base in an effort to measure (by apparent star displacement), the auroral display's height above the Earth. The movement of the Ross Ice Shelf in the vicinity of Little America III was clocked, at one-third of a mile per year. Paul Siple continued the studies of human adaptation to Antarctic climate which in 1939 had earned him a Clark University Ph.D.; the now well-known concept and term "wind chill," as a danger factor for persons exposed to cold weather, is an invention of Siple's. The youth who had begun his Antarctic sojourns as penguin-skinner, pup-trainer, and general handyman had come a long way.

Flag on Supporting Party Mountain
*"Tomorrow we shall raise our American flag with appropriate
ceremony if that is OK with you"—radiogram from Laurence
Gould to Byrd, December 20, 1929. Members of the Antarctic
Service Expedition (1939–41) took this kind of action on a much
more comprehensive scale.*

As the frigid polar darkness gave way to an Antarctic summer's
perpetual sun, planes, tractor trains, and dog teams fanned out
across the icy land to survey, geologize, and stake claims. (One of
the husky teams was driven by Jack Bursey, who had been among
the First Little Americans eleven years before, and who eventually
was to spend 42 months and three full winters in the Antarctic;
thus does the silent southern land draw its transient inhabitants
back again and again.) Like Gould's men a decade earlier, but on
a much wider scale, the scientist-explorers of the U.S. Antarctic
Service raised flags and placed papers containing their signatures
within cairns. Into bedrock, at the foot of (Ashley) McKinley Peak

in the Ford Range, and elsewhere, they set brass markers furnished by the General Land Office—thereby making the American stamp upon the Antarctic continent as unmistakable as Hitler's two years before. Over at East Base, the American settlers forged ahead with a similar program, inspiring in Finn Ronne in particular the desire to come back to that same area again. And then, suddenly, it all ended.[9]

On March 5, 1940, back in Washington, the House Appropriations Committee in a money-saving mood struck from the Interior Department's budget of approximately $119 million the relatively small sum—$250,000—for which FDR had asked in order to keep East and West Bases in operation for the next fiscal year. Leaving himself an escape hatch as usual, President Roosevelt in his formal orders to Admiral Byrd had included an instruction to work out with his executive committee a contingency plan for evacuating the new American settlements on the Antarctic continent, "in the event that the [U.S. Antarctic] Service is not a continuing project." However, it is unlikely that Roosevelt and Byrd expected their eviction notice to be so rude. "Has Admiral Byrd," committee chairman Jed Johnson of Oklahoma shockingly asked, "some advertising and radio contracts from which he expected to make a fabulous sum of money out of this expedition?"

Navy Lieutenant-Commander R.A.J. English, who had skippered the *Bear of Oakland* on the Second Expedition and who functioned in the U.S. Antarctic Service as executive secretary, publicly denied this unfair and demagogic charge. Polar exploration, as has been noted in previous chapters, had not historically been an enterprise that even paid its own way, let alone made a fortune for the explorers. But this congressional committee, so vigilant over the people's money that it had even struck from that same Interior Department budget an item for the hallowed Jefferson Memorial then being built beside the Potomac, was not about to be put off. The Congress could not be expected to cut farm parity payments and the WPA as it was doing, Representative Johnson argued, "in order to keep the Byrd Expedition at the South Pole for an indefinite period." Furthermore, Chairman Johnson doubted that "the land is worth our trip there to investigate." In vain did Lieutenant-Commander English try to remind the Oklahoma Democrat that the purchase of ice-bound Alaska had similarly been derided in Congress at the time as "Seward's Folly." The U.S. Antarctic Service in 1940 was up against the same mind-set that NASA would encounter in the mid-1970s: why *should* we send a space probe to Pluto or a manned vehicle to Mars? The notion that government funds not spent on "impractical" scientific ventures somehow become available instead for the public welfare can be most beguiling, and when such an attitude is strongly held by a legislator it will brook no argument.

On April 6, 1940, President Roosevelt asked that the cut be restored, and the Senate—as usual less volatile than the House of Representatives—duly put the appropriation for East and West Base back into the bill. Then on April 9 the German war machine rolled into Denmark and Norway, and a month later the Nazi forces attacked the Low Countries. The *Wehrmacht* was literally at the gates of Paris when the Interior Department's appropriation bill went to conference, and the news that the House conferees had refused to accept the item for Antarctica was necessarily shoved into the back pages. Jed Johnson's squabble with Franklin Roosevelt and Richard Byrd had been dwarfed by the tragic majesty of events. On June 19, while the new French government of Marshal Pétain awaited Hitler's armistice terms, Congress passed a deficiency appropriation providing the smaller sum ($171,000) for which Admiral Byrd had asked should it become necessary to evacuate all the Americans from Antarctica.[10]

The *North Star* and the *Bear* returned to the Bay of Whales in January of 1941. Little America III was abandoned, and then the two ships proceeded toward East Base, but found the harbor there so ice-choked that Richard Black's people had to be moved out by air. Space was at such a premium on board the rescuing aircraft

Killer Whales in the Bay of Whales
They had a playful habit of chasing boats or coming up under ice floes with dogs and men aboard.

that the East Bay colonists had to shoot their dogs. Overall, Paul Siple summed up, "It was a sad ending to an ambitious program." In the longer run of history, however, it may have been just as well that no attempt was made to maintain a North American presence in Antarctica during the early and middle 1940s. Had it remained on the scene and consummated FDR's plan for a permanent colony, the United States could easily have been drawn into an embarrassing quarrel amongst its own wartime allies. Such a quarrel, if long continued, could have given postwar Antarctica a much less happy history than it has in fact enjoyed.

While Dr. Ritscher's German expedition was sailing toward Antarctica, Cordell Hull and Mexico's foreign minister Ezequiel Padilla had been circulating through the corridors of an inter-

American conference at Lima, lining up delegates' support for a declaration (adopted December 24, 1938) that would reaffirm the absolute sovereignty of all the American states and express their determination to defend themselves against all foreign intervention. In further support of that stand, Secretary Hull proposed in 1940 that the American republics extend the Monroe Doctrine to the South Pole. This was a move at least as logical, in the dawning age of circumpolar air travel, as FDR's contention in 1941 that Iceland was strategically a part of the Western Hemisphere (even though that island, under its ancient name Ultima Thule, had been known and depicted on *Old* World maps since the time of the Roman Empire)! But such a proposal had some awkward diplomatic implications.

The intrusion against which Hull and Padilla sought to guard was, of course, that of the Axis powers. The "foreign intervention" that most concerned the American states nearest to Antarctica, however, was not German but British. The U.S. Antarctic Service's East Base, in particular, lay within a territory which H. M. Government since 1908 had been calling the Falkland Islands Dependencies. To the Falklands themselves, off the southeastern Argentine coast, Britain laid claim by virtue of a treaty in 1770 with Spain. At least two Latin-American states insisted, however—with considerable support in Roman law as it had been applied in the seventeenth and eighteenth centuries to international affairs—that that treaty between George III of England and Charles III of Spain had granted to the United Kingdom no such right.

On November 6, 1940, President Pedro Aguirre Cerda of Chile announced that, inasmuch as it was "the duty of the State to fix, with exactitude, its territorial limits," he therefore now decreed that "all lands, islets, reefs of rocks, glaciers, already known or to be discovered, and their respective territorial waters," lying between Longitudes 53° and 90° West, belonged to the Republic of Chile. Argentina, with even greater self-assurance, declined even

to make such a formal proclamation of ownership, on the ground
that the Antarctic pie-slice between 74° West and 25° West had
always belonged to that Republic, as an inheritance from the old
Spanish viceroyalty of Buenos Ayres. To be sure, the Argentine
and Chilean claims overlapped not only with Britain's but also
with each other's. Nevertheless, if Pope Alexander VI's demarca-
tion line of 1493 that split the New World between Portugal and
Spain ran all the way to the South Pole, as South American statecraft maintained, the United States could not endorse the Antarctic claims of its British war partner without violating those of its
sister Western Hemisphere nations; and, of course, vice versa.[11]

"There is a certain futility in interposing the lean and ascetic
visage of the law in a situation which first and last is merely a
question of power," one scholarly study of the legal and diplomatic history of the centuries-old Falkland Islands quarrel sadly
concludes. Had the warring nations in the 1940s left Antarctica to
the seals and penguins the entire question might have remained
antiquarian. But that was not fated to happen; in a truly global
conflict, even remote and peaceful Antarctica must be swept in.
First the missionary, then the trader, then the gunboat; so runs the
old proverb describing the progress of imperialism. Antarctica had
been spared the missionary stage. The traders had been hovering
around her shores for 150 years; hampered, to be sure, by the absence of any human natives to swindle or exploit (one group of
New Zealand entrepreneurs in 1927 had proposed to remedy that
defect by peopling certain of the sub-Antarctic islands with Eskimos). The gunboats finally crossed the Antarctic Circle during the
Second World War.[12]

Operating out of French-claimed Kerguelen, a craggy, fjorded
island 1300 miles north of the Antarctic mainland, the German
U-boat *Pinguin*—an appropriate name for an Antarctican
voyager!—captured at one stroke an entire Norwegian whaling
fleet as it lay quietly at anchor off the shore of Queen Maud Land.

In May 1941, H.M.S. *Cornwall* found and sank the *Pinguin,* but its sister submarines *Komet* and *Atlantis* continued to cruise the Antarctic Ocean, from time to time darting northward to sink an Allied merchantman or plant mines in one of the harbors of Australia. Alarmed lest the Germans establish themselves on the Antarctic continent itself, perhaps with Argentine cooperation—for the then government of Argentina, despite all declarations of inter-American solidarity, was not unfriendly to Nazi Germany—Britain in 1943 secretly sent a small naval force to Deception Island, which Chile, Argentina, and Britain all officially claimed. This black, gloomy, sunken crater off the Antarctic Peninsula—"'an unlikely volatile marriage of fire and ice,'' as Jacques Cousteau has called it—was an anchorage long known to Antarctic sealers and explorers; as noted in chapter 1, Sir Hubert Wilkins at the time of Little America's founding had flown from Deception Island in what the newspapers billed as a challenge to Byrd. The British tars from H.M.S. *Carnavon Castle* found and removed a bronze tablet installed just the year before by the crew of the Argentine ship *Primero de Mayo,* and hoisted the Union Jack; the following year the Argentines returned the favor. British, Chilean, and Argentine scientists and military people have been on the Antarctic Peninsula continuously ever since, calling it Graham Land or Tierra O'Higgins or Tierra San Martín depending on the speaker's nationality, and watching one another as much as they have the ice formations or the aurora. In this most unpromising way, the permanent occupation and settlement of Antarctica began.[13]

Somehow, in the midst of a desperate and bitter war, the non-ideological work of scientific investigation still went on. At the urging of Sir James Wordie, who had been Shackleton's chief of scientific staff on the attempted trans-Antarctican crossing of 1914–16, that first British shore party on Deception Island in 1943 included surveyors, geologists, biologists, and meteorologists as well as members of the Royal Navy. From that modest beginning, points out Sir Vivian Fuchs—who in 1957–58 *did* succeed in crossing Antarctica—has grown an extensive British Antarctic scientific program that continues to the present day.[14]

The scientists of the U.S. Antarctic Service, also, had a chance to reap the harvest of their findings before America entered the world conflict. At the American Philosophical Society's autumn general meeting, on November 21 and 22, 1941, twelve invited papers were read by expedition members, covering divers areas of Antarctic research. However, "only a fortnight after the Autumn Meeting," noted Admiral Byrd, "came that fateful December 7, and as a consequence practically all of the members of the expedition entered the armed forces of their country." Indeed, West Base leader Paul Siple had been recruited half a year earlier; upon his return from Little America III Siple had stepped off U.S.S. *Bear* on a rainy April day in Boston to find a man waiting for him from the Army Quartermaster Corps, to seek his expert assistance in the development of special cold-weather clothing. In a more modest way the polar explorers were learning what abstruse mathematical physicists had already discovered; that a total war economy has a place for even the most seemingly innocent kinds of scientific inquiry. Siple's work on the physiological effects of wind-chill and on the proper design of polar garments, begun with the admirable Scout's merit badge motive of helping to save life, would now enable soldiers more efficiently to fight.[15]

The skills of many other sometime Little Americans proved useful in the global struggle. Larry Gould was chief of the Arctic Section of the Arctic, Desert and Tropic Information Center, U.S. Army Air Force. Two members of Gould's 1929–30 dog sledge party , Ed Goodale and Norman Vaughan, served together in the Air Force in northeastern Canada. Another member of that pioneering geological party, Freddy Crockett, was decorated for heroic rescues of ferry plane crews, and later served in General Donovan's OSS. Aerologist Henry Harrison took four years' time out from his job as a United Airlines flight dispatcher to serve as tech-

nical adviser to the Commanding Officer, Air Force Weather
Wing. Ashley McKinley received the Legion of Merit for excep-
tional services in testing and developing Air Force cold-weather
equipment. George Hamilton Black ended up as a Master Sergeant
with five rows of chest ribbons, and Harold June was recalled from
a civilian airline job in South America to serve again in uniform.
Rear Admiral Byrd himself, ironically, spent part of the war in the
steam-heated islands of the South Pacific—"about as far, climat-
ically speaking, as it was possible to get from his beloved Antarctica." Decorating the explorer after the war for Navy activities that
had taken him to (among other places) New Zealand, Tonga,
France, Germany, and the deck of U.S.S. *Missouri* for the surrender ceremony, Fleet Admiral Chester Nimitz jokingly remarked:
"Many people think he is still at the South Pole." [16]

Perhaps the most rousingly adventurous wartime career of any
former Little American was that of Bernt Balchen. In charge of
Bluie West One, an Air Force base in Greenland where large
planes were being ferried across to Europe, Colonel Balchen participated in hair-raising, sometimes landing-gear-less, takeoffs and
pancake landings on the Greenland ice cap. Then, as Norway's
King Olaf V afterward acknowledged, "in our darkest days he
helped to nourish and sustain the resistance in Norway," haz-
ardously slipping into and out of Oslo from neutral Sweden to
direct the actions of the anti-Nazi underground. But as the war
progressed, the nature of the adventure changed. At the very end
of the war's European phase, on May 3, 1945, the Norwegian-
born pilot who had been the first person to fly to the South Pole
found himself at dinner with Lukim Grigge, commandant of a temporarily Soviet-held airfield in Norway's far north. Seated next to
Balchen, a high-ranking visitor from Moscow graphically described
one possible outcome of the war in Norway: the Russian forces in
the north driving to Narvik, while Zhukov in the south pushed
into Denmark, thereby bringing two wings of the Red Army
together in a pincers that would enclose Balchen's entire homeland

behind the Iron Curtain! Then, even more menacingly, Colonel Grigge—having become a bit maudlin on vodka—raised his glass: " 'Colonel American Balchen, we drink to you,' he said thickly. 'But one day in the Arctic we will be fighting you.' And he clinked his glass against mine."

Bernt Balchen as a young man had flown as a volunteer for the Finns, when they were winning their independence from Russia at the end of the First World War. For him, therefore, this was the resumption of an old quarrel. But the episode also symbolically illustrates the radically and rapidly changing perception of Soviet power in 1945 from the viewpoint of the United States and the European West. The old Mercator projection maps that used to hang on American schoolroom walls, with the Western Hemisphere selfconsciously located in the center of the map and the rest of the world pushed out to the edges behind two sheltering oceans, were now giving place in the public imagination to polar projection maps, on which the land-masses of Siberia and North America glowered at each other across the North Pole. "Doves" as well as "hawks," when arguing about the new Cold War confrontation, often echoed Colonel Grigge's grim, drunken prophecy of Arctic combat. In announcing on December 29, 1947, that he was going to run as an independent candidate for President in the next election, FDR's former vice-president Henry A. Wallace called for a large protest vote against the Republicans' and Democrats' bipartisan get-tough-with-Russia policy, which Wallace believed was "making inevitable the day when American soldiers will be lying in their Arctic suits in the Russian snow." [17]

Inevitably the Cold War gave a more martial color to polar exploration in the immediate postwar years. In the 1920s and 1930s, bucking through the ice pack in order to make bivouac on Antarctica's bleak shores had been a peaceful, if hazardous, undertaking. By the late 1940s, in sinister contrast, such activity seemed to have become a novel mode of military preparedness. Although old polar hands like Larry Gould continued to express hope that Ant-

arctica would become a force for peace, on occasion a veteran
Little American would voice the new militancy. Sigmund Gutenko, who had learned how to make pemmican from Dr. Dana
Coman and who had cooked at Little America III, as he spoke on
fund-raising campaigns in 1947 for a new private expedition (to be
led by Finn Ronne) sometimes digressed from his prepared discussion of Antarctic food problems to point out to his audiences how
unprepared America was for conflict at the North Pole: "Now we're
wide open for a left hook over the top of the world."

The U.S. government's own next venture toward the bottom of
the world took the form of an impressive military exercise. As
America's Navy contracted from a wartime peak strength of
4 million men and women toward a peacetime roster that was still
twice the size of this country's *combined* armed forces before the
outbreak of World War II, plenty of ships and sailors were available for Navy spectaculars. One such force, symbolically named
"Crossroads," gathered on July 1, 1946, at Bikini Atoll for the
fourth detonation—and the first public demonstration—of an
American atomic bomb. Another, surnamed "Highjump," was set
in motion by Fleet Admiral Nimitz at the behest of Richard Byrd
and of hard-driving Navy Secretary James Forrestal, on August
26, 1946, in a directive (classified until 1955) that set forth both
scientific and military purposes. Highjump was to train personnel
and test equipment under polar conditions; to determine whether
an air base could be established on ice, "with particular attention
to later application of such techniques to operations in interior
Greenland" (not far from the newly ominous Russians); and to
serve as a means for "consolidating and extending United States
potential sovereignty over the largest practicable area of the Antarctic continent."[18]

In retrospect, however, this move was not a prologue to sovereignty but a swan song. Within a decade, Americans would be
joining hands with Russians to check the imperial rush to the
south. In 1946, however, the Navy's Antarctic armada, even

though it was hastily assembled from ships some of which had been literally headed for mothballs (including U.S.S. *Mount Olympus,* the flagship) and despite being staffed with green crew members many of whom had never been to sea before, made a brave display indeed. Twelve Navy ships, plus an icebreaker borrowed from the Coast Guard, carried 4700 people to Antarctica— more, probably, than all who gone there in the southern continent's entire previous history. These were a far cry from the wooden warships on which Charles Wilkes's squabbling officers and scientists had sailed, or the creaking *City of New York* and the evermore rolling *Eleanor Bolling* that had founded Little America in 1929. The *Mount Olympus* contained a radio room with stations for fifty radio operators; the submarine *Sennet* carried lighting equipment for photographing ice floes from the underside; and the 35,000-ton aircraft carrier *Philippine Sea* brought along half a dozen twin-engined R4D airplanes, better known—and fondly remembered—by an entire generation of commercial air travelers as DC-3s. The expedition "had at its command all the technical developments in aviation and exploration that came about during the last months of the war," magazine correspondent Thomas R. Henry wrote; "many of which—never used in combat—were like swords turned into plowshares." A destroyer's fire control director, for example, originally intended to be used in bombarding invasion beaches, could just as readily be employed in offshore mapping. (Such improvised plowshares could, of course, just as readily be turned back into swords.)

The fleet divided into three Task Groups, two of which were to circumnavigate and photo-map the Antarctic continent while the Central Group, after making rendezvous on December 30 at Scott Island, threaded its way through the pack that guards the Ross Sea. "A stiff breeze rippled patches of water between the floes and sang in the rigging and radar screens overhead," wrote correspondent Walter Sullivan of the *New York Times,* as the ships moved forward "though a wonderland of blinding beauty. Here

and there an Adélie penguin stood in the powdery snow, display-
ing more curiosity than alarm at the passing procession.'' Then,
two days in, the pack ice began to show its teeth. Thin-skinned
modern naval vessels had never ventured into the Antarctic pack
before, mindful of how the *Titanic* disaster had shown what ice
can do to steel. Now, following the 6600-ton icebreaker
Northwind, ''the ship captains steered like taxicab drivers'' along
the tortuous route. The submarine had to give it up and be escorted
out; the others, after a close brush with icebergs—whose movement could be tracked with radar, a weapon not available to the
settlers of Little America I, II, and III—sailed clear of the pack on
January 14, 1947, and came up to the legendary white wall of the
Ross Ice Shelf.

U.S.C.G.S. *Northwind*, in the lead, suddenly disappeared except for its masthead and radar antenna. The ship had slipped into
the entrance to the Bay of Whales. Ten miles from side to side
when Amundsen came there in 1911, the Bay had shrunk to a
width of 300 yards. Quiet and oblivious of humanity's warlike
scurryings for the past six years, the walls of the Ice Shelf had
continued ponderously to move together; Paul Siple estimated
from his previous studies that they would collide in another six
months, wiping out the Bay of Whales. In the meantime, however,
the Task Group had a job to do. The *Northwind* broke out literally
millions of tons of sea ice to form a harbor for unloading; ''as the
task proceeded,'' Sullivan wrote, ''the bay became filled with
eight-foot ice cubes which churned in the wake of the *Northwind*
as though in a gigantic cocktail shaker.'' The men swarmed ashore
and put up a tent city, which became known as Little America IV.

Little America III had moved nearly two miles since Paul Siple
had seen it last. Apart from a brief visit by Siple and two other
West Base veterans, who lowered themselves into the old science
building and fixed themselves a nostalgic lunch from six-year-old
meat, bread, and butter, there was no attempt to dig out and re-use
the old structures, since the Fourth Little Americans only expected

Erratic on Ross Ice Shelf
*This boulder was quarried out by glacial action and will one day
be dropped into the Ross Sea.*

to be there for six weeks. (Just in case a plane should be forced
down in the interior so that a rescue party had to winter over, however, a cache was laid down under a Quonset hut at the site of
Little America III.) The main energies of the shore party were
turned to constructing a 5000-foot airstrip for the planes that
waited on board the *Philippine Sea* at the northern edge of the
pack, seven hundred miles away.[19]

For sheer audacity, this venture rivalled Bernt Balchen's dogged
aerial climb up to the south polar plateau eighteen years before.
Planes as large as these had never been launched from an aircraft
carrier. They had not enough clearance for their 110-foot wing
span, so that instead of a normal take-off down the length of the
flight deck they would have to make a shorter, diagonal run from
forward of the superstructure—bolstered by JATO (jet assisted

take-off) bottles locked onto their undersides. Furthermore, the *Philippine Sea* would need to get up sufficient speed for the launch. At six minutes between planes, at a launch speed of thirty knots, the carrier would need eighteen miles of open water. If either skinny flank touched a submerged ice-mass at that velocity, "her thin hull would be peeled back like a sardine can"—dumping 2000 men into the lethally cold ocean water of Antarctica. Once launched, the planes could not return; even more than on the First Byrd Antarctic Expedition this was literally a case of "the Ross Shelf or bust."[20]

Late in the evening of January 29, 1947, the ship's bugler sounded "flight quarters." The plane crews threw in water-tight bags, each containing a complete change of dry clothing—potentially the difference, in case they ditched, between life and death. The destroyer *Brownson* took up its station, ready to race to the rescue should one of the planes fall into the Ross Sea. "As a cold, wet wind ripped across her flight deck and was further stirred up by prop wash from the twelve engines, *Philippine Sea* leapt through the water." At 2:30 A.M., Admiral Byrd shook hands with the carrier's commanding officer; a green light flashed; the chocks were pulled; and the first plane rolled along the deck and jumped into the sky with fifty feet of flight deck to spare. Homing in on the *Mount Olympus*'s powerful radio beacon, the first of the R4Ds touched down six hours later at Little America, its wheels digging shallow troughs in the snow as the plane settled on its skis. Shortly all six airplanes were lined up in a neat row at "Little America Municipal Airport"—and just in the nick of time. The wind was already whipping across the improvised airfield, and before another day was out the tent city was cowering under an Antarctic blizzard.

As weather permitted, Admiral Byrd had the wheels removed from the planes' landing gear and dispatched the aircraft on missions of exploration. The Bay of Whales froze over and the fragile Navy ships moved out, leaving the ice party to be picked up later by the sturdy *Northwind*. On February 15, Byrd flew up Shackleton Glacier and across the polar plateau on the 180th meridian, arriving for the second time in his life at the South Pole. His actual goal was the yet unsighted region on the other side—the "Pole of Inaccessibility," that point in the midst of the Antarctic heartland which is equidistant from all the continent's coasts. DC-3s, stout though they were, had not the range for that kind of flying; still, it should be possible to see at least a few score miles into the unknown. Accordingly, the Admiral radioed back to Little America that he was proceeding "beyond the pole"—and that innocent remark was seized upon by some of the True Believers who dwell in the midst of our complicated scientific civilization, and by them woven into a fantasy far more colorful and outrageous than John Campbell's comparatively hard-headed story "Who Goes There?"[21]

The old "hollow earth" theory, which had helped to stimulate an earlier impulse toward polar exploration, had never quite died out. Since there is no way one can fly "beyond" the top or bottom of the world, adherents of that theory assumed, Byrd must therefore have flown inside the earth, and out again. Since the Earth's extremities are concave rather than convex, it follows that "the North and South Poles have never been reached because they do not exist"—a conclusion which would have surprised Peary and Amundsen. Ever since 1947, according to this line of reasoning, the government has sought to suppress what Byrd's discovery actually was.

If this sounds like the more arcane kind of UFO lore, it is. Those supposed "spacemen" who zip through the skies and sometimes contact us, it seems, are really from inside the planet (they originally migrated there from Atlantis, led by the Biblical Noah as refugees from a primeval nuclear war). The Eskimos, and perhaps also the Chinese, came from within the hollow Earth; in addition to the polar openings, subterranean tunnels with exits in Tibet and in the jungles of Brazil, possibly also under the Great Pyramid of Gizeh, lead to that inner world. The Central Sun at Earth's core which gives light and heat to a high underground civilization is also the real source of the aurora. "In comparison with the superior Subterranean People," Raymond Bernard sums up in his book *The Hollow Earth: The Greatest Geographical Discovery in History Made by Admiral Richard E. Byrd in the Mysterious Land Beyond the Poles; The True Origin of the Flying Saucers,* "surface dwellers are barbarians, and their proud 'civilization' is a state of mechanized barbarism"—and at that point, quite unexpectedly, the nonbelieving reader's condescension is shaken. "Until they learn to relinquish war forever," the writer goes on, "to destroy and bury all nuclear weapons, . . . and until they reorganize their economic and financial system on a basis of equity and justice, they will be unworthy to contact the inhabitants of the Subterranean World."[22]

We used to measure human unworthiness by the standards of heaven rather than of the nether regions, but the principle remains the same. The line between truth and madness in our time has become fine indeed. Since 1947, in a different way from that envisaged by the UFO–hollow Earth people, their fundamental point that we mechanized barbarians must abandon war and shape up our economic system has indeed come into special association with the polar regions. As will be seen in the concluding chapter that follows, Antarctica, with its historic knack for reducing human survival questions to their starkest essence, has become a focus both for our planet's deepest fears and for its highest hopes.

Even in those militant forties, however, other impulses were at work in Antarctica besides nationalism. One small signal of what might be coming was an incident at the beginning of the last privately financed American expedition to the southern continent, Finn Ronne's shoestring, one-ship venture, which arrived in Antarctica the month after Admiral Byrd's second flight over the Pole. On March 12, 1947, Ronne, his wife, and three other members of the Ronne Antarctic Research Expedition rowed through brash ice from their ship's anchorage in Marguerite Bay toward Stonington Island, where they planned to use the buildings at East Base that the U.S. Antarctic Service expedition had closed up in 1941. As their boat neared the rocky beach, a big ruddy Englishman wearing a thick brown sweater and laced rubber boots walked down the gravel to the shore and gave them a hail. He was Major K. S. Pierce Butler, commanding Base E of the Falkland Islands Dependencies Survey, whose buildings stood only two hundred yards from the abandoned American East Base. The Major invited them in for tea, and that meeting went off fairly cordially. When Ronne announced that his people intended to raise the American flag, however, Butler exclaimed: "I say, I can't allow that! This is British territory!"

An absurd exchange of formal messages followed. Butler, signing himself "Magistrate, Marguerite Bay," inquired on behalf of H. M. Government the reason for the United States flag's being flown. Ronne replied that his expedition, reoccupying buildings put there in 1940 by the U.S. Government, had "reflown the American flag on the American-built flagpole at the American camp." Butler, following time-hallowed British precedent, referred to the Antarctic Peninsula as "Grahamland"; Ronne, just as patriotically, called it "Palmer Land." But the story had a happier ending than was usual in Antarctica during the 1940s. Discovering that although the Americans were stronger in air power the British were stronger in dog power, Ronne and Butler decided upon a Joint British-American Weddell Coast Party, and by the end of Ronne's stay Great Britain's Secretary of State for the Colonies was thanking the Ronne Antarctica Research Expedition for an air search and rescue of three lost British explorers.

"You know," Major Butler told one of Ronne's men, who was seeing to it that the Stars and Stripes flew day and night even in Antarctic blizzards, "there's nothing personal about all this flag nonsense; I'm just trying to carry out orders. As far as I'm concerned you can fly it all you like. Like Ronne, I came out here because I wanted to.'' If the people who came to Antarctica because they wanted to could somehow gain leverage upon the process by which they were sent there, the swords might yet be turned into plowshares in that bleak southern land.[23]

The Ronne expedition was also a breakthrough in quite another way: Edith Ronne and Jennie Darlington were the first women in Antarctic history to winter over. Socially, Antarctica had always had an atmosphere something like that of a segregated private men's club (''I like the masculinity of the explorer's world,'' a male member of that expedition was later to say). The decision for this breakthrough had therefore met with furious resistance. While still at sea, seven expedition members had signed a letter threatening to leave as a group when the ship called at Valparaiso, Chile, en route to its goal if Commander Ronne broke this ancient sailors' taboo. To meet this hostility took a rare combination of tact and moral courage, in those days when the ''feminine mystique'' was unchallenged back home in America. In the course of that long, dark winter next door to what seemed like ''a men's locker room,'' Jennie Darlington worked her way through to acceptance, even to the point of sharing in ''the sharp awareness, the intense exhilaration'' that came with that hitherto most macho of Antarctic occupations, driving a sledge team. When her huskies came to a halt in a swirl of snow, barking joyfully, Darlington ''felt for the first time I was a small part of the real Antarctic.'' On the yet-unpeopled seventh continent it was one small step for a woman, one giant step for womankind.[24]

9

The Dinosaur
at the
Bottom
of the World

The expeditions which have been sent to explore unknown seas have contributed largely to the stock of human knowledge, and they have added renown to nations, lustre to diadems. Navies are not all for war. Peace has its conquests, science its glories; and no navy can boast of brighter chaplets than those which have been gathered in the fields of geographical exploration and physical research.

The great nations of the earth have all with more or less spirit undertaken to investigate certain phenomena touching the sea, and, to make the plans more effectual, they have agreed to observe according to a prescribed formula. The observations . . . were made by fellow-laborers under all flags.
—*Matthew Fontaine Maury,* The Physical
Geography of the Sea, *8th edition (1859)*

Little America, the sheltered hollow on the Ross Ice Shelf into which Richard E. Byrd and Bernt Balchen first skied in 1929, no longer exists. Shackleton had been right; the Bay of Whales was geologically a brief halt in the irresistible forward march of the Ross Ice Shelf. When the lone icebreaker U.S.S. *Atka,* scouting a year ahead of the Navy's ''Operation Deepfreeze,'' arrived off the towering front of the Barrier on January 14, 1955, near what ought to have been Discovery Inlet—found by Scott in 1902, and usually considered a stable feature of the landscape—no such indentation was to be seen. As the icebreaker sailed eastward toward Little America, the *Atka*'s navigator ruefully had to confess that according to the latest available chart of the coastline his sun shots placed the ship ten miles inland; and his observations, it turned out, were absolutely correct. A section of the Ice Shelf as large as Long Island had calved away, and the harbor at the Bay of Whales was no more.

A helicopter pilot and a newspaper representative flew in to look for Little America IV, the populous temporary town which in 1947 had welcomed the DC-3s. Near the brink of the ice cliffs they spotted two rows of tent poles protruding a few inches above the surface; one row broke off abruptly at the Ice Shelf's edge. "The camp," Walter Sullivan wrote, "had been cut in two as though by a gigantic meat cleaver," and the planes that had once been lined up with such military precision at "Little America Municipal Airport" had vanished. Maneuvering out over the ocean, Sullivan and helicopter pilot Albert Metrolis saw a dark horizontal line running across the front of the Shelf, seven and a half feet below the clifftops. It marked where the surface level had been, when Little America IV was in use eight years before:

> Soiled by our boots and vehicles, it now showed up in cross section on the face of the ice cliffs. Nearby a tent hung clinging from the face of the cliff. It too had been buried until the great calving exposed it to view for a brief reincarnation. Something which resembled a folded army cot hung free from one of the tent floor beams, casting its shadow on the powdery white face of the cliff. A torn fragment of red cloth blew in the wind.
>
> It was evident that the ice cliffs were disintegrating gradually. The belt of bright green water at their foot was slushy with newly fallen ice fragments and the crest of the cliffs was "smoking" with snow which blew off the surface of the ice shelf and curled down in white clouds that dissolved in the sea 100 feet below. Sooner or later erosion of the shelf was bound to spill the rest of the camp into the sea.

Little America III, however (West Base), was still there. Landing to investigate, another helicopter party found, two feet below the Barrier surface, the escape hatch in the roof of the Quonset hut within which the men of "Highjump" in 1947 had deposited their emergency cache. Light of gasoline lanterns glittered back from delicate, undisturbed ice crystals; "never had a quonset hut—that drab structure born of World War II—been decked out in such glory." Leaving a note for future visitors, of whom there would

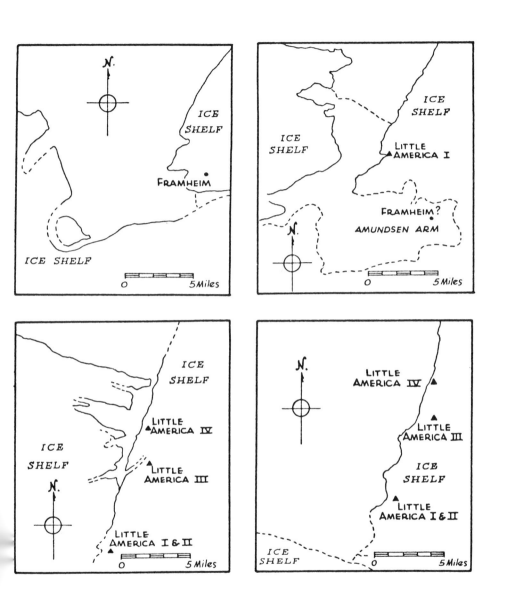

The Changing Bay of Whales

The Changing Bay of Whales.
From Walter Sullivan, Quest for a Continent (London: Secker
and Warburg, 1957), p. 221. Used by permission.

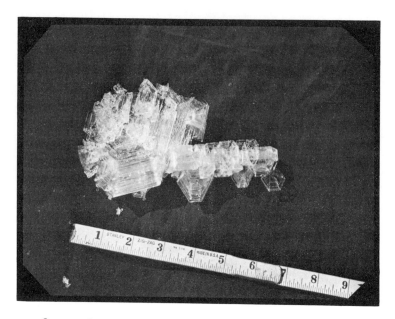

Ice crystals
Undisturbed for generations in the silent darkness of an ice cave,
these beautiful formations have had the leisure to grow.

probably be none before Nature finished the destruction it had
begun, the men from the *Atka* stole away. "Wispy streamers of
drifting snow skimmed over the ice sheet, and as we left they had
already begun to bury the camp entrance."[1]

In the following Antarctic summer season came the probing
ships of the Navy's "Operation Deepfreeze," under the opera-
tional command of Admiral George Dufek but with the overall
supervision of Admiral Byrd, to find a site for a proposed Little
America V. The old Bay of Whales location was now clearly out
of the question; "the walls of the Barrier were sheer perpendicular
uprights more than one hundred feet high." The ships moved on to
Japanese-discovered Kainan Bay, thirty miles eastward. But on
December 26, 1955, Paul Siple and Richard Byrd paid a last nos-

talgic visit by helicopter to Little America I and II. The three 70-foot radio towers of the first Expedition now barely protruded above the surface, and the tips of five telephone poles were all that remained of the second. "Though I had spent so many years of my life here," Siple mused, "there was little time for regrets." The helicopter, piloted by West Base veteran Murray Wiener, rose high over the Barrier to search for a new Little America. A fortnight later, on January 8, 1956, Siple and Byrd flew toward the Pole of Inaccessibility, where the Soviets were planning to place a scientific station, and then back along the meridian of 90° East toward the geographic pole. It was the 68-year-old Admiral's third flight over the South Pole and, as it turned out, his last. To his deep disappointment, the Admiral was never to step down upon the sastrugi at the place where Amundsen and Scott had walked in the Antarctic summer of 1911–12.

Siple saw Byrd for the last time at the house on Brimmer Street in Boston on October 3, 1956. By that time the former Scout had been named Scientific Leader of an American base to be established at the pole itself. "Paul," the old explorer confessed, "living at the South Pole would have been the high point of my life. But since I can't go, there is no one else I'd rather see taking my place than you." Bidding the Admiral farewell and proceeding south to set up the new South Pole station—named, rightly and inevitably, Amundsen-Scott—Paul Siple learned by radio on March 12, 1957, that Richard Evelyn Byrd was dead. Stunned, Siple went out into the cold and put the flag at half-mast, where it remained until the sun sank into the Antarctic winter night. The Moses of America's Antarctic frontier had not made it all the way to his Promised Land.[2]

If Little America had undergone profound physical transformation since Richard Byrd and Bernt Balchen first walked into it on skis in 1929, the change in its political environment had been equally revolutionary. One illustration of how sharply the times had changed in Antarctica since the Second World War was a message sent by Byrd, ten days after his last flight over the Pole and just before his departure from Antarctica forever, to a Russian expedition that was then headed southward in the mighty ice ship *Ob*. "Welcome to Wilkes Land," Byrd radioed. "We recently flew over interior in vicinity of your planned inland bases. . . . We would like to exchange weather information. Siple joins me in sending our best wishes for success in our international effort in science." In 1956 this seemed a natural friendly gesture, akin perhaps to the "howdy, stranger" tradition on the North American frontier: if the other fellow isn't going for his gun, be prepared to shake his hand. A decade earlier, such words might have branded the Admiral as "soft on Communism."[3]

To be sure, the Soviet Union—like the United States—reserved its own rights in Antarctica. Pointing out in a memorandum of June 10, 1950, "the outstanding services of Russian navigators in the discovery of the Antarctic," and noting also that nine-tenths of the world's whale catch—in which the USSR was a major participant—came from Antarctic waters, the Soviets declared that they could "not recognize as legal any decision on the regime for the Antarctic taken without their participation." At the time—two weeks before the outbreak of the Korean War!—this would have sounded to many in the West like just another case of Soviet muscle-flexing. Actually, the two superpowers' legal positions on Antarctica were closer to each other than to the formal stands taken by Chile, Argentina, and Great Britain. High scientific and diplomatic statecraft might therefore generate a truly multinational solution to the Antarctic problem; legally acceptable to the Soviets because they participated in the decision, and legally acceptable to the Americans because they had never accepted any other nations' unilateral claims. To secure such a solution, however, the Soviets would have to back off from a previous assertion by some of their scientists that Admiral Bellingshausen's discoveries ought to be called the "Russian sector of the Antarctic mainland," and the

Americans would have to shelve the Roosevelt Administration's venture into Antarctic imperialism as merely another of FDR's experimental aberrations.[4]

The first concrete step toward that multinational solution was taken on April 5, 1950, at a dinner party in Silver Spring, Maryland, at the home of physicist James E. Van Allen (after whom the "Van Allen belts" of radiation surrounding the Earth are named; thus was polar study already phasing into the exploration of space). It was a bad time to be proposing international collaboration, especially in science. Joe McCarthy had already raised his hue and cry against suspected Communists in the State Department, and a British court had just sentenced the nuclear physicist Klaus Fuchs to fourteen years for atomic espionage. Nevertheless, abundant historical precedent existed for nations to work together on scientific problems. At Kerguelen Island in 1874, a chance to measure the transit of Venus across the sun—the first such chance since the eighteenth century—had attracted American, British, German, and French scientist-explorers. Similarly, the voyage of Captain Scott aboard the *Discovery* in 1902 had been scientifically coordinated with an expedition led by the German explorer Erich von Drygalski—even though Scott and Drygalski had also paid their dues to nationalism by respectively naming features of the Antarctic terrain Edward VII Land and Kaiser Wilhelm II Land. There had been an International Polar Year in 1882–83, and a second in 1932–33; on that fifty-year timetable a third could be expected in the early 1980s. But why wait? asked geomagnetism specialist Lloyd Berkner, who had been radio engineer on board the *City of New York* during the first voyage to Little America. Science could make immediate use of the new, war-born technology: rockets, for sounding far more deeply into the Antarctic stratosphere than Haines's and Harrison's hand-reeled, candle-lit weather balloons; longer-ranging aircraft; tractors that would be capable of withstanding the rigors of the cold far better than Pete

Demas's modest ice flotilla of 1934. The time to tackle Antarctica on a massive scale, Berkner and the other scientists present agreed, was now.

The worldwide scientific establishment had never quite broken down, even at the worst stages of the Cold War. Fairly quickly, the International Council of Scientific Unions was able to organize a planning commission for a third polar year. Scheduled to take place in 1957–58, these Arctic and Antarctic investigations would coincide with one of the regular eleven-year peaks in sunspot activity, and therefore with spectacular auroral displays. But the Earth's magnetic field is not confined to the poles; why not expand the inquiry to include the entire planet? That suggestion, made by the World Meteorological Organization, was acted upon; and what was to have been the Third International Polar Year thus mutated into what has been called "the greatest peacetime activity in man's history," the International Geophysical Year.[5]

Under the loose authority of a *Comité Special de l'année Geophysique Internationale,* representatives of those nations which planned to do work in Antarctica—Argentina, Australia, Chile, France, Japan, New Zealand, Norway, South Africa, the United Kingdom, the United States, and (most crucially) the USSR (all countries with previous experience on or near the southern continent)—convened in Paris between July 6 and 10, 1955, to decide where they would place their scientific stations. There, "in a continual rush from one meeting room to another," U.S. delegation member Paul Siple recalled, "we discussed such matters as methods for communicating between stations, mutual aid among all the stations, and . . . the kinds of equipment, such as planes, dog teams and radios, we would be able to make available in case of emergency." The Russians arrived at the conference with detailed mapping and surveying proposals, and a plan for a station at the South Pole—which was overruled on the ground that the Pole had already been spoken for by the Americans. The Soviets undertook to build a base at the Pole of Inaccessibility instead. Thus the

United States and the Soviet Union nudged each other into the heart of Antarctica, much as in the next decade they would race each other into space.[6]

When this Antarctic Conference took place the post-Stalin (and, one must add, post-Truman) thaw in international relations was well under way. Dwight Eisenhower, on December 8, 1953, had made his dramatic "Atoms For Peace" address to the United Nations, pledging to search for "the way by which the miraculous inventiveness of man shall not be dedicated to his death, but consecrated to his life." At an international scientific congress at Geneva, meeting in August 1955—the same summer in which the IGY's Antarctic Conference met in Paris—literally tons of previously secret information on nuclear energy flooded the sessions, turning Geneva into what one reporter termed "the greatest scientific irrigation project of modern times," as Russian and U.S. scientists frantically scribbled newly declassified data onto their papers right up to the moment they delivered them. Despite this thaw in international scientific communication, however, all was not yet sweetness and light in Antarctic diplomacy. In 1952, Argentine bullets had whizzed over the heads of a British landing party attempting to set up a weather station at Hope Bay—probably the first shots ever fired in anger in Antarctica. In May 1955 the United Kingdom tried to sue Chile and Argentina before the World Court, charging repeated encroachments upon British Antarctic claims. (The case collapsed when both South American countries declined, on grounds of national sovereignty, to let the Court take jurisdiction).[7]

Tensions such as these were inevitably felt at the Paris IGY meeting. Nations with existing Antarctic bases grumbled at proposals that "foreign" scientists be permitted to establish bases on what they regarded as home territory. The objection applied as much to the Americans, who wanted to place their Ellsworth Station near an already existing Argentine facility on the Filchner Ice Shelf, as to the Russians, whose stations would be on territory

claimed by Australia—which at that time did not have diplomatic
relations with the Soviet Union. G. R. Laclavère, the very able international civil servant who presided over the Antarctic Conference, patiently untied the knot by stressing the technical, nonpolit-
ical purpose of the meeting, and secured at the end a unanimous
resolution endorsing his view "that the overall aims of the Conference are entirely scientific." The spirit of Laclavère's declaration—that nations should tackle the practical problems of technology and logistics which lay before them, while remaining silent on
the questions of sovereignty upon which they could not agree—
became the working philosophy of the IGY.[8]

Even before this formal assignment of the research stations,
some of the nations concerned were already on the scene in Antarctica, enlarging their old bases or scouting out new locations for
the scientific work they were going to do. We have already noted
the visit of U.S.S. *Atka* to Little America in January 1955. That
same summer the powerful new diesel-electric icebreaker *General
San Martín,* built in West Germany for the Argentine Navy, sailed
from Buenos Aires into a relatively unknown sector of the Weddell
Sea; an area regarded with special interest by countries participating in the International Geophysical Year, Frigate Captain Luis
R. A. Capurro poisnted out, "on account of its being the other
way to reach the South Pole."[9] By December 1955, from the
Filchner Ice Shelf clear out around the bulge of East Antarctica
through Wilkes and Adélie Lands and on into the Ross Sea at Mc-
Murdo Sound, French, Australian, British, Soviet, and American
expeditions were knocking at the ramparts of Antarctica. Adding
these IGY ventures together with the already existing British and
Latin American stations up on the Antarctic Peninsula there were,
by the time the sun went down in 1956, about thirty groups settling in for the winter night. "Antarctica," Walter Sulllivan of the
New York Times rather sadly wrote, "was no longer a continent of
solitude."

One of the winter parties dug in at Kainan Bay, thirty miles east from what remained of the first four Little Americas. Some day this Little America V, as the ice shelf continued its implacable march, must also break away and drift off to the north. Its planners and builders felt certain, however, that it would remain safe throughout the International Geophysical Year. From Little America V, on January 14, 1956, with half a dozen men, two Sno-Cats, and one Weasel, Lieutenant-Commander Jacob Bursey of the U.S. Coast Guard—a Little America I veteran, who a quarter-century previously had been helping Paul Siple force-feed the First Expedition's penguins—pushed inland toward the Rockefeller Mountains, locating and flagging a trail for a tractor train, which during the following Antarctic summer season would bring in the supplies for Byrd Station, an IGY base far within the interior of Marie Byrd Land.

Little America V itself was to be Weather Central for all of Antarctica during the IGY. Its first wintering-over group included a Russian meteorologist, Vladimir Ivanovich Rastorguev, whose American counterpart, Gordon Cartwright, wintered over at Mirny, the main Soviet Antarctic base. Conventional Cold War attitudes, at least among Antarctic settlers, were changing. During a pause in Adelaide in the course of his return trip to the United States, the American exchange meteorologist was cornered by Australian newspapermen who asked him whether the Soviet research station at Mirny was really a cover for a missile-launching site and submarine base. According to Soviet Estonian playwright Juhan Smuul, who was also returning home from Mirny, "Mr. Cartwright replied with a categorical 'No!' "[10]

Even the Soviet Sputnik, which when it went into earth orbit on October 5, 1957, generated alarmed cries in the U.S. of "missile gap" and demands for an instant upgrading of American education, was taken more calmly in Antarctica. Sputnik was a plowshare as well as a sword; in addition to advancing Russia's military missile program, the beeping satellite was also a Russian contribution to the science program of IGY. Asked about Sputnik by Dick

Chappell, his American bunkmate at Little America V, Vladimir Rastorguev "said simply, 'Well, Deek, someone had to put it up there first.' " Paul Siple, as he put some of his crew at the South Pole on a round-the-clock observation schedule, tape-recording Sputnik's pulse rate, "wondered why ours wasn't up also."

Richard Chappell, incidentally, was an American Boy Scout, who had been selected to come to Antarctica in much the same manner as Paul Siple nearly three decades before. Chasing after skua gulls in an effort, usually fruitless, to band them with U.S. Fish and Wildlife Service markers, and serving in other ways as a Junior Scientific Aide to the IGY scientists at Little America V, Chappell rarely got to wear his Scout uniform in Antarctica. But he put it on for a brief visit to Mirny, because he "wanted the Russians to know what a Boy Scout was." One of his Soviet hosts, seeing him bearded and splendid in Explorer Scout green, with three service stars over his left pocket indicating his years of activity in Cub Scouts, Boy Scouts, and Explorers, mistook the youth for an American three-star general. It was almost a parody of the serious, low-down encounter with Soviet militarism Bernt Balchen had reported a dozen years before.[11]

On July 1, 1957, when the International Geophysical Year officially began, Little America was no longer what it had been in 1929, the solitary American town on an empty continent. Half a dozen other U.S. IGY stations were in operation. Science journalist Richard Lewis referred to them as "the Seven Cities of the seventh continent": Little America V; Byrd Station, 450 miles inland from Little America over a twisting tractor trail called U.S. Minus 66; McMurdo Station, established on the hallowed ground at Hut Point where Scott had wintered in 1902–4; Amundsen-Scott, at the pole itself; Ellsworth Station, on the Filchner Ice Shelf fifty miles west of Britain's Shackleton Base (whence Sir Vivian Fuchs's Commonwealth Trans-Antarctic Expedition would soon move inland to realize Shackleton's old dream of crossing the southern continent by land); Wilkes Station, in the Windmill Islands along the all-but-unexplored coast of Wilkes Land; and, finally, Hallett Station, a sandspit jutting into the Ross Sea near the tip of Cape Adare, the only flat place on that coast for many precipitous miles. The first job at Hallett Station, one of the intruders reported, was to "move two acres of penguins so we could build a base." (Hallett's previous residents protested vigorously; after all, they had been living there for at least 1400 years, as scientists know from studying their ancestors' bones.) [12]

Although Little America V was the focus of American IGY work it was not to be the logistical center of American Antarctic enterprise, as Little Americas I, II, and IV had been. Doubts had been expressed, during the planning stage in Washington, as to whether a snow-compacted runway at the new Little America would stand up under repeated heavy use. Accordingly, U.S. Antarctic headquarters shifted from Amundsen's historic area to Scott's, on the solid land over at McMurdo Sound. The Navy had no doubt that large planes, flying direct from New Zealand, could land there on the bay ice.

Larry Gould, now director of the U.S. IGY Antarctic program, as he returned to Antarctica in the admiral's quarters aboard U.S.S. *Curtiss*—a luxurious contrast to the *Eleanor Bolling!*— found an enormous difference between the bustling activity at Mc-Murdo and the village life he had known 26 years earlier at Little America I: bright orange buildings all above the ground, not buried in the snow; many caterpillar tractors, pulling long lines of sledges up the ice from the ships toward the station; a row of old Navy destroyers, taken out of mothballs in New Jersey and frozen into McMurdo Sound to serve as quick, temporary storage for gasoline and oil; and a steel welder working on an oil storage tank who, Deepfreeze's commander Admiral George Dufek told Gould, was at that moment the highest-paid man in Antarctica.

Byrd Station was established from Little America by tractor train, as planned. Once built, however, it was completely supplied by air from McMurdo. Amundsen-Scott, at the South Pole, was *built* from McMurdo, entirely by air drop—a revolutionary advance in technology, accompanied by a great deal of waste. The Advance Party which was to receive and sort out the initial stores won one last moral victory for traditional Antarctic folkways; mistakenly set down by air eight miles from the actual geographic pole, they had to trek the rest of the way to the drop site with their dogs. Thereafter, however, mighty Air Force C-124 Globemasters emphatically brought in the modern age.[13] Food, lumber, machinery, and expensive scientific equipment, flown up over Scott's classic route via the Beardmore Glacier, rained from the skies upon the South Pole. Some parachutes failed to open, and their cargoes "streamed in," smashing to pieces or burying themselves in the snow, sometimes never to be found again. On occasion a parachute would open but remain attached to its package, which thereupon "would take off like a powered sled and disappear over the horizon." Surrounding the station, as Navy Seabees put its buildings together, "was an enormous pile of litter—broken crates, piles of cans, and assorted trash, which made the glamorous south pole look like the corner of a city dump," Richard Lewis sadly observed, adding that of course the scar would be covered by the next season's snowfall.

Paul Siple, whom old Victor Czegka had taught never to lay a tool down and walk away lest it sink into the snow and be lost forever, found this wanton wastefulness distressing. He realized that "these young titans of modern Antarctica" were members of a new generation, "accustomed to the opulence of the military services" and operating by a philosophy that was "an outgrowth of World War II practices, to get the job done and to hell with conserving supplies." Siple had to concede that they were supplying and building his South Pole station with breathtaking speed. Nevertheless it bothered him, in that woodless land, to see a board that might have a few nails in it "burned as trash like yesterday's newspaper." It was not the resources-and-energy-conserving ethic he had learned in Scouting, and it did not seem to him to be an appropriate lifestyle for Antarctica.

After March 21, 1957, when the sun went down (earlier of course at the South Pole than at any of the other IGY bases) it was a different story. "Face to face with raw nature so grim and stark that our lives could be snuffed out in a matter of minutes," the eighteen people wintering over at Amundsen-Scott Station, Siple wrote, "were like men who had been fired off in rockets to take up life on another planet." They had their radio contacts with the Navy, with the other IGY stations (U.S. and foreign), and—via ham radio phone patches—with their families and friends at home. They had the moral support and example of those who had come to Antarctica before them, including an eerie, posthumously-received message from Admiral Byrd, who had asked that it be sent to them at the beginning of the long winter night ("Your work . . . may well mark the beginning of permanent occupancy of the Antarctic Continent. . . . Good luck and my affectionate greet-ings"). None of this outside encouragement, however, could abate for one moment the appalling reality that surrounded them. The wind; the landmarkless dark; the potential of fire; and, especially, the necessity of living in a closed-in community of "men in a box," with no possibility of relief or escape—all this was much as it had been in the old days at the Bay of Whales. (In one respect at least it was less rigorous: with the temperature ranging as low as one hundred below, nobody suggested letting the fire go out at night and opening the door.)[14]

The winter passed; the sun came up again; the scientific program went on. Just before midday on January 4, 1958, Sir Edmund Hillary, who with the Sherpa Tenzing Norkay had been first to climb Mount Everest only five years before, came driving into camp after a 1250-mile tractor journey from New Zealand's Scott Base (adjacent to McMurdo). Hillary had been laying depots for the Commonwealth Trans-Antarctic expedition under Vivian Fuchs, which was working its way in from the opposite side of the continent at the head of the Weddell Sea. Two weeks later Sir Vivian himself arrived, wearing on a leather thong around his neck the watch that had belonged to Captain Scott, and followed by a brave procession of orange Sno-Cats, a Weasel, and loaded dog sledges, flying the flags of four Commonwealth nations, crevasse markers, trail pennants, and the flag of the city of Bristol, England. As they approached the South Pole—the quest for which had cost men of other generations so much in energy and life— thirty people came out of the station, all armed with cameras. A planeload of VIPs, including Admiral Dufek, had flown up from McMurdo. "There was such a press of photographers and recorders," Fuchs wrote at the end of the day, "that it was quite difficult to move about." For all the hazards Paul Siple's wintering-over party had had to face during the previous night season, civilization had definitely come to Antarctica.

When the International Geophysical "Year"—stretched out to eighteen months—came officially to an end on December 31, 1958, Antarctic Weather Central was transferred to Melbourne, Australia, and Little America V was closed down. According to Professor Gould it was no longer useful. All the scientific work that could only be done there had been done, and—not being located on solid rock, like McMurdo Station and New Zealand's adjoining Scott Base—"it was a little dangerous." Shackleton's caution against the use of the Bay of Whales was finally being heeded, fifty years later. Nostalgic scientists and Seabees protested the closing in letters to their Congressmen, but the Navy stuck to its guns.[15]

In addition to Little America V, the United States prepared also to give up some of its other IGY bases. It turned over Ellsworth Station to Argentina, for example, and Wilkes Station to Australia. But there was no intention, this time, of pulling out of Antarctica entirely. In the eighteen months of IGY, there had barely been time to scratch the surface of what was still there to be studied. Even before the International Geophysical Year ended, therefore, scientists in the participating countries were setting up organizational machinery for continuing their work in Antarctica. At The Hague, between February 3 and 5, 1958—while Sir Vivian

Fuchs's Commonwealth trans-Antarctic party, now far past the Pole, paused on the trail to tighten vehicle tracks and lubricate gearboxes before tackling the last major crevassed area on its journey across the polar plateau—a body came into existence which was to become known as the Scientific Committee on Antarctic Research. In addition to representatives from the scientists' international professional associations, the Committee had delegates from each country "actively engaged" in Antarctic research. ("Actively engaged" for this purpose meant being involved in operations that required people to winter over.) That first meeting of SCAR wrote a constitution and elected officers, assessed a modest budget from its member nations (with Argentina, the U.S., and the Soviet Union paying the most), and worked out a plan for the scientific exploration of Antarctica in the years following the IGY. G. R. Laclavère, of France, who had been so instrumental in the birth of IGY itself, became the organization's first president; he was followed, in 1963, by Laurence Gould.

"Science is no respecter of political boundaries," Gould wrote in 1971, "and SCAR has played an important role in all of the international scientific projects involving worldwide observation." Those political boundaries, however, would not vanish merely because the observers found them an inconvenience while taking seismic soundings of the ice cap or banding skua gulls. There would have to be a firm legal basis for the scientists' freedom of access to Antarctica; and so came into being the Antarctic Treaty of 1959—"the first such document in history formed to protect a scientific program." [16]

There was nothing historically inevitable about this decision to internationalize Antarctica. The United States, under other circumstances, might have continued along the path of empire as marked out by Franklin Roosevelt and Cordell Hull. In fact the distinguished Australian Antarctic explorer Sir Douglas Mawson, not long before his death in 1958, strongly endorsed just such a course. "I am still sorry that America has not laid claim to the big

Whale in the Bay of Whales

unclaimed central Pacific sector [of Antarctica]," Mawson wrote
in a letter to Larry Gould. Since the coastline of that unclaimed
sector was one of the most inaccessible parts of the southern continent, perhaps New Zealand—compensated by boundary adjust-
ments elsewhere—would grant the United States territorial access
across the Ross Shelf to Marie Byrd Land. If the Antarctic continent were "tied up to a limited number of sovereignties of good
repute and mutual regard," Mawson argued, it "could then be ad-
ministered on good lines conjointly for the benefit of all and especially of the inhabitants (penguins, birds, seals, etc.)." Otherwise,
"if every nation had a hand in it, some of the life there may soon
become extinct."

Sir Douglas wrote out of the highest motives. At least two nations having a hand in Antarctic administration were at that moment allowing their hunting fleets to harry the blue whale out of

existence. Still, Mawson's words carry a disquieting echo of the paternal advice by Kipling to the Americans at the time of the Philippine Insurrection: that they should "take up the white man's burden" for the good of the benighted natives. (The flipper-waving, blubber-wrapped natives of Antarctica, in dignified silence, refrained from comment upon this condescending attitude.) Did those "sovereignties of good repute and mutual regard," as of 1958, include Japan and the Soviet Union? Or, for that matter, Chile and Argentina? [17]

Had the Americans yielded to Mawson's suggestion, they would have locked themselves once more into the "Western European equation," as William Appleman Williams calls it, which "holds that discovery is defined by penetration, conquest, possession, and exploitation: that knowing comes down to owning." For a scientist, however, knowing has purposes that go beyond ownership. American scientific exploration in Antarctica during the International Geophysical Year, Thomas O. Jones points out, had "brought in a clientele with a legitimate long-term interest," backed by the fiscal and managerial support of the National Science Foundation. The age of prowess, in which particular Antarctic exploits—like U.S. and Soviet space shots—had been defined, Plains Indian fashion, as "counting coup," had yielded during the IGY to "a comparatively long period (1955 to 1959) of widespread U.S. presence not dependent upon the efforts of a single explorer or upon military ventures." "We do not want Antarctica to become an object of political conflict," President Eisenhower declared. "We propose that Antarctica shall be open to all nations to conduct scientific or other peaceful activities there." Accordingly the United States, on May 2, 1958, formally invited the other IGY Antarctic nations to meet in Washington to negotiate a treaty for Antarctica. Signed by the negotiators on December 1, 1959, the Antarctic Treaty went into force in 1961.

The regime for Antarctica under the Antarctic Treaty is a culture developed under laboratory conditions rather than allowed to grow in the wild. Scientific internationalism, like any other kind—e.g., the world fellowship symbolized in the Olympic Games—has limits beyond which it tends to break down. Even though "science and the consequences of scientific discovery recognize no boundary lines or national barriers," international lawyer Charles E. Martin has pointed out, "nations will compete in scientific development in the areas of security and power," as the nuclear weapons programs of the United States and the Soviet Union continue to demonstrate. Genuinely cooperative scientific progress could take place only in situations where these demands of power and security did not apply. Therefore, from the standpoint of the "constructive and peace-keeping foreign policy" which the Eisenhower Administration in its best moments attempted to forge, the existence of Antarctica was a God-sent opportunity. There at the ends of the Earth, where nations had a great deal to gain by cooperation—in the eminently practical field of weather prediction, for example—and, so far as anyone could then tell, very little to lose, it proved possible to put together a functioning international entity which could serve as the pilot model for a more comprehensive world social order.[18]

In effect the self-denying ordinances of the IGY were continued and extended. The signers of the Antarctic Treaty promised not to use their activities on the southern continent to advance any further claims of national sovereignty. (They did not, however, renounce any of their previously existing claims; the sovereignty question was simply shelved for the thirty years during which the Treaty was to be in force, and it would have to be faced again when the document came up for renewal.) The participants pledged themselves not to build any fortifications, carry out any military maneuvers, or test any weapons; they would use their armed forces only for logistic support of the stations, and for taking field parties wherever the scientists wanted to go. They would dump no radioactive wastes and ignite no nuclear explosions. Particularly striking, in view of the security fetish that has plagued the civilized world since the end of the Second World War, was the provision that "all areas of Antarctica, including all stations, installations and equipment within those areas, and all ships and aircraft at points of discharging or embarking cargoes or personnel in Antarctica, shall be open at all times to inspection" by observers chosen by any of the member nations. The Soviet Union, which again and again has balked at international agreements over exactly this issue of free inspection, has whole-heartedly cooperated with these terms. Antarctica has become, in Joseph Dukert's apt phrase, a land of "many flags, no borders," where "the struggle between man and man," as Antarctic votary Charles Neider puts it, "must be set aside so that mankind can better understand and endure nature."[19]

The treaty structure at some points is vulnerable. Nothing was said in the Antarctic Treaty, for example, about the discovery and development of mineral resources and fossil-fuel reserves. An "oil rush" to the Antarctic Peninsula—which may now be in the making—would put the trans-Andean sector of that borderless land under very considerable strain. Objections have also been raised in some Third World countries to the exclusive control of Antarctica by a "club" composed of the Antarctic Treaty nations; such countries have brought objections of the same kind against the "have" nations in general. Also possible now is an "actual settlement" of Antarctica even by Charles Evans Hughes's strict and narrow definition—i.e., by outright colonization. "I used to be able to say that Antarctica has never been the home of man," Larry Gould told his University of Arizona class in glacial geology on February 13, 1978, "but within the last two weeks it has become the home of a baby." Congratulating the proud parents of the first human native Antarctican, born at Argentina's Esperanza Station (Hope Bay), Argentine President Jorge Gonzáles Videla declared that the birth "reaffirms not only the role of the family in our society but also the inalienable role of Argentines in those far lands." The announcement soon afterward of the first wedding ever to take place in Antarctica, also at Hope Bay, gave further force to the President's words. When the Antarctic Treaty came up for renewal the Argentines were evidently prepared to raise some sharp questions, and "if it is not renewed," Professor Gould predicted, "this whole miserable business of international claims will rise again."[20]

In the absence or abeyance of such claims during the intervening thirty years, the Antarctic cosmopolis that science and statecraft patiently constructed after the IGY has functioned very impressively. "Even at the times of greatest tension in the terror-filled sixties—the Cuban missile crisis and the invasion of Czechoslovakia, for example—Russians, Americans, Britons and others have continued their work in the Antarctic undisturbed," the *New York Times* editorialized at the tenth anniversary of the Treaty in 1969. "In this coldest of the continents . . . . the Cold War was abolished." Especially noteworthy as a human achievement has been the unbroken continuation of exchange residencies at those far southern stations. Antarctic wintering-over lore is filled with tales of friction among people of the same nationality, having no ideological differences to complicate matters. The modern conveniences undreamed-of by Scott and Shackleton—hot showers, abundant lighting, and the like—have never quite made up for the fact that once people have settled in for the winter there is no way they can get away from one another. But, typically, an American planning to winter over at Vostok in 1971 was "not worried about the possible complexity of personal relations with the Russians in so small and isolated a station. There were going to be good people and some not so good, as there had been during his summer at the Pole and his winter at Byrd," American bases both. As he cheerfully prepared to make charcoal at Vostok by burning crate boards so that he could throw an American-style steak dinner for the Russians on the Fourth of July, Dale Vance epitomized the Antarctic spirit at its best. "Here in the Antarctic's barren wastes," Jacques Cousteau said of a 1973 visit to Deception Island, "different species have come to tolerate each other," and those barren wastes' human tenants—who, after all, constitute only *one* species—have profited from the nonhuman natives' example.[21]

The most serious crisis in Antarctica during the first two decades under the Treaty was not political but environmental. To some extent the seven cities of the seventh continent repeated the history of frontier boom towns in nineteenth-century America. Just as "construction along the river fronts proceeded with no thought for scenic protection" in the early years of Pittsburgh and Louisville, so at McMurdo Station "we have been somewhat unappreciative of our 'million-dollar view' of the Royal Society Range, having obscured it with a maze of telephone poles and wires." More serious, because of its impact on the fragile Antarctic ecology, was the condition of the bottom of McMurdo Sound, which had become littered with beer cans, fuel lines, discarded clothing, airplane parts, and much else. Sponges in the Sound were "particularly sensitive to being covered," two oceanographers reported in 1970, "and even beneath such seemingly insignificant materials as cardboard and clothing all the sponges are dead." Smog, no less, had become noticeable in Antarctica; "on some occasions, smoke from burning trash has reduced visibility on the Williams Field runway." McMurdo Station, nonexistent prior to Operation Deepfreeze in 1956, was already in need of urban renewal![22]

Its inhabitants tackled their problems with zest—and found, as town dwellers have in other parts of the world, that a solution can sometimes be even more appalling than the original problem. In particular, they sought to abate the nuisance of petrochemical fuels by substituting supposedly clean and abundant nuclear energy. Economically that decision was highly plausible; diesel fuel in 1960 cost the Navy 12 cents per U.S. gallon, but it was worth 40 cents a gallon by the time they had transported it in to McMurdo and $6 a gallon by the time it got to the South Pole. Accordingly, Congress authorized Antarctica's first nuclear reactor, which was installed at McMurdo Station in the Antarctic summer of 1961–62.

In addition to providing light and power, the heat from the reactor could be used to distill sea water into fresh; after having scraped the hills bare for miles around, McMurdo was actually running out of fresh snow.

Old Antarctican Paul Siple reportedly was delighted at the prospect of atomic power:

> When I first came here Antarctica was the cleanest place in the world. But we had to bring fire with us, and that meant smoke and soot.
>
> Diesels were a big improvement so far as power goes, but they still covered the camps with black dust. I think morale will get a boost from the use of nuclear power. It produces no smoke, and this place is prettier without it.

It may have been prettier, but nuclear reactor PM-3A—which Mc-Murdoites irreverently christened "Nukey Poo"—was by no means economical; in its first year of operation the reactor was shut down for an eight-week stretch during which emergency diesel fuel had to be flown in by helicopters, each burning a quantity of aviation gas nearly as great as the amount of fuel it carried. The plant continued intermittently to break down, and the energy it was producing turned out to be very expensive indeed. Since it is all but impossible to pour and cure concrete in Antarctica's subzero temperatures, the spent fuel from the reactor had to be housed in a large excavation back-filled with crushed gravel, which heated up and therefore melted some of the ice contained in the surrounding sodium-rich volcanic rock. Carried by the meltwater into the excavation, the dissolved sodium was turned into radioactive sodium-24. Solving *that* problem, by blowing air through the gravel to carry away the excess heat, the Navy found that the air was being irradiated also, so that its argon was being converted into radioactive argon-41. When Nukey Poo was finally shut down, in the Antarctic summer of 1972–73—at a cost exceeding what the manufacturer had received to build it—investigation disclosed leakage of radioactive effluent into the underlying soil. The Ant-

Geological Party at foot of Queen Maud Mountains, 1929
*Shows good exposure of Beacon Series of rocks. "No symphony I
have ever heard, no work of art before which I have stood in awe
ever gave me quite the thrill that I had when I reached out after
that strenuous climb and picked up a piece of rock to find it sandstone." (Laurence M. Gould, radio message to Commander
Byrd, December 29, 1929.)*

arctic Treaty forbade the dumping of *any* radioactive waste, so that
the Navy now had to shovel out thousands of tons of contaminated
earth and ship it away. "No one could have guessed 14 years
ago," a recent account sums up, "that the concluding act for this
reactor—a reactor which was going to revolutionize Antarctic living and provide electricity for only two-thirds the cost of diesel
generated power—would be two shiploads of dirt being sent half
way around the world." All the while, clean and virtually inex-
haustible geothermal energy might have been available; the smoking cone of Mount Erebus was only forty miles away.[23]

Antarctica was still full of wonderful surprises, however, for those who came with awe and love to that harsh and beautiful land. Larry Gould received just such a surprise when he came back to Antarctica late in 1969, to help celebrate the tenth anniversary of the Antarctic Treaty and the fortieth of Byrd's initial flight to the South Pole. Gould on December 7, 1929, at an outcrop high in the Queen Maud Mountains, had held in his hands one of the keys to Antarctic (and planetary) history (see chapter 5); now, over on the other side of the Victoria Range, new keys were falling into the hands of other geologists. A busy round of travel—a flight on November 29 along the Barrier to Little America and then south over Byrd's route (and "my sledge route too of course as far as Liv Gl[acier]") to lay a wreath at the Pole; a ceremony next day around Byrd's statue near the chapel at McMurdo; visits to the historic huts of Scott and Shackleton, to one of the strange ice-free "dry valleys," and to an Adélie rookery—did not distract Gould from what his scientific colleagues were doing elsewhere in Antarctica. On December 4, 1969, he wrote in his diary of "highly productive fossil finds" over at Coalsack Bluff, where Edwin Colbert's field party had that very day unearthed bones identified as *Lystrosaurus,* a fresh-water reptile that dated from the lower Triassic, early in the age of the dinosaurs. "This is the one specific fossil that establishes sharp stratigraphic relationships among the major southern hemisphere land masses," Gould wrote; "one of the great fossil finds of all time." He promptly got on radio to the National Science Foundation in Washington to tell them so.[24]

Scott's men and Gould's had found coal. Antarctica abounded in fossil ferns, tree stumps, and other evidence of a time when there was no snow and the land was covered with tropical green. Either the entire planet had at one time been warmer; or the poles had moved; or Antarctica itself had moved. Old World savants (Wegener, in Germany; Du Toit, in South Africa) had theorized of "continental drift," from a formerly continuous landmass from which all the present continents had broken off and moved away. American geologists, however, skeptical of the existence of a

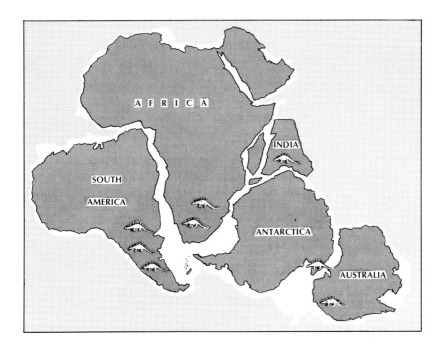

Ancient supercontinent of Gondwanaland, showing approximate locations of fossils of lystrosaurus. The Triassic reptile could have walked to Antarctica from Southern Africa. Adopted from John G. McPherson, Footprints on a Frozen Continent *(London: Methuen, 1975), pp. 150–51, and Edward H. Colbert,* Wandering Lands and Animals *(New York: Dutton, 1973), p. 60, fig. 26.*

source of sufficient energy to move those landmasses, had inclined to the view that the present continents have always been approximately where they are now. Fossils that paleontologists had found in similar rock strata all over the globe must therefore be the remains of animals that got from one continent to another over transient land bridges, the long way around. "But there was no 'long way around' to Antarctica," paleontologist Edwin Colbert objected. "There would seem to have been no possible land connection between Antarctica and South America" in the Age of Reptiles. The Triassic fossil he had just found, however, was identical to *Lystrosaurus* fossils previously discovered in southern Africa, in rocks stratigraphically similar to those where Colbert's men were working in 1969. But if the continents had lain undisturbed for most of Earth's history, there was no way *Lystrosaurus* could have gotten across from Africa to Antarctica. As Gould said afterward to his geology students in Arizona, "I don't think reptiles can build rafts."[25]

Colbert's discovery meant that historical geology was about to undergo a revolution as profound as that which Copernicus brought to astronomy. If the southern continents were once all fitted together into an ancient supercontinent, *Lystrosaurus* could have walked to Antarctica—a dubious decision on its part, inasmuch as Antarctica later fissioned off and drifted down to its present location, in the process becoming too cold for dinosaurs. Evidence other than from the fossil record was piling up also. The new subscience of plate tectonics, some of the data for which was coming from ships sounding the sea bottom near Antarctica, gave the geologists the hypothetical energy source they needed to account for the continents' having moved. "The American geological family," Professor Gould told his class, "has acted in a ridiculous fashion toward continental drift," resisting the theory to the point of not even holding conferences on the subject until the proofs became overwhelming. Perhaps that resistance was a subtle, scientifically rationalized version of American isolationism.

If an animal fossil species came into a stationary, sharply defined North American continent over a land bridge, it was an immigrant, and presumably subject to America's usual scrutiny of foreigners. But if it could move freely across a continuous landmass that only later was to break up and disperse, then at that far-off time the flora and fauna must have moved and mingled promiscuously across a primal continent where one could not even distinguish the existence of "New" and "Old" Worlds. The oneness of Earth in space, as astronauts and cosmonauts have seen it from their modules, seems matched by a oneness of Earth in time, as the post-IGY scientists have perceived it in Antarctica. When F. Scott Fitzgerald lamented (at the end of *The Great Gatsby*) that the European explorers and colonists of early America were "face to face for the last time in history with something commensurate to [their] capacity for wonder," he evidently overlooked the scientific wonder that lay waiting at the bottom of the world.

Prologue

1. This unexpectedly poetic passage occurs in an eassy with the prosy title "Description of a new Crustaceous Animal found on the Shores of the South Shetland Islands, with Remarks on their Natural History," by James Eights, which first appeared in the *Transactions of the Albany Institute*, 2 (1833–32): 53–69. A modern audience owes the resuscitation of this essay, and a rediscovery and appreciation of the work of its author, to an article by Joel W. Hudspeth, "James Eights of the Antarctic (1798–1882)," in Louis O. Quam and Horace D. Porter, eds., *Research in the Antarctic* (Washington: American Association for the Advancement of Science, 1971), pp. 3–40. This quotation is at p. 30.

2. *Time*, August 2, 1976, p. 23; Richard S. Lewis, *A Continent for Science: The Antarctic Adventure* (New York: Viking Press, 1965), p. 191; F. Michael Maish, "U.S.–Soviet Exchange Program at Vostok," in Richard S. Lewis and Philip M. Smith, eds., *Frozen Future: A Prophetic Report from Antarctica* (New York: Quadrangle Books, 1973), p. 341.

3. Anna Gertrude Hall, *Nansen* (New York: Viking Press, 1940), p. 51; John G. McPherson, *Footprints on a Frozen Continent* (London: Methuen, 1975), p. 50; George A. Llano, "A Survey of Antarctic Biology: Life Below Freezing," in Lewis and Smith, *Frozen Future*, p. 224.

4. Apsley Cherry-Garrard, *The Worst Journey in the World* (New York: Lincoln MacVeagh, The Dial Press, 1930), Introduction, p. xvii; Saint Augustine, *The City of God*, Gerald G. Walsh, S.J., et al., trans. (Garden City, N.Y.: Image Books, 1958), p. 367; Vincent H. Cassidy, *The Sea Around Them: The Atlantic Ocean, A.D. 1250* (Baton Rouge: Louisiana State University Press, 1968), p. 160.

5. Lewis, *Continent for Science*, p. 7; Philip I. Mitterling, *America in the Antarctic to 1840* (Urbana: University of Illinois Press, 1959), pp. 11–12; Brooke Hindle, *The Pursuit of Science in Revolutionary America* (Chapel Hill: University of North Carolina Press, 1956), pp. 99–100, 146–65.

6. James Cook, *A Voyage toward the South Pole, and Round the World, Performed in His Majesty's Ships the RESOLUTION and ADVENTURE, In the Years 1772, 1773, 1774*, and *1775* . . . (London: printed for W. Strahan and T. Cadell, 1777), Vol. 1, pp. ix, xxxvi, 258, 267–68. The standard biography of Cook, a monument of scholarship, is J. C. Beaglehole, *The Life of Captain James Cook* (Stanford, Ca.: Stanford University Press, 1974).

7. Mitterling, *America in the Antarctic*, p. 21; Kenneth J. Bertrand, *Americans in Antarctica 1775–1948* (New York: American Geographical Society, 1971), p. 67; Frank Debenham, ed., *The Voyage of Captain Bellingshausen to the Antarctic Seas, 1819–21* (London: Hakluyt Society, 1945), 1:420; Laurence M. Gould,

"Emergence of Antarctica: The Mythical Land," in Lewis and Smith, *Frozen Future,* p. 15.

8. *Voyage of Captain Bellingshausen,* 1:13–29, 112, 425.

9. James Monroe, seventh Annual Message, Dec. 2, 1823, in James D. Richardson, ed., *A Compilation of the Messages and Papers of the Presidents* (Washington: Bureau of National Literature, 1912), 2:788; John Quincy Adams, first Annual Message, Dec. 6, 1825, *ibid.,* pp. 878, 882.

10. Two substantial accounts of the Wilkes Antarctic expedition must be read against each other: David B. Tyler, *The Wilkes Expedition: The First United States Exploring Expedition 1838–1842* (Philadelphia: American Philosophical Society, 1968), which generally follows Charles Wilkes's own interpretation of events, and William Stanton, *The Great United States Exploring Expedition of 1838–1842* (Berkeley: University of California Press, 1975), which draws in large measure upon the diaries of Wilkes's disaffected subordinates and is far more critical than Tyler.

11. Mitterling, *America in the Antarctic,* p. 105; Edgar Allan Poe, "MS. Found in a Bottle," in Poe, *Tales* (New York: Grosset & Dunlap, n.d.), pp. 336, 332.

12. Thomas Philbrick, *James Fenimore Cooper and the Development of American Sea Fiction* (Cambridge: Harvard University Press, 1961), pp. 229, 232; James Eights, "On the Icebergs of the Ant-Arctic Sea," *American Quarterly Journal of Agriculture and Science,* 4 (1846):20–24, as reprinted in Quam and Porter, *Research in the Antarctic,* pp. 5–9.

13. Finn Ronne, *Antarctic Conquest: The Story of the Ronne Expedition, 1946–1948* (New York: G. P. Putnam's Sons, 1949), p. 97; Stanton, *U.S. Exploring Expedition,* pp. 320, 365, 296. American scientists in the nineteenth century seem to have been a good deal more theoretically oriented than we have usually assumed; they represented themselves as more utilitarian than they actually were in order to get their work financed, and they conceded a lead in theoretical work to Old World scientists only because the Europeans "had been studying their rocks longer." George H. Daniels, *American Science in the Age of Jackson* (New York: Columbia University Press, 1968), pp. 7, 9, 25, 32.

14. James Weddell, *A Voyage Towards the South Pole Performed in the years 1822–24, Containing an Examination of the Antarctic Sea,* reprinted with a new introduction by Sir Vivian Fuchs (Devon, Great Britain: printed for the U.S. Naval Institute, 1970), p. 36; Stanton, *U.S. Exploring Expedition,* pp. 101, 103.

15. James Clarke Ross, *A Voyage of Discovery and Research in the Southern Antarctic Regions* (London, 1847) as reprinted in Charles Neider, ed., *Antarctica: Authentic Accounts of Life and Exploration in the World's Highest, Driest, Windiest, Coldest and Most Remote Continent* (New York: Random House, 1972), p. 176; Una Pope-Hennessy, *Edgar Allan Poe, 1809–1849: A Critical Biography* (New York: Haskell House, 1971), p. 289.

16. Admiral Lord Mountevans, R.N., *The Antarctic Challenged* (New York:

John de Graff, Inc., 1955), p. 27; Walter Sullivan, *Quest for a Continent* (London: Secker & Warburg, 1957), p. 33.

17. Lennard Bickel, *Mawson's Will* (New York: Stein & Day, 1977), p. 24; Thomas Philbrick, *James Fenimore Cooper,* pp. 260–61; Jack London, *White Fang* (1906), as quoted in Earle Labor, *Jack London* (New York: Twayne Publishers, 1974), p. 136.

18. Hamlin Garland, *The Trail of the Goldseekers* (1899), as quoted in *ibid.,* p. 36.

19. Frederick A. Cook's diary for January 23, 1898, as quoted in Ian Cameron, *Antarctica: The Last Continent* (Boston: Little, Brown, 1974), p. 137.

20. Edward Wilson, *Diary of the Discovery Expedition to the Antarctic Regions 1901–1904* (London: Blandford Press, 1966), p. 111; L. B. Quartermain, *South to the Pole: The Early History of the Ross Sea Sector, Antarctica* (London: Oxford University Press, 1967), p. 84. Funds for the balloon operation were raised in part by public subscription; Quartermain notes that "a polite note of thanks to a lady who had given £5 is preserved in the Mitchell Library, Sydney." *Ibid.,* p. 141.

21. Sir Ernest Shackleton, *The Heart of the Antarctic* (Philadelphia: J. B. Lippincott, 1909), 1:72–75; Lord Mountevans, *Antarctic Challenged,* pp. 62–63. Laurence Gould agrees with Lord Mountevans: "Alas! If he [Shackleton] had but stopped here and made his quarters the pole would have been his." Gould, penciled annotations in personal copy of Shackleton's book (subsequently donated to the University of Arizona library), p. 73.

22. Thorstein Veblen, "The Place of Science in Modern Civilization," as reprinted in Perry Miller, ed., *American Thought: Civil War to World War I* (New York: Rinehart and Company, 1954), p. 306; Waldemar Kaemppfert, "Lifting the Veil from the Antarctic," *New York Times,* March 18, 1928, x, 21. A recent literary retelling of the Amundsen-Scott story is Kare Holt, *The Race: A Novel of Polar Exploration,* tr. by Joan Tate (New York: Delacorte Press, 1976). This is not so much a novel as the kind of fictionized biography that used to be in good repute. The author has read, and quotes accurately from, the polar literature, and then extrapolates from particularly revealing passages into the protagonists' minds. As a historical conjecture about these highly controversial events it is, perhaps, as plausible as a more conventional historical reconstruction of the diaries and memoirs might have been. Nevertheless, a historian becomes uneasy when the high point of this analysis is reached in an imagined *conversation* between Scott and Amundsen, at a time when the leaders were at their respective winter camps—four hundred miles apart, at opposite ends of the Ross Ice Shelf!

23. Scott as quoted in Quartermain, *South to the Pole,* p. 196; Amundsen as quoted in his own memoir *My Life as an Explorer* (Garden City, New York: Doubleday, Page, 1927), pp. 69–70; Scott's journal as quoted in Edward Ponting, *The Great White South; or, With Scott in the Antarctic, being an account of Experience with Captain Scott's South Pole expedition and of the Nature Life of the*

Antarctic (New York: Robert McBride and Company, 1929), p. 290. See also the excerpts from Roald Amundsen, *The South Pole,* and Leonard Huxley, ed., *Scott's Last Expedition,* in Neider, *Antarctica: Authentic Accounts,* pp. 199–224 and 227–67. An excellent recent biography of Captain Scott is Elspeth Huxley, *Scott of the Antarctic* (New York: Atheneum, 1978).

24. Duncan Carse, Introduction to F. A. Worsley, *Shackleton's Boat Journey* (London: The Folio Society, 1974), pp. 10–11; *Time,* December 19, 1977, p. 96. Evidence that interest in Antarctica had not entirely faded in those intervening years of the anti-hero is the selection as a Book-of-the-Month of Alfred Lansing, *Endurance: Shackleton's Incredible Voyage* (New York: McGraw Hill, 1959); 1959 was the year of ratification of the Antarctic Treaty, which brought the southern continent to a new focus of attention, not so much heroic as scientific and internationalist. See chapter 9.

25. Cartoon in *Columbus Dispatch,* reprinted in *Literary Digest,* 93 (June 25, 1927):15; Max Valier, "The Rocket-ship of the Future," *ibid.,* p. 93.

1. Ross Ice Shelf or Bust

1. Bernt Balchen, *Come North With Me* (New York: E. P. Dutton, 1958), p. 167. A good recent description of Spitsbergen is Gordon Young, "Norway's Strategic Arctic Islands," *National Geographic,* 154 (August, 1978): 266–83.

2. Byrd evidently told this story afterward to several of his colleagues in the Little America venture. Paul Siple, *90° South: The Story of the American South Pole Conquest* (New York: Putnam, 1959), p. 38; Laurence McKinley Gould, personal interview, October 19, 1977. Byrd himself implied however that the Little America expedition was not (in Siple's words) "begun as an impulsive remark," but was a "plan which I had secretly worked out," although he had not spoken of it until the meeting with Amundsen; Richard Evelyn Byrd, *Little America* (New York: Putnam, 1930), p. 24. When Byrd later announced his intentions at a small formal Polar Legion dinner in Washington, Amundsen's reaction seems to have been more blasé: "Byrd can fly to the South Pole, if he wants to, but what is the use?" Lincoln Ellsworth, *Beyond Horizons* (New York: Book League of America, 1938), p. 120.

3. Alden Hatch, *The Byrds of Virginia* (New York: Holt, Rinehart, & Winston, 1969), p. 304; Bernt Balchen, "The Strange Enigma of Admiral Byrd," typed manuscript included in correspondence between Balchen and L. M. Gould, 1949–59, in Laurence M. Gould Papers, Center for Polar and Scientific Archives, RG 401, National Archives.

4. Richard E. Byrd, "Why I Am Going to the South Pole," *World's Work,* 55 (December 1927): 158; Byrd, *Little America,* p. 25; *New York Times,* March 11, 1928.

5. "We considered Hearst a bitter enemy due to newspaper rights and contracts made by the Com. [i.e., Commander Byrd] to the New York Times." Epaminondas J. Demas, manuscript diary "Byrd Antarctic Expedition 1928," vol. 2 (Nov. 19, 1928–July 4, 1929), entry for June 1, 1929; in Epaminondas J. Demas Papers, Center for Polar and Scientific Archives, RG 401, National Archives.

6. *Literary Digest,* 97 (June 23, 1928):50; Earl Hanson, "The 'Race to the South Pole,' " *The Nation,* 127 (October 24, 1928): 418–20; Laurence M. Gould, personal interview, Dec. 5, 1977. There was, nonetheless, more worry among members of the Little America expedition about Wilkins and his plans than Byrd cared to acknowledge. "Wilkins was a favorite subject of conversation both at sea and later at Little America," aerologist Henry T. Harrison observed (in a letter to the author, April 15, 1978). After the South Pole flight was over, Harrison wrote in his diary: "Everyone breathes more freely with the polar flight out of the way and Sir Hubert Wilkins and his threat to beat us to the pole are practically forgotten." "Local color at Little America during First South Pole Flight," typed excerpt from diary of Henry T. Harrison, in Harrison Papers, Center for Polar and Scientific Archives, RG 401, National Archives.

7. *New York Times,* March 18, III, p. 1; *ibid.,* March 13, 1928, p. 1; J. Olin Howe, "The Bottom of the World," *Popular Mechanics,* 49 (February 1928): 195.

8. Byrd, *Little America,* p. 29; Siple, *90° South,* p. 39; picture caption, *Literary Digest,* 98 (September 15, 1928): 34; Harry Adams, *Beyond the Barrier with Byrd: An Authentic Story of the Byrd Antarctic Expedition* (Chicago: Goldsmith Publishing Company, 1932), pp. 26, 187; *New York Times,* July 13, 1928, p. 2. The diary of expedition member Henry T. Harrison confirms Melville's respect for nautical superstition, in an entry made while the *City of New York* was at sea: "Mac caught an albatross in morning but Capt. ordered it turned loose saying it was 'bad luck to kill one.' " Henry T. Harrison manuscript diary (photocopied pages by the kind courtesy of Mr. Harrison), entry for Nov. 17, 1928.

9. *New York Times,* July 15, 1928, III, p. 9; Byrd, *Little America,* p. 28; Laurence M. Gould, classroom lecture in Geosciences 254, University of Arizona, February 17, 1978; Arnold Clarke, Manuscript diary, entry for February 22, 1929, in Arnold H. Clarke Papers, Center for Polar Archives, RG 401, National Archives; Adams, *Beyond the Barrier,* pp. 59, 60; Arnold Clarke diary, entry for February 21, 1929, Clarke Papers.

10. Byrd, *Little America,* p. 28; "Personal Record or Diary of L M Gould, Geologist and Geographer, Byrd Antarctic Expedition, beginning Sept 28, 1928," xerox and transcript [of original in Vilhjalmur Stefannson Collection, Dartmouth College Library], initial entry, p. 2, in Laurence M. Gould Papers, Center for Polar and Scientific Archives, RG 401, National Archives. In fairness to Byrd it should be noted that Tromsoe, Norway, by the kinds of transportation available in 1928, was not the easiest place to get to; sending someone to check

the ship out at dockside might have taken more time and trouble than it was worth.

11. V. I. Cooper, "Stocking Up an Expedition's Larder," *Scientific American,* 139 (November 1928): 433–35; *New York Times,* August 26, 1928, p. 1; *ibid.,* July 2, p. 1; *ibid.,* July 26, p. 1; *ibid.,* Sept. 12, p. 29; *Literary Digest,* 98 (Sept. 15, 1928): 34; *New York Times,* July 31, 1928, p. 8; *ibid.,* August 15, p. 23; *ibid.,* Aug. 4, p. 4.

12. Francis Dana Coman to Major Cyrus Wood, Medical Corps, August 23, 1928; Coman to Cornelius H. Tuszynski, vice-president of Davis & Beck, August 22, 1928; The Bay Company to Richard E. Byrd, August 10, 1928; Francis D. Coman to Rogers Brothers Seed Company, August 23, 1928; Coman to Smith, Kline & French, August 23, 1928. In file of correspondence received, Dana Coman Papers, Center for Polar and Scientific Archives, RG 401, National Archives.

13. Bernt Balchen, *Come North With Me,* p. 152; Cooper, "Stocking Up," pp. 433–34; *New York Times,* August 25, 1928, p. 7. Donations, as of mid-September—after the *City of New York*'s departure, and prior to the *Eleanor Bolling*'s—were listed at $435,000; expenditures, $343,000, with some costs (for example, that of transporting the sledge dogs across the continent and embarkation and of reconditioning the two ships) not yet accounted for. Figures furnished by Byrd to the *New York World,* as quoted in *Literary Digest,* 98 (September 15, 1928): 48, 50.

14. Byrd, *Little America,* pp. 38–39, 20, 10; Byrd, "How I Pick My Men," *Saturday Evening Post,* 200 (April 21, 1928): 12, 13, 58; *Literary Digest,* 98 (September 15, 1928): 34, citing the *Brooklyn Eagle, Boston Globe,* and (p. 36) *Washington Star;* typed memo, Byrd to Coman, dated 4:30 P.M. July 30, 1928, in file of correspondence received, Dana Coman Papers.

15. Byrd had nevertheless begun recruiting actively long before any formal announcements were made. William C. Haines, the expedition's meteorologist, stated later that Byrd on the ship coming back from Spitsbergen, where Haines had served in a similar capacity, asked him. "Bill, how about going to the Antarctic with me?" Haines, however, that early in the game, "didn't really think Byrd was in earnest about it." Typescript from story in *St. Louis Post-Dispatch,* June 10, 1948, by F. A. Behymer, "Colorful Life as Weather Observer: William C. Haines tells of career in meteorology," p. 2. This typescript is in the correspondence file, William C. Haines Papers, Center for Polar and Scientific Archives, RG 401, National Archives.

16. *New York Times,* March 11, 1928, p. 2; Byrd, "How I Choose My Men," p. 58; Byrd, "Why I Am Going to the South Pole," p. 162; Laurence M. Gould, personal interview, December 5, 1977. Before sailing, Commander Byrd declared himself well satisfied with the results; Byrd, "Crusaders," *Saturday Evening Post,* 201 (September 22, 1928): 6–7, 169–70, 173–74, 177.

17. Roald Amundsen, *My Life as An Explorer* (Garden City: Doubleday,

1927), p. 237; Gould interview, December 5, 1977 (however, Gould also adds that the psychiatric screening for present-day scientific expeditions in Antarctica is "very important," an acknowledgement that times do change); Henry T. Harrison to the author, September 17, 1978.

18. James E. West, Chief Scout Executive, Boy Scouts of America, "The Selection of a Boy Scout for the Byrd Expedition Expedition," appendix to Paul Siple, *A Boy Scout With Byrd* (New York: Putnam, 1931), 153–64; *New York Times,* August 21, 1928, p. 27 (under "Amusements"!); *ibid.,* Aug. 22, p. 12; *ibid.,* Aug. 23, p. 14.

19. *Ibid.,* August 25, p. 1; *ibid.,* August 24, p. 19; Russell Owen, "Byrd's Ship Sails with 32 Adventurers on First Lap of Her Antarctic Voyage," *ibid.,* Aug. 26, 1928, pp. 1, 17.

20. W. A. MacDonald in *Boston Transcript,* as quoted in *Literary Digest,* 98 (September 15, 1928): 46–47.

21. *New York Times,* August 27, 1928, p. 1; *ibid.,* September 17, p. 1; Arnold Clarke diary, entry for September 16, 1928, Clarke Papers; Adams, *Beyond the Barrier,* pp. 42, 61; *New York Times,* September 20, 1928, in story by William T. Christian, "Adventure Besets Byrd Ship's Voyage"; Epaminondas J. Demas manuscript diary, Vol. 1, entry for September 20, 1928, Demas Papers.

22. Byrd, *Little America,* pp. 11, 9; Amundsen, *My Life as an Explorer,* p. 36.

23. Finn Ronne, *Antarctic Conquest* (New York: Putnam, 1949), p. 6; Byrd, *Little America,* pp. 12–13, 6, 7; Malcolm Anthony, "Silent Lady," *American Magazine,* 110 (July 1930): 68–69, 86.

24. Byrd, *Little America,* pp. 7, 8. This entire chapter in Byrd's account of the first Antarctic expedition, titled "Notes From a Journal," may have been as close as its author ever came to dropping his public mask. "Sometimes," one formerly close associate has written, "I think the secrets of the Poles are easier to solve than the mystery of this man." Bernt Balchen, "The Strange Enigma of Admiral Byrd," typed manuscript, p. 2. In correspondence file, Gould Papers.

25. *Washington Star* and *Tacoma Ledger* as quoted in *Literary Digest,* 98 (September 15, 1928), p. 34; but compare the balancing quote, in *ibid.,* from the *Houston Post-Dispatch,* which argued that the million dollars ought to have been spent on educational loan funds instead: "Spent on Antarctic exploration it will return nothing of value to the world." The quote from the *Salt Lake Telegram* is in *Literary Digest,* 100 (March 9, 1929): 8.

26. Byrd, *Little America,* p. 9; Epaminondas J. Demas diary, vol. 1, entry for October 10, 1928, Demas Papers; Byrd, *Little America,* p. 21.

27. L. B. Quartermain, *South to the Pole: The Early History of the Ross Sea Sector, Antarctica* (London: Oxford University Press, 1967), pp. 299, 290; Byrd, *Little America,* p. 20.

28. Laurence M. Gould, "Personal Record or Diary," entry for November 3, 1928 at Papeete, Gould Papers; William Stanton, *The Great United States Explor-*

ing Expedition of 1838-1842 (Berkeley and Los Angeles: University of California Press, 1975), *passim.*

29. E. J. Demas diary, vol. 2, entry for November 25, 1928, Demas Papers; Siple, *90° South,* p. 39.

30. Herman Melville, *Moby-Dick,* chap. XXXV; Siple, *A Boy Scout With Byrd,* p. 14.

2. They Named It Little America

1. *New York Times,* November 4, 1928, III, p. 6; *Encyclopaedia Britannica* (Chicago: William Benton, 1959), 8:740; *Times Atlas of the World,* 5th ed., revised (London: Times Books, 1957), Plate 11; Ian Wards, ed., *New Zealand Atlas* (Wellington: A. R. Shearer, government printer, 1976), p. 33.

2. Paul A. Siple, *90° South: The Story of the American South Pole Conquest* (New York: Putnam, 1959), pp. 39–40. "Perhaps no Boy Scout ever so belied his name," Russell Owen observed of Siple. "He worked hard, kept his mouth shut, listened without comment to the ribaldry that went on about him, and never took part in it. He has the poise of a much older and experienced man." Owen, *South of the Sun* (New York: John Day, 1934), pp. 57–58.

3. Siple, *90° South,* p. 39; "Report on Fairchild Cabin Monoplane NX-8006, 'Stars and Stripes,' " carbon copy (marked in pencil "Demas") of typescript, p. 5, in Epaminondas Demas Papers, Center for Polar and Scientific Archives, RG 401, National Archives.

4. Owen, *South of the Sun,* pp. 12, 13, 24.

5. Laurence M. Gould, lecture in Geosciences 254, University of Arizona, February 27, 1978; Gould, "Personal Record or Diary . . . beginning Sept. 28, 1928," Xerox copy, entries for December 12 and 16, 1928, in Laurence M. Gould Papers, Center for Polar and Scientific Archives, RG 401, National Archives.

6. Russell Owen, "Byrd's Pilots Mind Balky Wheel in Ice," datelined *City of New York,* December 21 (transmission resumed after previous day's message had been lost by fading), *New York Times,* December 24, 1928, p. 6.

7. Walter Sullivan, *Quest for a Continent* (London: Secker & Warburg, 1957), pp. 100, 282.

8. "When I went down in 1928 they took 30,000 blue whales. Now there are probably no more than a thousand left." Laurence M. Gould, lecture in Geosciences 254, University of Arizona, February 13, 1978.

9. Bernt Balchen, *Come North With Me* (New York: E. P. Dutton, 1958), p. 163; Siple, *90° South,* p. 40.

10. *New York Times,* December 27, 1928, pp. 1, 2 (two stories); William James, *Essays on Faith and Morals* (Cleveland: World Publishing Company, 1962), pp. 311–28, esp. p. 326.

11. Parker's remark is as cited in *New York Times,* December 27, p. 1.

12. Paul A. Siple, *A Boy Scout With Byrd* (New York: Putnam, 1931), pp. 30–31; Russell Owen, *South of the Sun,* p. 55. On the foibles of penguins, see further Thomas R. Henry, *The White Continent* (New York: William Sloane, 1950), pp. 175–89.

13. *New York Times,* December 27, 1928, p. 2; Siple, *A Boy Scout With Byrd,* pp. 32–33.

14. Laurence M. Gould, "The Ross Shelf Ice," *Bulletin of the Geological Society of America,* 46 (September 30, 1935): 1367–93, esp. the map showing the changing boundaries of the Bay of Whales, Fig. 2, p. 1376; Gould, "Personal Record," entry for December 28, 1928, Gould Papers.

15. Richard Evelyn Byrd, *Little America* (New York: Putnam, 1930), pp. 90, 91 (citing his own journal).

16. *New York Times,* March 18, 1928, X, p. 21; R. L. Duffus, "Covering the News of Frozen Antarctica," *ibid.,* February 10, 1929, X, p. 4; Russell Owen, *The Conquest of the North and South Poles: Adventures of the Peary and Byrd Expeditions* (New York: Random House, 1952), p. 172.

17. Siple, *90° South,* p. 41; Laurence M. Gould, personal interview, December 5, 1977; Richard E. Byrd, "Crusaders," *Saturday Evening Post,* 201 (September 22, 1928):170; Epaminondas J. Demas, manuscript diary "Byrd Antarctic Expedition 1929," Vol. 2 (Nov. 19, 1928–July 4, 1929), entries for December 31, 1928 and January 1, 1929, Demas Papers. Professor Gould believes there never was any real doubt that Siple would stay, having eminently proven his worth. Gould, personal interview, April 12, 1978.

18. Laurence M. Gould, manuscript diary titled "L. M. Gould BAE I, beginning Jan 6, 1929," Vol. 1 (through August 1, 1929), entry for Jan. 2, 1929, Gould Papers; Byrd, *Little America,* pp. 92–95.

19. Owen, *South of the Sun,* p. 56; E. J. Demas, manuscript diary, Vol. 2, entries for January 11 and January 20, 1929, Demas Papers (Demas misspelled Creagh's name as "Craig").

20. Laurence M. Gould manuscript diary, Vol. 1, entries for January 8, 10, 11, and 22, 1929, Gould Papers.

21. Byrd, *Little America,* pp. 101–2, 14, 103–5; Henry T. Harrison manuscript diary, entry for January 15, 1929, copied by Mr. Harrison and kindly included in a letter to the author, September 17, 1978; Gould, manuscript diary "BAE I," Vol. 1, entry for Jan. 20, 1929, Gould Papers.

22. Owen, *South of the Sun,* p. 54; Terris Moore, reviewing Mike Banks, *High Arctic* (London: J. M. Dent, 1957), in *Appalachia,* 32 (June 15, 1958):135.

23. Arthur T. Walden as interviewed by John T. Brady, "Dog Heroes of the White Hell," *Popular Mechanics,* 54 (September 1930):380, 382. Professor Gould is skeptical of the detail about Byrd's having told the airplane pilots to keep a lookout for the lost dog, because a dark object on snow from any distance tends to become invisible against its background. Laurence M. Gould, personal interview, April 14, 1978.

24. Gould, manuscript diary "BAE I," Vol. 1, entry for January 25, 1929,

Gould Papers; Byrd, *Little America,* pp. 117–25. On closer inspection these peaks proved less impressive: "To anyone expecting a great mountain range the Rockefellers are rather disappointing;" moreover, their rock formations ultimately proved "barren of any interesting or important mineralization." Laurence M. Gould, "Some Geographical Results of the Byrd Antarctic Expedition," *Geographical Review,* 21 (April, 1931):178, 179.

25. Gould, lecture in Geosciences 254, University of Arizona, February 17, 1978. Rockefeller responded handsomely to Byrd's tribute: "Just back from Egypt. I have learned of the honor you have done me in giving a mountain range the name Rockefeller. . . . But your own safety and the safety of your men is worth more than all the mountain ranges in the world." Radiogram dated 0330 March 16 [1929], in file of memoranda and radiograms, Arnold H. Clarke Papers, Center for Polar and Scientific Archives, RG 401, National Archives.

26. Byrd, *Little America,* pp. 125, 132; Owen, *South of the Sun,* pp. 70–71; Arnold H. Clarke manuscript diary, entry for Feb. 20, 1929, Clarke Papers. Even though he was in fact chosen to winter over, Clarke remained a loyal partisan of his ship: "This business of staying on the ice may have it's attractions and rewards, but the honor of having been one of the Bolling Crew willl not easily be surpassed."

27. *New York Times,* March 5, 1929, p. 3; Byrd, *Little America,* p. 124.

28. Gould, "Some Geographical Results," p. 178; Gould, manuscript diary "BAE I," Vol. 1, entries for March 10, 14, and 15, 1929.

29. Harold June's diary as quoted in Ian Cameron, *Antarctica: The Last Continent* (Boston: Little, Brown, 1974), p. 197; Gould, "Some Geographical Results," pp. 178, 179; Henry Harrison manuscript diary, entry for March 22, 1929, copied by Mr. Harrison and kindly included in a letter to the author, September 17, 1978.

30. George J. Dufek, *Operation Deepfreeze* (New York: Harcourt, Brace, 1957), p. 117. The Fokker's engine and propeller, however, had been salvaged and brought back to Little America on Byrd's second expedition, just before it left Antarctica early in 1935. Richard F. Byrd, *Discovery: the Story of the Second Byrd Antarctic Expedition* (New York: G. P. Putnam's Sons, 1935), pp. 337, 357.

3. Wintering Over

1. Richard E. Byrd, *Little America,* (New York: Putnam, 1930), pp. 149, 196; Ian Cameron, *Antarctica: The Last Continent* (Boston: Little, Brown, 1974), p. 195.

2. Laurence M. Gould, personal interview, January 13, 1978; Gould, *Cold: The Record of an Antarctic Sledge Journey,* (New York: Brewer, Warren & Putnam, 1931), p. 42.

3. Bernt Balchen, "The Strange Enigma of Admiral Byrd," p. 11, typescript

in file of correspondence between Balchen and L. M. Gould, 1949–1959, in Laurence M. Gould Papers, Center for Polar and Scientific Archives, RG 401, National Archives; Byrd, *Little America,* p. 197. On this kind of point, diaries and reminiscences of other members of the expedition are necessarily incomplete as a historical source. However, without Byrd's own papers, which have not hitherto been available to scholars, any personal judgment about Admiral Byrd must be to a great extent a matter of inference and conjecture.

4. This description of the layout of living arrangements at Little America is collated from Byrd, *Little America,* esp. p. 233, a useful and detailed map; Paul A. Siple, *A Boy Scout With Byrd* (New York: Putnam, 1931), which gives the clearest extant description of the several houses; Laurence M. Gould, manuscript diary titled "L. M. Gould BAE I, beginning Jan 6, 1929," Vol. 1 (through August 1, 1929), entry for March 2, 1929, Gould Papers, which sorts out the expedition members by residence; Siple, *90° South: The Story of the American South Pole Conquest* (New York: Putnam, 1959), p. 41; Gould, *Cold,* p. 55; Bernt Balchen, *Come North With Me* (New York: E. P. Dutton, 1958), p. 179; and Russell Owen, *South of the Sun* (New York: John Day, 1934), p. 92.

5. Byrd, *Little America,* p. 201; "Report on Fairchild Cabin Monoplane NX-8006, 'Stars and Stripes,' " carbon copy (marked in pencil "Demas") of typescript in Epaminondas Demas Papers, Center for Polar and Scientific Archives, RG 401, National Archives; Siple, *A Boy Scout With Byrd,* pp. 76–79; Laurence M. Gould, personal interview, December 5, 1977. Gould has a photo of Al Smith in his office, along with other Antarctic memorabilia. It is the same picture that appears in this book.

6. Owen, *South of the Sun,* pp. 95, 239; Owen, "What Byrd's Men Do in the Antarctic Night," *New York Times,* May 19, 1929, X, p. 4; Byrd, *Little America,* p. 198.

7. This account of the expedition's daily routine is collated from Owen, "What Byrd's Men Do"; Laurence M. Gould, *Cold,* pp. 54–59; Gould, manuscript diary "BAE I," Volume I, entry for June 16, 1929, Gould Papers; Owen, *South of the Sun,* p. 145; Byrd, *Little America,* pp. 199–200, 269; *New York Times,* Feb. 14, 1929; and Paul A. Siple, *A Boy Scout With Byrd,* p. 87. Henry Harrison adds that he and Haines made 414 such balloon runs during their 14 months at Little America. Harrison to author, September 17, 1978.

8. Jerome Alexander, "Physicochemical Phenomena in the Antarctic," *Science,* n. s. 72 (November 7, 1930):478; Byrd, *Little America,* pp. 207, 232; Arnold H. Clarke manuscript diary, entry for May 17, 1929, in Arnold H. Clarke Papers, Center for Polar and Scientific Archives, RG 401, National Archives.

9. Owen, *South of the Sun,* p. 108; F. A. Behymer, "Colorful Life As Weather Observer—William C. Haines Tells of Career in Meteorology," *St. Louis Post-Dispatch,* June 10, 1948, typed transcript in William C. Haines Papers, Center for Polar and Scientific Archives, RG 401, National Archives; Byrd, *Little America,* p. 193; Siple, *A Boy Scout With Byrd,* p. 95.

10. Gould, *Cold,* pp. 57–58; Byrd, *Little America,* p. 226. On some of these

walks Commander Byrd asked other expedition members—a different one each time—to accompany him, and these walks of Byrd's have been the subject of considerable controversy. Was he functioning as a father-figure, to hear and counsel his men concerning their personal problems? Or did he use these private talks as a means for psychological manipulation and control? Compare Siple, *A Boy Scout With Byrd,* p. 86; Richard E. Byrd, *Alone* (New York: Putnam, 1938), p. 16; Bernt Balchen, "The Strange Enigma of Admiral Byrd," pp. 10–12, in correspondence file, Gould Papers; Laurence M. Gould to Bernt Balchen, April 12, 1958, copy in correspondence file, Gould Papers; Arnold H. Clarke manuscript diary, entry for August 26, 1929, Clarke Papers; Epaminondas Demas diaries (leatherbound pocket notebook covering Jan. 11, 1929 to Nov. 26, 1929, and larger diary, Vol. 3, covering July 5, 1929 to March 1, 1930), entries for July 28, 1929, Demas Papers.

11. Russell Owen, "What Byrd's Men Do in the Antarctic Night," as cited in note 6; Siple, *90° South,* p. 41; Byrd, *Little America,* p. 221; Gould, manuscript diary "BAE I," Vol. 1, entry for June 11, 1929, Gould Papers; Laurence M. Gould, *Cold,* p. 48. De Ganahl, however, apparently had had some previous experience with radio; his name appears on several bylined *Times* stories sent from the *Bolling* en route in 1928.

12. Owen, "What Byrd's Men Do"; Arnold Clarke manuscript diary, entry for July 10, 1929, Clarke Papers; Byrd, *Little America,* p. 224; Owen, *South of the Sun,* p. 121; Gould, *Cold,* p. 59.

13. Russell Owen, "Sabbath Observed at Byrd's Camp," *New York Times,* May 13, 1929, p. 4; Byrd, *Little America,* p. 220; Gould, *Cold,* p. 49.

14. Gould, *Cold,* p. 44; Laurence M. Gould, personal interview, May 1, 1978; Victor Czegka, biographical statement (dated April 20, 1972), in Victor Czegka Papers, Center for Polar and Scientific Archives, RG 401, National Archives; Gould, personal interview, April 12, 1978.

15. Laurence M. Gould, personal interview, January 13, 1978; Owen, *South of the Sun,* p. 258; *New York Times,* April 1, 1929; *Publisher's Weekly,* 116 (August 24, 1929):722; *ibid.,* 117 (June 14, 1930):2920–22; Gould, *Cold,* pp. 64–65.

16. Owen, *South of the Sun,* p. 146; Byrd, *Little America,* pp. 224–25; Epaminondas Demas, larger manuscript diary, Vol. 2, (covering Nov. 19, 1928 to July 4, 1929), entry for July 2, Demas Papers.

17. Robert L. Nichols, "More on Antarctic Historic Huts," *Appalachia,* 33 (December 15, 1961): 558–59; Byrd, *Little America,* p. 220; Gould manuscript diary "BAE I," Vol. 1, entry for Sunday [April 7], 1929, Gould Papers; *New York Times,* July 28, 1929, p. 12; Siple, *A Boy Scout With Byrd,* pp. 91–92; Gould, *Cold,* p. 49.

18. *New York Times* editorial, April 9, 1929, p. 30; Gould diary, entry for May 13. Since the *Times* bracketed its own statement with a highly poetic passage on the *aurora borealis* from Nansen's *Farthest North,* which ended "Is not all

life's beauty high, and delicate, and pure like this night?'' the newspaper's insistence upon the miraculousness of ordinary radio chatter seems particularly crass.

19. Gould diary, entries for May 13 and June 25, 1929. Henry Harrison adds: "It was a 40 mph gale from Northeast—first blizzard from that direction." Harrison to author, September 17, 1978.

20. Thirty years later, apropos of the Navy's decision to permit liquor on the Antarctic Continent for Operation Deepfreeze I, Paul Siple made the quite incredible statement that "in the past we had always forbidden liquor on expeditions. There was no way to know how men already keyed up would react under its influence and a group of isolated individuals battling the elements had sufficient problems without adding to their burden." Siple, *90° South,* p. 112. The diaries and memoirs of his bunkmates simply do not bear him out: "Siple's memory on this point was *very* bad," comments Henry Harrison (in a letter to the author, September 17, 1978). "He may have been thinking of his fellow officer on BAEII''—the second Little America expedition in 1934—"who went on a Carrie Nation tear one night and destroyed the complete liquor supply of the camp according to a pretty reliable source." On this point see further below, chapter 6.

21. Gould, manuscript diary "BAE I," Vol. 1, entry for May 12, 1929, Gould Papers; Owen, *South of the Sun,* p. 101.

22. Epaminondas Demas, larger manuscript diary, Vol. 2, entry for May 17, 1929, Demas Papers; Laurence M. Gould, manuscript diary "BAE I," Vol. 1, entry for May 27, 1929, Gould Papers; Owen, *South of the Sun,* p. 111; Gould, manuscript diary, entry for July 6; Demas, larger manuscript diary, vol. 3, entries for July 5, July 6, and July 12, Demas Papers.

23. Owen, *South of the Sun,* p. 141; Laurence M. Gould, manuscript diary, Volume 2, (red leather notebook hand labeled "L. M. Gould, B. A. E. I, Beginning Aug. 9, 1929''), first entry, Gould Papers; Owen, *South of the Sun,* pp. 145, 160; Gould diary, vol. 2, entry for August 21, 1929.

4. Into the White Wilderness

1. Russell Owen, *South of the Sun* (New York: John Day, 1934), pp. 159–60; Richard E. Byrd, *Little America* (New York: Putnam, 1930), p. 271. The phrase "deep shadow of the world" is Sverre Strom's.

2. Laurence M. Gould, handwritten comment on an earlier draft of this manuscript, May 20, 1978; Byrd, *Little America,* p. 272; Paul A. Siple, *A Boy Scout With Byrd* (New York: Putnam, 1931), p. 96; Gould, manuscript diary, Vol. 2 (red leather notebook hand labeled "L. M. Gould, B.A.E. I, Beginning Aug. 9, 1929''), entry for August 23, 1929, in Laurence M. Gould Papers, Center for Polar and Scientific Archives, RG 401, National Archives; Owen, *South of the Sun,* p. 167.

3. Epaminondas Demas, small manuscript diary (red leather pocket notebook

covering Jan. 11, 1929 to Nov. 26, 1929), entries for Aug. 31, Sept. 2, Sept. 3, Sept. 4, and Sept. 14, in Epaminondas Demas Papers, Center for Polar and Scientific Archives, RG 401, National Archives; "Report on Fairchild Cabin Monoplane NX-8006, 'Stars and Stripes,' " carbon copy (marked in pencil "Demas") of typescript in Demas Papers; Owen, *South of the Sun*, p. 184.

4. Siple, *Boy Scout with Byrd*, pp. 116–19.

5. Byrd, *Little America*, pp. 282, 286, 294.

6. Henry T. Harrison manuscript diary (photocopied pages by the kind courtesy of Mr. Harrison), entry for October 29, 1929; John Kenneth Galbraith, *The Great Crash* (Boston: Houghton Mifflin, 1961), pp. 103–4, 116.

7. Byrd, *Little America*, p. 221; Russell Owen, "Even Antarctic Felt Crash; Byrd Aide a Loser, but Grins," *New York Times*, November 1, 1929, p. 2. The *Times* at that point was itself treating the Crash rather lightheartedly. Its page one headline read "Stocks up again on flood of buying; thousands of orders flood into brokers' offices before the opening at noon."

8. Frederick Lewis Allen, *Only Yesterday* (New York: Bantam Books, 1952), p. 304; Russell Owen, *South of the Sun*, p. 223; Henry Harrison diary, entries for October 30, November 1, and November 4, 1929, courtesy of Mr. Harrison.

9. Laurence M. Gould, *Cold: The Record of an Antarctic Sledge Journey* (New York: Brewer, Warren, & Putnam, 1931), p. 125; Gould, large (8″ x 11″) ledger-paper notebook autographed on flyleaf "L. M. Gould Byrd Antarctic Expedition Southern Sledging Party Log," entry for November 4, 1929, in Laurence M. Gould Papers, Center for Polar and Scientific Archives, RG 401, National Archives; Byrd, *Little America*, p. 303; Harrison diary, entry for Nov. 5, 1929, courtesy of Mr. Harrison.

10. Laurence M. Gould, sledging party log, entry for Nov. 7, 8, 10, and 11, 1929, Gould Papers; Gould, classroom lecture in Geosciences 254, University of Arizona, Feb. 17, 1978; Gould, *Cold*, pp. 76–78, 84, 87.

11. Laurence M. Gould, sledging party log, entries for November 13 and 14, 1929, Gould Papers; Henry T. Harrison diary, entry for November 13, courtesy of Mr. Harrison; E. J. Demas, small manuscript diary, entry for Nov. 15, Demas Papers (in his larger diary, Vol. 3, covering July 5, 1929–March 1, 1930, Demas wrote up later at his leisure and entered as of November 15 a description of the motor tuneup work); Russell Owen, *South of the Sun*, p. 227.

12. Henry T. Harrison diary, entry for November 17, 1929, courtesy of Mr. Harrison; Laurence M. Gould, sledging party log, entries for Nov. 17 and 18, Gould Papers; Byrd, *Little America*, pp. 311–12.

13. Henry Harrison diary, entries for Nov. 18, 19, and 20, 1929, courtesy of Mr. Harrison.

14. Byrd, *Little America,*, pp. 329, 319; Owen, *South of the Sun*, p. 236; Siple, *Boy Scout With Byrd*, p. 109.

15. Laurence M. Gould, sledging party log, entries for November 19, 22, and 23, 1929, Gould Papers; Henry T. Harrison diary, entries for Nov. 22, 23, 24,

25, 26, and 27, 1929, courtesy of Mr. Harrison; Arnold H. Clarke manuscript diary, entry for Thursday, November 26, 1929, in Arnold H. Clarke Papers, Center for Polar and Scientific Archives, RG 401, National Archives.

16. Byrd, *Little America,* pp. 326–27; W. L. G. Joerg, *The Work of the Byrd Antarctic Expedition, 1928–1930* (New York: American Geographical Society, 1930), p. 39.

17. Arnold Clarke to Mr. Henry (otherwise unidentified), December 1, 1929 (mailed from San Francisco, April 15, 1930), carbon copy in file of correspondence, news clippings, and reports, Clarke Papers; Henry T. Harrison diary, entry for Nov. 28, 1929, courtesy of Mr. Harrison; *New York Times,* Nov. 29, 1929, p. 2; *ibid.,* Nov. 30, p. 3. Balchen evidently cut short his nap; the Harrison diary indicates that he had all three motors going by 2:45.

18. Altimeter readings on this and other flights in Antarctica in 1929 were notoriously unreliable. Balchen later gave a figure of 8200 feet—"just about the Ford's ceiling with its present loading"—for this moment just before June dumped the first food sack. Bernt Balchen, *Come North With Me* (New York: E. P. Dutton, 1958), p. 189.

19. Here is another statistic that does not square. Commenting on this passage Henry Harrison writes: "As an airline dispatcher for two years, I remember that we assumed 6 pounds per gallon for gasoline. 200 pounds therefore would represent about 33 gallons." Harrison to author, September 17, 1978. Perhaps Byrd meant that if June had opened the dump valve of the fuselage tank he would have had to let go its entire contents—more than necessary to make their ceiling.

20. Byrd, *Little America,* pp. 328–45; Joerg, *Work of the Byrd Expedition,* pp. 1, 37–51; Balchen, *Come North With Me,* pp. 187–91; *New York Times,* Nov. 30, 1929; *ibid.,* Dec. 1, 1929; Paul A. Siple, *90° South: The Story of the American South Pole Conquest* (New York: Putnam, 1959), p. 46. The portion of the Joerg book cited here is essentially a transcript of the account of the flight which Byrd wrote at Little America immediately upon his return, as it appeared in the *New York Times* for December 2, 3, and 4, 1929. Minor discrepancies between this account and that which appears in Byrd's *Little America* I have usually resolved in favor of the early version, which was presumably fresher in memory.

21. Henry T. Harrison diary, entry for November 30, 1929, courtesy of Mr. Harrison; Laurence M. Gould, sledging party log, entry for Nov. 30, 1929, Gould Papers; Gould, "Some Geographical Results of the Byrd Antarctic Expedition," *Geographical Review,* 21 (April 1931):186; Gould, *Cold,* pp. 168–70.

5. "I'd Go Back Tomorrow"

1. Laurence M. Gould, large (8″ x 11″) ledger-paper notebook autographed on flyleaf "L. M. Gould Byrd Antarctic Expedition Sledging Party Log," entry for January 5, 1930, in Laurence M. Gould Papers, Center for Polar and Scientific

Archives, RG 401, National Archives; Gould, *Cold: The Record of an Antarctic Sledge Journey* (New York: Brewer, Warren, & Putnam, 1931), pp. 172–73, 223, Gould, "Some Geographical Results of the Byrd Antarctic Expedition," *Geographical Review,* 21 (April 1931): 188; sledging party log, entry for December 5, 1929, Gould Papers.

2. Epaminondas Demas, larger manuscript diary, Vol. 3 (covering July 5, 1929–March 1, 1939), entry for December 4, 1929, in Epaminondas Demas Papers, Center for Polar and Scientific Archives, RG 401, National Archives; *New York Times,* December 7, 1929.

3. Harold June as interviewed on the *second* Byrd Antarctic Expedition by Little America's radio station KFZ (32nd broadcast, June 27, 1934), typescript carbon in John N. Dyer Papers, Center for Polar and Scientific Archives, RG 401, National Archives.

4. Richard E. Byrd as quoted in *New York Times,* Dec. 7, 1929; Earl Hanson, "What Use Antarctic Exploration," *World's Work,* 59 (April 1930):70; Isaiah Bowman as quoted in *New York Times,* December 8, 1929.

5. The Secretary of State [Hughes] to the Norwegian Minister [Bryn], April 2, 1924, full text as reprinted in Appendix to Laurence M. Gould, *The Polar Regions in their Relation to Human Affairs* (New York: American Gerographical Society, 1948), p. 53; *New York Times,* April 6, 1929; *ibid,* November 29, 1929.

6. Message from Richard E. Byrd to the Editor of the *London Evening Standard* as sent via Little America's radio station WFA on April 15, 1929, typewritten carbon copy (as posted on the expedition bulletin board) in file of correspondence, news clippings, and reports, Arnold H. Clarke Papers, Center for Polar and Scientific Archives, RG 401, National Archives.

7. Editorial in *Dunedin Star,* May 22, 1929, as copied by Little America's radio personnel, in file of correspondence, news clippings and reports, Clarke Papers.

8. Gould, *Cold,* p. 205. A good discussion of the overlapping international Antarctic claims may be found in Thomas R. Henry, *The White Continent* (New York: William Sloane, 1950), pp. 246–57.

9. Sledging party log, entry for December 7, 1929, Gould Papers; Gould, *Cold,* p. 183 (the date December 8 in this later account is evidently a misprint); *New York Times,* December 9, 1929, p. 3; smaller log (4½" x 11") of handwritten drafts of radiograms, dispatch #53-1929 (sent on December 29, 1929), Gould Papers.

10. Gould, "Some Geographical Results of the Byrd Antarctic Expedition," p. 189; Gould, "Structure of the Queen Maud Mountains, Antarctica," *Bulletin of the Geological Society of America,* 46 (June 30, 1935):979; Gould, *Cold,* p. 184; *New York Times,* December 8, 1929. See also chapter 9.

11. Sledging party log, entries for December 7 and 8, 1929, Gould Papers; Gould, *Cold,* pp. 185, 190; Gould, "Some Geographical Results," pp. 189, 194; Gould, lecture in Geosciences 254, University of Arizona, February 17, 1978.

12. Sledging party log, entries for December 11, 12, 13, and 15, 1929 (and,

undated on an unused back page, an unmistakable bridge game score), Gould Papers; radio log, hand draft of message from Laurence M. Gould to Richard E. Byrd (undated, but evidently sent on December 15, 1929), Gould Papers; *New York Times,* December 22, 1929, p. 2.

13. Radio log, undated message received by sledging party from Little America, Gould Papers. On the G.I.-style griping that showed up in camp after the South Pole flight was over and the majority of the group were idle, see extracts from a letter by Frank T. Davies in *BAE I News,* a newsletter privately circulated among the surviving members of the first Byrd Antarctic Expedition; *BAE I News,* 2 (November 29, 1975):9, in Henry T. Harrison Papers, Center for Polar and Scientific Archives, RG 401, National Archives.

14. *Congressional Record,* 71st Congress, 2nd Session, Vol. 72, Part I, pp. 912–13, 1001, 1078; *Wahington Post,* December 19, 1929; *New York Times,* Dec. 19, 21, and 22, 1929; editorial in *ibid.,* December 23, 1929, p. 22.

15. Gould, *Cold,* pp. 207–9; radio log, dispatch #30 (1929) [sent December 20, 1929], Gould Papers; Gould, "Some Geographical Results," pp. 192–93; sledging party log, entries for December 20 and 21, 1929, Gould Papers. The last-named entry, the party's leader noted on the next page of the log, was a replica of the note the party had placed that day in the cairn on Supporting Party Mountain. Quoting from it in *Cold,* p. 209, Gould updated the "Commander" to "Admiral," a rank which in legal fact Byrd held by the time the note was placed, Congress having adjourned shortly after noon in Washington—about five in the morning Little America time.

16. Gould, *Cold,* pp. 220–21; radio log, dispatches #34-29 and 36-29 (sent on December 27, 1929), and dispatch #52-29 (sent December 29, 1929), Gould Papers; sledging party log, entries for December 26 and 28, 1929, and January 7, 1930, Gould Papers; *New York Times,* December 31, 1929, p. 3.

17. Harry Adams, *Beyond the Barrier with Byrd: An Authentic Story of the Byrd Antarctic Exploring Expedition* (Chicago: Goldsmith Publishing Company, 1932), pp. 190–91; sledging party log, entries for December 31, 1929, and January 4 and 5, 1930, Gould Papers; Gould, *Cold,* p. 241; Arnold Clarke manuscript diary, entry for January 5, 1930, Clarke Papers; Richard E. Byrd, *Little America* (New York: G. P. Putnam's Sons, 1930), p. 367, quoting radiograms form Captain Melville.

18. *Ibid.,* pp. 366, 368, 376, 380; radio log, draft of radiogram from Laurence M. Gould to Professor W. H. Hobbs, Universtiy of Michigan, sent as dispatch #7-1930, Gould Papers; Laurence M. Gould, personal interview, May 1, 1978.

19. Paul A. Siple, *A Boy Scout With Byrd* (New York: Putnam, 1931), pp. 140, 128–30. It was probably just as well, from a humane point of view, that so many of the birds escaped. Antarctic penguins do not do well in captivity; they die of infections from which in their native habitat, some scientists believe, they may be protected by an antibiotic in the krill they feed upon. Laurence M. Gould, personal interview, December 5, 1977.

20. Siple, *A Boy Scout With Byrd,* p. 138; sledging party log, entry for Jan-

uary 18, 1930, Gould Papers; radio log, unnumbered last message (sent January 18, 1930), Gould Papers.

21. Laurence M. Gould manuscript diary, Vol. 2 (red leather notebook hand labeled "L. M. Gould, B. A. E. I, Beginning Aug. 9, 1929"), entry for January 24, 1930, Gould Papers. There is a long gap in this diary between the Geological Party's departure early in November 1929 and its return to Little America in January 1930, a gap which is filled by Gould's entries in the sledging party log, in the radio log, and his geological field notebook.

22. Adams, *Beyond the Barrier,* pp. 192–94; Russell Owen, *South of the Sun* (New York: John Day, 1934), pp. 284–85.

23. Byrd, *Little America,* p. 387; Siple, *A Boy Scout With Byrd,* p. 144; Gould, manuscript diary, Vol. 2, entry for February 19, 1930. The entry closed with a passage Gould may have added later, consisting of the concluding lines of a poem that had also been a favorite among Antarcticans of the Scott-Shackleton generation:

> *Do you recall that sweep of savage splendor*
> *That land that measures each man at his worth*
> *And feel again in memory half fierce, half tender,*
> *The brotherhood of men who know the south.*

24. Richard E. Byrd, *Discovery: The Story of the Second Byrd Antarctic Expedition* (New York: Putnam, 1935), p. 1; Epaminondas Demas manuscript diary, Vol. 3, entries for February 19 and February 9, 1930, Demas Papers. Henry Harrison comments: "Don't mind Pete! He spells like that today." Harrison to author, September 17, 1978.

25. Laurence M. Gould, personal interview, October 19, 1977. Admiral Byrd later commented on the "stampede to the altar" that followed the return of the expedition: "Of the forty-one men with me at Little America, thirty were bachelors. Several married the first girls they met in New Zealand; most of the rest got married immediately upon their return to the United States. Two of the bachelors were around fifty years old, and both were married shortly after reaching home." Richard E. Byrd, journal entry for May 12, 1934, as published in Byrd, *Alone* (New York: Putnam, 1938), p. 143.

6. A Ghost Town Returns to Life

1. Bernt Balchen, *Come North With Me* (New York: E. P. Dutton, 1958), pp. 194–95, 197–99; Balchen, "The Strange Enigma of Admiral Byrd," p. 16, typed manuscript included in correspondence between Bernt Balchen and L. M. Gould, 1949–1959, in Laurence M. Gould Papers, Center for Polar and Scientific Archives, RG 401, National Archieves.

2. John E. Caswell, "Ellsworth, Lincoln," *Dictionary of American Biography,* Supplement Five (New York: Charles Scribner's Sons, 1977), pp. 205–7; Lincoln Ellsworth, *Beyond Horizons* (New York: Doubleday, Doran, 1937), pp. 250–55.

3. Richard E. Byrd, *Discovery: The Story of the Second Byrd Antarctic Expedition* (New York: Putnam, 1935), pp. 60–61; Paul A. Siple, *90° South: The Story of the American South Pole Conquest* (New York: Putnam, 1959), p. 50; Byrd, *Alone* (New York: Putnam, 1938), p. 17.

4. The information on Arnold Clarke and Leland Barter is taken from Henry T. Harrison, "Some Facts About Members of Winter Party, Byrd Antarctic Expedition I," typescript furnished me by the kind courtesy of Mr. Harrison. Henry Harrison functions as a kind of alumni secretary for the veterans of the First Byrd Antarctic Expedition. His painstaking labor of compiling the post-Antarctican careers of the First Little Americans is gratefully acknowledged.

5. Siple, *90° South,* p. 52; letter to the editor, *New York Times,* March 15, 1930, p. 18; *NEA Journal,* 20 (April 1931): 116–18, (May 1931): 151–52.

6. Kenneth J. Bertrand, *Americans in Antarctica, 1775–1948* (New York: American Geographical Society, 1971), p. 314; A. J. Lepine to Victor Czegka, August 3, 1933, Victor Czegka Papers, Center for Polar and Scientific Archives, RG 401, National Archives; Peter J. Anderson, "Richard Evelyn Byrd—Polar Explorer," *The Iron Worker,* 28 (Autumn 1974):8.

7. Epaminondas J. Demas, red leather pocket notebook "National Diary 1933," entries for December 16, 29, and 31, 1933; Paul A. Siple, typewritten entry dated October 30, 1933, in loose diary entries, Paul A. Siple Family Papers, Center for Polar and Scientific Archives, RG 401, National Archives.

8. Demas, large red board-bound "Collins Trader's Diary 1934," entries for January 12, 13, 14, and 16, 1934, in Epaminondas Demas Papers, Center for Polar and Scientific Archives, RG 401, National Archives; Ellsworth, *Beyond Horizons,* pp. 264–67.

9. Byrd, *Discovery,* pp. 67, 71; Demas, 1934 manuscript diary, entry for January 14, 1934, Demas Papers; Siple, *90° South,* p. 53.

10. Richard E. Byrd, in script for the Second Byrd Antarctic Expedition's tenth radio broadcast on January 20, 1934, originating from the *Jacob Ruppert* at the Bay of Whales with call letters KJTY, carbon copy in file of radio scripts, John N. Dyer Papers, Center for Polar and Scientific Archives, RG 401, National Archives; Byrd, *Discovery,* p. 72.

11. Thomas C. Poulter in script for the expedition's thirteenth broadcast, February 10, 1934, originating from Little America with call letters KFZ, carbon copy in file of radio scripts, John N. Dyer Papers. At the appointed time Byrd and Poulter *spoke* the lines attributed to them in these scripts, but whether or not they *wrote* them is a matter for some conjecture. Most if not all of the scripts appear to have been put together by Charles J. V. Murphy of CBS, and they have a stylistic unity and a professional radio writer's touch—musical bridges, the cueing of

recorded sound effects, et cetera—from which one may infer a fair amount of ghost writing.

12. Siple, *90° South*, p. 55; script of tenth radio broadcast, January 20, 1934, carbon copy in Dyer Papers; Byrd, *Discovery*, pp. 73, 75.

13. Laurence M. Gould, "The Ross Shelf Ice," *Bulletin of the Geological Society of America*, 46 (September 30, 1935 [read before the Society on December 27, 1934]:1378–79 and Fig. 2, p. 1376; Byrd, *Discovery*, p. 78.

14. *Ibid.*, pp. 79–97; Siple, *90° South*, p. 55; John N. Dyer in script for expedition's twelfth broadcast, February 3, 1934, carbon copy in file of radio scripts, Dyer Papers.

15. Byrd, *Discovery*, p. 98 (quoting his own journal for February 3, 1934); Byrd, Dyer, and Charles J. V. Murphy in script for twelfth broadcast, February 3, 1934, carbon copy in file of radio scripts, John N. Dyer Papers.

16. Byrd, *Discovery*, p. 101; Siple, *90° South*, p. 112; Louis J. Potaka in script for sixteenth broadcast, February [misprint for March] 3, 1934, carbon copy in file of radio scripts, John N. Dyer Papers. Medical diagnosis by hospital corpsman J. M. Sterrett was sent on the 15th broadcast, on Feb. 24; KFZ then stood by for an eminent New York surgeon's reply.

17. Charles J. V. Murphy in Byrd, *Discovery*, pp. 183, 190, 192, 204. Chapters X, XI, and XII of *Discovery*, detailing events in Little America while Admiral Byrd was away at Advance Base, were written by Murphy, and each is initialed at the end "C.J.V.M."

18. Scripts for 13th broadcast, February 10, 1934; 17th broadcast, March 10, 1934 (reenacting an actual debate that had taken place the evening of March 4); 28th broadcast, May 26, 1934; 29th broadcast, May 30, 1934; 30th broadcast, June 6, 1934; 32nd broadcast, June 27, 1934. Carbon copies in file of radio scripts, Dyer Papers.

7. To Walden Pond with Gasoline Engines

1. S. Edward Roos, "The Submarine Topography of the Ross Sea and Adjacent Waters," *Geographical Review*, 27 (October 1937):574–83; Quin A. Blackburn, "Some Geographical Results of the Second Byrd Antarctic Expedition, 1933–35; III, The Thorne Glacier Section of the Queen Maud Mountains," *ibid.*, pp. 598–614; Paul A. Siple and Alton A. Lindsey, "Ornithology of the Second Byrd Antarctic Expedition," *Auk*, 54 (April 1937):147–59; Alton A. Lindsey, "The Weddell Seal in the Bay of Whales," *Journal of Mammalology*, 18 (May 14, 1947):127–44; Thomas C. Poulter, "The Scientific Work of the Second Byrd Antarctic Expedition," *Scientific Monthly*, 49 (July 1939):5–20 (Poulter's account borrowed heavily, sometimes word-for-word, from others cited); George A. Llano, "A Survey of Antarctic Biology: Life Below Freezing," in Richard S. Lewis and Philip M. Smith, eds., *Frozen Future: A Prophetic Report*

from Antarctica (New York: Quadrangle Books, 1973), pp. 205–229, esp. p. 207.

2. Eleanor Bolling Byrd as quoted (for the *New York Herald-Tribune*) by Ishbel Ross, in "Wanted: New Poles for Byrd to Conquer," *Literary Digest,* 106 (July 5, 1930):380; Egbert W. Nieman and Elizabeth C. O'Daly, *Adventures for Readers,* Book Two (New York: Harcourt, Brace and World, n.d.), pp. 442–55.

3. Laurence M. Gould, personal interview, February 27, 1978; Paul A. Siple, *90° South: The Story of the American South Pole Conquest* (New York: G. P. Putnam's Sons, 1959), p. 56; Charles J. V. Murphy, "Alone," *American Magazine,* 120 (September 1935):100, 16. Alden Hatch, in an account of Admiral Byrd's life based on extensive interviews with members of the Byrd family, concluded that Byrd's elaborate explanation of why Advance Base had to be staffed with only one person was no more than a rationalization: "If his logic seems somewhat strained, it was." Alden Hatch, *The Byrds of Virginia* (New York: Holt, Rinehart and Winston, 1969), p. 336.

4. Murphy, "Alone," p. 17; Richard E. Byrd, *Discovery: the Story of the Second Byrd Antarctic Expedtition* (New York: G. Putnam, 1935), p. 141; Byrd, *Alone* (New York: Putnam, 1938), pp. 5, 7.

5. H. H. Railey, "Solitary Explorer," *Saturday Review of Literature,* 19 (November 5, 1938):10; Thomas Poulter's statement as it appears in script of 28th broadcast over Little America's radio station KFZ, May 26, 1935, carbon copy in file of radio scripts, John N. Dyer Papers, Center for Polar and Scientific Archives, RG 401, National Archives; Byrd's statement as read by Charles J. V. Murphy on 20th broadcast, March 31, 1935, carbon copy in file of radio scripts, Dyer Papers.

6. Siple, *90° South,* p. 57; Richard E. Byrd, *Alone,* p. 30; Byrd, *Discovery,* pp. 151–52; Epaminondas Demas, manuscript diary for 1934, entries for March 16, 17, 19 and 20, 1934 (afterward transcribed on a typewriter by Demas, who included the typed pages with the diary), in Epaminondas J. Demas Papers, Center for Polar and Scientific Archives, RG 401, National Archives.

7. Byrd, *Discovery,* p. 161; Epaminondas Demas manuscript diary, entries for March 21 and March 23, 1934, Demas Papers; Siple, *90° South,* p. 58; Byrd, *Alone,* pp. 37–42; Innes-Taylor as quoted in Murphy, "Alone," p. 97. Murphy comments: "On this he staked his life; and in the end it all but brought him down."

8. Byrd, *Alone,* pp. 49, 53; Siple, *90° South,* p. 58; Byrd manuscript diary as quoted in Murphy, "Alone," p. 17; Epaminondas Demas manuscript diary, entries for March 25, 28, and 30, Demas Papers.

9. Paul Siple as interviewed by C. J. V. Murphy, in script of 20th broadcast, March 31, 1934, carbon copy in file of radio scripts, John N. Dyer Papers; Byrd, *Alone,* pp. 64–67, 87, 125; Murphy, "Alone," p. 100.

10. Byrd, *Alone,* pp. 133, 64, 74, 163–64; Murphy, "Alone," pp. 98 (quoting Byrd's diary entry for April 14, 1934), 100 (quoting Byrd's diary entry for

May 12), 102. Murphy's account gave May 29, rather than the 31st, as the date when Little America's radio log showed the 20-minute gap while Byrd was out in the tunnel. This is evidently an error.

11. Byrd, *Alone,* pp. 169, 166, 181, 186; Charles J. V. Murphy, "A Fight for Life," *American Magazine,* 120 (October 1935):32 (quoting Byrd's diary for June 20, 1934); *ibid.,* p. 33 (quoting Byrd's diary for June 4, 1934).

12. Paul Siple's statement as it appears in script of 29th broadcast, May 30, 1934, carbon copy in file of radio scripts, John N. Dyer Papers; J. A. Pelter's statement as it appears in script of 30th broadcast, June 6, 1934, carbon copy in Dyer Papers; Murphy, "A Fight for Life," p. 33, quoting Byrd's diary entry for June 6, 1934; *ibid.,* quoting Byrd's diary entry for June 8; *ibid.,* p. 98, quoting Byrd's diary entry for June 10.

13. Byrd, *Alone,* pp. 206–7, 221–22, 223; Byrd, *Discovery,* p. 211; Murphy, "A Fight For Life," p. 98. Murphy's account gave July 18–23, Byrd July 23–29, as the time of full moon; Byrd's, according to the 1934 *World Almanac,* was right.

14. 33rd broadcast, June 30, 1934, carbon copy in file of radio scripts, John N. Dyer Papers; Murphy, "A Fight For Life," p. 99; Byrd, *Alone,* pp. 226, 237, 245.

15. Murphy, "A Fight For Life," p. 100; Byrd, *Discovery,* pp. 236, 237, 238 (written by Murphy); William C. Haines to Thomas Poulter, typed flimsy dated August 9, 1934, in file of radiograms, William C. Haines Papers, Center for Polar and Scientific Archives, RG 401, National Archives; Poulter to Haines, message #2 KFY, typed flimsy dated Aug. 13, 1934 at 1830, in file of radiograms, Haines Papers; script of 40th broadcast over KFZ, August 15, 1934, carbon copy in file of radio scripts, John N. Dyer Papers.

8. New Dealers and Cold Warriors in the Great White South

1. John W. Campbell, Jr. ["Don A. Stuart," pseud.], "Who Goes There?", *Astounding Science-Fiction,* 21 (August 1938):60–97. The modern Gothic writer Howard Phillips Lovecraft, stimulated by accounts of the first Byrd Antarctic Expedition, also tried his hand at fiction with an Antarctic setting, in a short novel deriving some of its themes from Edgar Allan Poe's south polar fantasy *The Narrative of A. Gordon Pym;* H. P. Lovecraft to Clark Ashton Smith, November 18, 1930, as printed in Lovecraft, *Selected Letters,* III, 1929–1931 (Sauk City, Wisconsin: Arkham House, 1971), p. 218. Lovecraft's imagined explorers follow the classic British route along the coast of Victoria-Land to McMurdo Sound, after which they establish by air a base above the Beardmore Glacier in Lat. 86° 7' S., Long. 174° 23' E. From thence they fly off into the unknown, discovering the

ruins of a settlement built in Antarctica's ancient tropical past by nonhuman im-
migrants from the stars. Its lower cellars are inhabited by giant albino penguins
and other, less wholesome tenants. H. P. Lovecraft, "At the Mountains of Madness," *Astounding Stories,* 16 (February 1936):8–32; 17 (March 1936):125–35;
(April):132–50.

2. Richard E. Byrd, "Is a Dark Age Ahead?", *The Rotarian,* 50 (March
1937):6–9; Thomas R. Henry, *The White Continent: The Story of Antarctica*
(New York: William Sloane Associates, 1950), p. 254; Laurence M. Gould, *The
Polar Regions in their Relation to Human Affairs,* Bowman Memorial Lectures,
Series 4 (New York: American Geographical Society, 1958), p. 16; Walter Sulli-
van, *Quest for a Continent* (London: Secker & Warburg, 1957), p. 126.

3. Text of King Haakon's proclamation as printed in Gould, *Polar Regions,*
Appendix, p. 45; text of Ritscher Expedition's final report as quoted in "New
Maps of the Antarctic," *Geographical Review,* 30 (January 1940):160.

4. Lincoln Ellsworth's visit to Little America II as described in Ellsworth,
Beyond Horizons (New York: Book League of America, 1938), p. 344; language
of Ellsworth's American Highland claim as quoted in Kenneth J. Bertrand, *Americans in Antarctica, 1775–1948* (New York: American Geographical Society,
1971), p. 403; Cordell Hull, *Memoirs* (New York: Macmillan, 1948), 1:758–59.

5. F. Alton Wade, "An Introduction to the Symposium on Scientific Results of
the United States Antarctic Service Expedition, 1939–1941," *Proceedings of the
American Philosophical Society,* 89 (April 1945):1. Most of that issue of the *Proceedings* was devoted to scientific monographs deriving from the Expedition's
work; several had been read as papers at the Society's Annual Meeting on November 21 and 22, 1941.

6. Paul A. Siple, *90° South* (New York: G. P. Putnam's Sons, 1959), p. 61;
New York Times, July 28, 1929, p. 12; Richard E. Byrd, *Alone* (New York: G. P.
Putnam's Sons, 1938), p. 133; photograph of Byrd with Roosevelt as reprinted in
Peter J. Anderson, "Richard Evelyn Byrd—Polar Explorer," *The Iron Worker,*
28 (Autumn 1974):12.

7. Text of President Roosevelt's order of November 25, 1939, to Admiral
Byrd, as printed in Bertrand, *Americans in Antarctica,* pp. 472–74; Siple, *90°
South,* pp. 63, 66. Professor Gould, who is certain FDR wanted a formal claim of
U.S. sovereignty over some Antarctic territory, adds: "But of course we put a
stop to all that" with the negotiation of the Antarctic Treaty in 1959. Laurence
M. Gould, personal interview, October 19, 1977.

8. Bertrand, *Americans in Antarctica* pp. 413–15, 423–24; Siple, *90° South,*
pp. 67, 69–73; Siple to Mr. and Mrs. Victor H. Czegka, July 9, 1940, radiogram
(via Army Amateur Radio System), in Victor Czegka Papers, Center for Polar
and Scientific Archives, RG 401, National Archives.

9. The semi-official narrative by R. A. J. English, "Preliminary Account of
the U.S. Antarctic Expedition 1939–1941," *Geographical Review,* 31 (July
1941):466–78, is disappointingly brief. For greater detail, see the articles in the

American Philosophical Society symposium on Antarctica cited in note 5, above, especially Paul A. Siple, "Geographic Exploration from Little America III, the West Base of the United States Antarctic Service Expedition 1939–41"; Finn Ronne, "Main Southern Sledge Journey from East Base"; Siple and Charles F. Passel, "Measurements of Dry Atmospheric Cooling in Subfreezing Temperatures"; and Vernon P. Boyd, "Motorized Surface Transport in the Antarctic."

10. *Washington Post,* March 5, 1940, p. 1; *New York Times,* March 5, 1940, pp. 1, 18; March 6, p. 46; April 6, p. 31; June 14, p. 11; June 19, p. 12. Bertrand, *Americans in Antarctica,* attributes the decision to evacuate the bases to the rapidly mounting international crisis rather than to congressional pique; but compare Siple, *90° South,* p. 72.

11. Gould, *The Polar Regions,* p. 21; text of Chilean Decree No. 1747 of 6 November 1940 as printed in *ibid.,* Appendix, pp. 39–40.

12. Julius Goebel, Jr., *The Struggle for the Falkland Islands* (Port Washington, N.Y.: Kennikat Press, 1971 [reprint of 1927 ed.], p. 468; L. B. Quartermain, *The Early History of the Ross Sea Sector, Antarctica* (London: Oxford University Press, 1967), p. 424.

13. Siple, *90° South,* pp. 75–76; Joseph M. Dukert, *This Is Antarctica,* rev. ed. (New York: Coward, McCann & Geoghegan, 1971), p. 95.

14. Sir Vivian Fuchs, "Evolution of a Venture in Antarctic Science: Operation Tabarin and the British Antarctic Survey," in Richard S. Lewis and Philip M. Smith, eds. *Frozen Future: A Prophetic Report from Antarctica* (New York: Quadrangle Books, 1973), pp. 234, 236; *International Court of Justice Pleadings, Antarctica Cases* (United Kingdom v. Argentina; United Kingdom v. Chile), pp. 28, 30, 31.

15. Richard E. Byrd, preface to the symposium on scientific results of the United States Antarctic Service Expedition (as cited in note 5), p. iii; Siple, *90° South,* p. 73.

16. Henry T. Harrison, "Some Facts About Members of Winter Party, Byrd Antarctic Expedition I," April 15, 1978, typescript furnished by the kind courtesy of Mr. Harrison; Alden Hatch, *The Byrds of Virginia* (New York: Holt, Rinehart, and Winston, 1969), pp. 365, 371.

17. Bernt Balchen, *Come North With Me* (New York: Putnam, 1958), p. 297; text of radio address by Henry A. Wallace announcing his 1948 presidential candidacy as published in the *New York Times,* December 30, 1947, p. 15. Ten years later, by which time U.S.-Soviet relations were considerably friendlier, at least where Arctic and Antarctic affairs were concerned, Bernt Balchen personally had not mellowed; he still saw the basic relationship as competitive, not cooperative. See Balchen's review of Terence Armstrong, *The Russians in the Arctic* (New York: Essential Books, 1958), *Saturday Review,* 41 (November 15, 1958):17.

18. Sigmund Gutenko as quoted in Jennie Darlington, *My Antarctic Honeymoon: A Year at the Bottom of the World* (Garden City, N.Y.: Doubleday and Company, 1956), p. 67; Sullivan, *Quest for a Continent,* pp. 173–74.

19. Henry, *White Continent*, p. ix; Bertrand, *Americans in Antarctica,* p. 485; Sullivan *Quest for a Continent,* pp. 176, 182; Siple, *90° South,* pp. 78–79.

20. William H. Kearns, Jr., and Beverly Britton, *The Silent Continent* (New York: Harper and Brothers, 1955), p. 170. Kearns, co-pilot of a PBM Martin Mariner flying boat operating from the seaplane tender *Pine Island* with the Eastern Task Group, survived an air crash—and thirteen days on the ice cap—in the Thurston Peninsula during the period when the Central Group was battling the ice pack. Bertrand, *Americans in Antarctica,* pp. 507–9; Sullivan, *Quest for a Continent,* chap 16.

21. Kearns and Britton, *Silent Continent,* pp. 171, 180; Sullivan, *Quest for a Continent,* pp. 233–34.

22. Raymond Bertrand, *The Hollow Earth: The Greatest Geographical Discovery in History made by Admiral Richard E. Byrd in the Mysterious Land Beyond the Poles; the True Origin of the Flying Saucers* (New York: University Books, 1969), pp. 20, 24, 190, 191.

23. Finn Ronne, *Antarctic Conquest* (New York: Putnam, 1949), pp. 42, 59, 60, 118, 162. Captain Ronne's autobiography, which may be in print by the time this book appears, should throw more light on the episode.

24. Robert L. Nichols, "Man-hauling in Antarctica," *Appalachia,* 34 (December 1962):207; Jennie Darlington, *My Antarctic Honeymoon: A Year at the Bottom of the World* (Garden City: Doubleday & Company, 1956), pp. 93, 270, 170–71. The masculine insecurity that so often goes with this kind of prejudice is painfully evident in the phrasing of the letter: "We, the undersigned, feel that it would jeopardize our physical condition and mental balance if the Ronne expedition consisting of twenty men were to be accompanied by one or more females for that period of time spent in the Antarctic." Or perhaps, more charitably, we may assume that these men were victims of the vulgarized American Freudianism then in vogue.

9. The Dinosaur at the Bottom of the World

1. Walter Sullivan, *Quest for a Continent* (London: Secker & Warburg, 1957), pp. 302–6, 309. The erosion continued; in 1963 part of Little America III was sighted sticking out of an iceberg in the Ross Sea. A Navy photograph of this ruin appears in Joseph M. Dukert, *This Is Antarctica,* 2nd rev. ed. (New York: Coward, McCann & Geoghegan, 1971), p. 12; another can be seen in Richard S. Lewis, *A Continent for Science: The Antarctic Adventure* (New York: Viking Press, 1965), p. 186.

2. Paul A. Siple, *90° South: The Story of the American South Pole Conquest* (New York: Putnam, 1959), pp. 118, 120. Not only did Admiral Byrd not fulfill his lifelong desire to set foot upon the South Pole; after his death a shadow was cast upon his achievements at the North Pole as well. Bernt Balchen argued that

within the times given for the takeoff from Kings Bay and return the airplane could not have traveled to the Pole and back, and that Byrd and Floyd Bennett had therefore not reached it at all. This assertion was included in Balchen's auto-biography *Come North With Me,* which was scheduled to be published in 1958, the year following Byrd's death. Balchen was persuaded to delete this and other anti-Byrd passages from the book, partly on the ground that he had waited to make the accusation until the Admiral was dead and could not reply. In 1971, however, the journalist Richard Montague in a book titled *Oceans, Poles and Air-men,* drawing upon and quoting from the unpublished portions of Balchen's manuscript, flatly stated that Byrd and Bennett did not fly over the North Pole. Pete Demas, however, who (like Balchen) had also been at Spitsbergen, wrote a ringing defense of Byrd. Demas challenged the Norwegian's figures, arguing that an error in the press reports of the time of takeoff (as between local time and GMT) allowed an ample period within which the plane could have, and presum-ably did, reach and return from the Pole. The *Encyclopaedia Britannica* in its 1974 edition has taken cognizance of the controversy, as has the *National Geo-graphic Magazine*—the latter on the ground that while it does not accept the Balchen-Montague charges, it is journalistically bound to report their existence. The episode has been an unhappy experience for surviving First Little Americans who admired both Balchen and Byrd. See Bernt Balchen, "The Strange Enigma of Admiral Byrd," typed manuscript included in correspondence between Bal-chen and L. M. Gould, 1949–1959, in Laurence M. Gould Papers, Center for Polar and Scientific Archives, RG 401, National Archives; Balchen, *Come North With Me* (New York: E. P. Dutton, 1958); file of correspondence regarding *Come North With Me,* 1958, Gould Papers (includes copies of letters from Paul A. Siple and Laurence M. Gould to Bernt Balchen, as well as correspondence with the publisher); thermofax copies of unpublished pages of *Come North With Me,* also in the Polar Archives; Richard Montague, *Oceans, Poles and Airmen: The First Flights over Wide Waters and Desolate Ice* (New York: Random House, 1971); E. J. "Pete" Demas, *Byrd's North Pole Flight,* duplicated typescript, n. d , copy in Epaminondas Demas Papers, Center for Polar and Scientific Archives, RG 401, National Archives; *The New Encyclopaedia Britannica* (Chicago, 1974), Macropaedia Vol. 3, p. 542 [compare previous edition, *Encyclopaedia Britannica* (Chicago, 1973), Vol. 4, p. 507]; *National Geographic Magazine,* 154 (Sep-tember 1978):302; Henry T. Harrison to the present writer, May 26 and Sep-tember 6, 1978; Laurence M. Gould, personal interview, January 11, 1979. Mr. Harrison has also kindly furnished me copies of his correspondence on this matter with Joseph R. Judge, associate editor of the *National Geographic,* and with Commander Richard E. Byrd, Jr. Further correspondence between Mr. Judge and E. J. Demas between August 26, 1978, and January 17, 1979, copies of which were made available to me by Professor Gould, convinces me that as of the present moment Demas—and therefore Byrd—has the better of the argument.

    3. Siple, *90° South,* p. 122. The cold-warring American press, however,

seems to have interpreted Byrd's message as an announcement that "we got there first". Détente in 1956, outside of Antarctica, had yet a long way to go. Sullivan, *Quest for a Continent*, p. 344.

4. Soviet memorandum on the Antarctic, 1950, text as reprinted in Laurence M. Gould, *The Polar Regions in their Relation to Human Affairs*, Bowman Memorial Lectures, Series 4 (New York: American Philosophical Society, 1958), Appendix, pp. 49–50; William H. Kearns, Jr., and Beverly Britton, *The Silent Continent* (New York: Harper and Brothers, 1955), p. 208.

5. Lewis, *Continent for Science*, pp. 62–63, paraphrasing an account by a participant in the meeting at Van Allen's home; Hugh Odishaw, Executive Secretary of the U. S. National Committee for the IGY, quoted in Laurence M. Gould, "The History of the Scientific Committee on Antarctic Research (SCAR)," as published in Louis O. Quam and Horace D. Porter, eds., *Research in the Antarctic* (Washington: American Association for the Advancement of Science, 1971), p. 48.

6. Siple, *90° South*, pp. 98–99. Siple's own interpretation of the South Pole decision seems more Cold Warrior than is historically warranted. According to Siple, the Americans up until that moment had not definitely committed themselves to a South Pole venture, but the Russian overture left them no choice but to go ahead. According to Hugh Odishaw, however, as relayed to me by Professor Gould, the United States had indicated where it was going to place its IGY stations at the Committee's meeting in Rome the previous year. Telephone conversation with Laurence M. Gould, February 4, 1979.

7. Dwight D. Eisenhower, *Mandate for Change* (Garden City: Doubleday & Company, 1963), p. 253; John Lear, "Ike and the Peaceful Atom," *The Reporter*, 14 (January 12, 1956):21; Kearns and Britton, *Silent Continent*, p. 212; *International Court of Justice Pleadings, Antarctica Cases* (United Kingdom v. Argentina; United Kingdom v. Chile), The Hague, 1955.

8. Laclavère as quoted in Laurence M. Gould, "The History of the Scientific Committee on Antarctic Research" (as cited in n. 5), p. 48. Professor Gould is of the opinion that M. Laclavère's leadership was absolutely crucial for the Antarctic Conference's success. Laurence M. Gould, personal interview, January 9, 1979.

9. "Dentro de las actividades científicas previstas en la Antártida para la realización del Año Geofísico Internacional 1957/1958, la zona correspondiente al Mar de Weddell es motivo de especial interés para varios de los países participantes. Esto es obvio ya que a través de este mar se ofrece la otra posibilidad de abordar el Polo Sur." Luis R. A. Capurro, *Expedición Argentina al Mar de Weddell, Diciembre de 1954 a Enero de 1955* [Argentinian Expedition to the Weddell Sea, December 1954 to January 1955] (Buenos Aires: Republica Argentina, Ministerio de Marina, 1955), p. ii. Texts also in English and German.

10. Sullivan, *Quest for a Continent*, p. 350; George J. Dufek, *Operation Deepfreeze* (New York: Harcourt, Brace, and Company, 1957), pp. 159, 99; Juhan Smuul, *Antarctica Ahoy! The Ice Book* (Moscow: Foreign Languages Pub-

lishing House [1963]), p. 211. The continuing official coolness between the Soviet Union and Australia did not deter a leading Soviet academician from writing a handsome eulogy to Australia's greatest Antarctic explorer, Sir Douglas Mawson, after a visit in Adelaide shortly before Mawson's death in 1958. E. M. Suzyumov, *A Life Given to the Antarctic,* tr. by Tina Tupikina-Glaessner (Adelaide: Libraries Board of South Australia, 1968), esp. p. 56.

11. Richard Lee Chappell, *Antarctic Scout* (New York: Dodd, Mead & Company, 1959), pp. 151, 194; Siple, *90° South,* p. 345. The scientists and military personnel involved in the IGY, well aware of Russian polar achievement since the time of the Tsars, did not need to be educated as to the technical and scientific competence of the Soviet Union. Sputnik had the subtle effect, however, of generalizing this awareness to the Western Hemisphere and Western European countries from which the Antarcticans had come. It is noteworthy that the American press, for example, immediately accepted the official Soviet announcement of Sputnik, and that nobody in this country tried to challenge it as just another piece of "Moscow propaganda." Nor could it be rationalized away as the result of Soviet espionage. "Those Russian spies must be *really* good," one science fiction editor mockingly wrote, "they stole a secret we didn't even have yet." John W. Campbell, Jr., "Project Vanguard Me Too," *Astounding Science Fiction,* 60 (January, 1958):7.

12. Lewis, *Continent for Science,* pp. 66, 71; maps of the "seven cities" as printed in Dufek, *Operation Deepfreeze,* pp. 212–18; Sir Vivian Fuchs and Sir Edmund Hillary, *The Crossing of Antarctica* (Boston: Little, Brown), p. 106; John R. T. Molholm, "Antarctic IGY Activities, 1956–1958," *Appalachia,* 32 (June 15, 1959):404. Unfortunately, Hallett Station's environmental impact seems to have been considerable: "The lack of nesting penguins in areas of intense [human] activity suggests the inability of the species to tolerate continuous disturbance." Leigh H. Fredrickson, "Hallett Station," in Richard S. Lewis and Philip M. Smith, eds., *Frozen Future: A Prophetic Report From Antarctica* (New York: Quadrangle Books, 1973), p. 417.

13. Laurence M. Gould, personal interview, January 19, 1979; Siple, *90° South,* p. 154, Lewis, *Continent for Science,* p. 71; Laurence M. Gould, telephone conversation, Feb. 4, 1979. Richard Bowers and his advance sledge party were not, however, the first people to come on foot to the South Pole since Scott's departure in 1912. Admiral Dufek touched down (briefly; it was −58°F!) at the Pole in an RD4 on October 31, 1956, about a month before Bowers's departure. Dufek, *Operation Deepfreeze,* p. 200; Lewis, *Continent for Science,* p. 70. Dufek, incidentally, had apparently ridiculed the inclusion of sledge dog teams on Operation Deepfreeze, "as a costly $40,000 concession to antiquated Antarctic expedition practices," to which Paul Siple retorted that the dogs "might one day prove to be good insurance compared with the hundreds of pairs of useless snowshoes the Navy had brought to the Antarctic." Siple, *90° South,* p. 154.

14. Lewis, *Continent for Science,* p. 71; Siple, *90° South,* pp. 155, 179–80, 244, 248, and chapters 23, 24, and 27.

15. Fuchs and Hillary, *Crossing of Antarctica,* pp. 201, 246; Laurence M. Gould, personal interview, November 7, 1978; Lewis, *Continent for Science,* p. 116. Paul Siple was airlifted out of Amundsen-Byrd Station on November 30, 1957, as the first IGY wintering-over party at the South Pole was replaced with a second, and so missed these historic meetings with Hillary and Fuchs. (Fuchs's party had just left Shackleton Base, on November 24.) Fuchs and Siple had, however, conversed at some length by radio from their respective stations. Siple, *90° South,* pp. 274, 335; Fuchs and Hillary, *Crossing of Antarctica,* p. 119.

16. *Ibid.,* p. 267; Laurence M. Gould, "The History of the Scientific Committee on Antarctic Research, (SCAR)," as cited in note 5, pp. 49–51, 54.

17. Sir Douglas Mawson's letter as quoted in Gould, *The Polar Regions in Their Relation to Human Affairs,* p. 32. Paul Siple also leaned toward a solution of the Antarctic problem far more limited in scope than the Antarctic Treaty, in the form of a joint U.S.-New Zealand condominium, stretching from France's Adélie Land claim "across West Antarctica to the Weddell Sea, save for the hotly contested northern half of the Palmer Peninsula." Siple, *90° South,* p. 363.

18. William Appleman Williams, "Another Frontier Another Tyranny," *In These Times,* May 31–June 6, 1978, p. 13; T. O. Jones, "The Antarctic Treaty," in Louis O. Quam and Horace D. Porter, *Research in the Antarctic,* pp. 60–61; Charles E. Martin, President of the American Society of International Law, as quoted in Arthur Krock, *Memoirs* (New York: Funk & Wagnalls, 1968), p. 299. Incidentally, Krock pointed out that one of the Senators who *opposed* ratification of the Antarctic Treaty was Harry Byrd of Virginia, the explorer's older brother. Might the political history of the Treaty have been different had the Admiral still been living?

19. Paul C. Daniels, "The Antarctic Treaty," in Lewis and Smith, *Frozen Future,* pp. 31–45; Finn Sollie, "The Political Experiment in Antarctica," *ibid.,* pp. 46–63; text of the Antarctic Treaty as printed in *ibid.,* Appendix I; Dukert, *This Is Antarctica,* chapter 6; Charles Neider, *Edge of the World: Ross Island, Antarctica* (Garden City, N.Y.: Doubleday, 1974), p. 1. The economic objections frequently raised against the American space program have not been much of a problem in polar work because Antarctica is much less expensive than space. The U.S. Antarctic program's annual budget in 1977 was only $37 million, and most of that was logistics; the science itself cost only $8 million. Laurence M. Gould, personal interview, October 19, 1977.

20. Charles Neider, "Conversation with Laurence McKinley Gould," transcript of taped interview, copy furnished me by the kind courtesy of the interviewee; Laurence M. Gould, lecture in Geosciences 254, University of Arizona, February 13, 1978; Charles Neider, letter to the *New York Times,* January 9, 1978; *ibid.,* February 19, 1978, p. 28. Incidentally, one of the two women with the Ronne Antarctic Research Expedition was expecting a child at the time that

expedition left Antarctica early in 1947. Had that party been forced to winter over again, as seemed quite possible at the time, the first human native of Antarctica would have had U.S. citizens as parents—on a spot claimed by Argentina, Chile, and Britain, with plausible cases that could have been made also for the United States and the Soviet Union! Jennie Darlington, *My Antarctic Honeymoon* (New York: Doubleday, 1956), pp. 250, 256, 264.

21. Editorial in *New York Times,* December 9, 1969; Dale Vance as interviewed by Charles Neider, in *Edge of the World: Ross Island, Antarctica,* p. 183; Jacques Cousteau in narration for a film made on Deception Island in 1973, one of a four-part sequence on Antarctica viewed by the present writer in a locally televised rerun, January 8, 1979.

22. Philip M. Smith, "Antarctic Engineering," in Lewis and Smith, *Frozen Future,* pp. 430, 429; Paul K. Dayton and Gordon A. Robilliard, "McMurdo Sound," *ibid.,* p. 411. Both articles included photographs vividly illustrating this pollution. Smith's article also noted that "tragically, many individuals at McMurdo have become alienated from the program's objectives." The two kinds of deterioration, environmental and social, are functionally connected.

23. Paul Siple as quoted in Dukert, *This Is Antarctica,* p. 152; Owen Wilkes and Robert Mann, "the Story of Nukey Poo," *Bulletin of the Atomic Scientists,* 34 (October 1978):32–36.

24. Laurence M. Gould, small pocket notebook hand-labeled "1969 Antarctic Diary," entries for November 27 and December 4, 1969, in L. M. Gould Papers, Center for Polar and Scientific Archives, RG 401, National Archives. I am aware that Lystrosaurus itself was not a dinosaur, and I hope that the use of that term in the title of the present chapter may be forgiven as a minor exercise of poetic license.

25. Edwin H. Colbert, "Antarctic Fossil Vertebrates and Gondwanaland," in Quam and Porter, *Research in the Antarctic,* p. 698; Colbert, *Wandering Lands and Animals* (New York: Dutton, 1973), pp. 18–32; Gould, lecture in Geosciences 254, University of Arizona, February 10, 1978; Gould, personal interview, October 19, 1977. "I might have found the bone," Professor Gould wistfully adds, "but the helicopter that was supposed to take me out there [to Coalsack Bluff] broke down."

Index

Numbers in italics refer to photographs

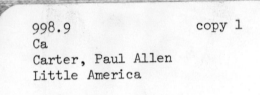